Theory and Applications
of Natural Language Processing

Series Editors:
Graeme Hirst
Julia Hirschberg
Eduard Hovy
Mark Johnson

Aims and Scope

The field of Natural Language Processing (NLP) has expanded explosively over the past decade: growing bodies of available data, novel fields of applications, emerging areas and new connections to neighboring fields have all led to increasing output and to diversification of research.

"Theory and Applications of Natural Language Processing" is a series of volumes dedicated to selected topics in NLP and Language Technology. It focuses on the most recent advances in all areas of the computational modeling and processing of speech and text across languages and domains. Due to the rapid pace of development, the diversity of approaches and application scenarios are scattered in an ever-growing mass of conference proceedings, making entry into the field difficult for both students and potential users. Volumes in the series facilitate this first step and can be used as a teaching aid, advanced-level information resource or a point of reference.

The series encourages the submission of research monographs, contributed volumes and surveys, lecture notes and textbooks covering research frontiers on all relevant topics, offering a platform for the rapid publication of cutting-edge research as well as for comprehensive monographs that cover the full range of research on specific problem areas.

The topics include applications of NLP techniques to gain insights into the use and functioning of language, as well as the use of language technology in applications that enable communication, knowledge management and discovery such as natural language generation, information retrieval, question-answering, machine translation, localization and related fields.

The books are available in printed and electronic (e-book) form:

* Downloadable on your PC, e-reader or iPad
* Enhanced by Electronic Supplementary Material, such as algorithms, demonstrations, software, images and videos
* Available online within an extensive network of academic and corporate R&D libraries worldwide
* Never out of print thanks to innovative print-on-demand services
* Competitively priced print editions for eBook customers thanks to MyCopy service http://www.springer.com/librarians/e-content/mycopy

More information about this series at
http://www.springer.com/series/8899

Carlos Ramisch

Multiword Expressions Acquisition

A Generic and Open Framework

Springer

Carlos Ramisch
Aix Marseille University
Marseille
France

ISSN 2192-032X   ISSN 2192-0338 (electronic)
ISBN 978-3-319-35754-6   ISBN 978-3-319-09207-2 (eBook)
DOI 10.1007/978-3-319-09207-2
Springer Cham Heidelberg New York Dordrecht London

Printed on acid-free paper

Springer is part of Springer Science+Business Media (www.springer.com)

To my parents

Preface

The work described in this book was mostly carried out between 2009 and 2012 in Grenoble (France) and Porto Alegre (Brazil) as part of my PhD.[1] For their guidance and support, I would like to thank my advisers, Aline Villavicencio and Christian Boitet, who are true inspirations for me. I would also like to thank the colleagues of the Federal University of Rio Grande do Sul (UFRGS) and of the University of Grenoble. I thank Eric Wehrli and Gaël Dias for their comments and suggestions as *rapporteurs* of my thesis, as well as the other members of the jury: Yves Lepage, Helena de Medeiros Caseli, Rosa Vicari, Renata Vieira and Mathieu Mangeot. I am thankful to my Springer editor, Federica Corradi dell Acqua, and the anonymous reviewers, who provided constructive feedback and helped improve my work.

This book is not as much a personal achievement as it is the result of a collective effort. Therefore, I am grateful to the people who contributed to it, in particular the co-authors of papers discussed in this book: Aline Villavicencio, Christian Boitet, Magali Sanches Duran, Evita Linardaki, Mathieu Mangeot, Cassia Trojahn dos Santos, Renata Vieira, Sandra Maria Aluísio, Maria José Finatto, Roger Granada, Marco Idiart, Lucelene Lopes, Helena de Medeiros Caseli, Laurent Besacier and Alexander Kobzar. I had interesting discussions and received valuable suggestions from Emmanuelle Esperança-Rodier, Paulo Schreiner, Rodrigo Wilkens, Valérie Bellynck, Sara Stymne, Lucia Specia, Agata Savary, Violeta Seretan, Dimitra Anastasiou, Preslav Nakov, Paul Cook, Kyo Kageura, Francesca Bonin and Muntsa Padró.

Many improvements in the mwetoolkit would not have been possible without the help of Sandra Castellanos, Maitê Dupont, Vitor De Araujo and Alexander Kobzar. I am specially indebted to Vitor for his programming skills and perspicacity. I would like to express my gratitude to all the anonymous users who downloaded the mwetoolkit and also to the non-anonymous ones who provided me with

[1]Funding: French Ministry of Higher Education & Research, CAMELEON (CAPES-COFECUB 707-11), AIM-WEST (FAPERGS-INRIA 1706-2551/13-7), LIG, PPGC UFRGS, LICIA lab.

valuable feedback: Spence Green, Julien Corman, Agnès Tutin, Olivier Kraif, Cleci Bevilacqua, Anna Maciel, Guilherme Pilotti and Lis Kenashiro.

For their help as proofreaders, I thank my sister Renata and my partner Antoine. Along with the other members of my family and my friends, they have been extremely patient and supportive, particularly during the redaction of my thesis. This book is dedicated to my parents, who are unconditional fans, and especially to my father, who always said I should write a book some day.

Marseille, France   Carlos Ramisch
April 2014

Contents

Acronyms

AM	Association measure
CP	Complex predicate
DTD	Document type definition
GS	Gold standard
LM	Language model
LNRE	Large number of rare events
LSF	Lexico-semantic function
LVC	Light verb construction
MAP	Mean averaged precision
MLE	Maximum likelihood estimation
MTT	Meaning-text theory
MWE	Multiword expression
MWT	Multiword term
NLP	Natural language processing
POS	Part of speech
P	Precision
PV	Phrasal verb
R	Recall
SVC	Support verb construction
SVM	Support vector machine
TP	True positive
VPC	Verb-particle construction
XML	Extended markup language

Association Measures	
dice	Dice's coefficient
ll	Log-likelihood ratio
mle	Maximum likelihood estimator
pmi	Pointwise mutual information
t-score	Student's t test statistic

Applications

IR	Information retrieval
MT	Machine translation
OCR	Optical character recognition
PB-SMT	Phrase-based statistical machine translation
SMT	Statistical machine translation
SRL	Semantic role labelling
WSD	Word sense disambiguation

Conferences

ACL	Annual Meeting of the Association for Computational Linguistics
COLING	International Conference on Computational Linguistics
EACL	European Chapter of the Association for Computational Linguistics
LREC	Language Resources and Evaluation Conference
NAACL	North American Chapter of the Association for Computational Linguistics

Corpora

BNC	British national corpus
EP	Europarl corpus
PLN-BR	Corpus of the project Processamento de Linguagem Natural—Brasil

Language Codes

el	Greek
en	English
fr	French
pt	Portuguese
pt-BR	Brazilian Portuguese

Symbols

*	Ungrammatical construction
?	Unnatural construction

Chapter 1
Introduction

This book is about *multiword expressions (MWEs)* and their treatment in *natural language processing (NLP)* applications. Building computer systems capable of dealing with MWEs is a hard and open problem, due to the complex and pervasive nature of these constructions in language. This chapter is a general introduction to this exciting research topic. We motivate and illustrate the importance of MWEs through many examples in several human languages. Then, we discuss the goals and scope of the computational framework for MWE acquisition presented in this book.

1.1 Motivations

Before we dig into linguistic formal definitions, real-world data and technical details, we would like to discuss the answers to the following three questions: what are MWEs, why do they matter for NLP, and what happens if we ignore them?

1.1.1 What Are Multiword Expressions?

The question of what counts as a multiword expression and what does not is a polemic one, and in Sect. 2.2 we will provide a set of definitions for the term, including the one adopted in this book. But for the moment, let us put the technicalities aside. Put simply, MWEs are habitual recurrent word combinations of everyday language (Firth 1957). For example, when we say that someone *sets the bar high*, we use it as a metaphor to say that his/her rivals will have a hard time trying to beat him/her. There is actually no physical bar in a high position. Someone who is not familiar with this particular expression cannot guess its meaning from

© Springer International Publishing Switzerland 2015

C. Ramisch, *Multiword Expressions Acquisition*, Theory and Applications
of Natural Language Processing, DOI 10.1007/978-3-319-09207-2_1

the meanings of the individual words. This is one of the most prototypical examples of MWEs: idiomatic expressions. Analogously:

- A *point of view* is not a good place to take a picture,
- A *loan shark* is not a fish,
- *By the way* is not a place,
- *White trash* is not something that you should throw in the rubbish bin,
- *Red wine* is actually purple while *white wine* is actually yellow,
- You can still walk when someone *stands on your feet*,
- You do not need a knife to *cut someone a break*,
- You do not need money to *buy someone some time*,
- Air will not become more available just because you *saved someone's breath*,
- A *French kiss* has nothing to do with the nationality of the kissers,
- An *open mind* is (fortunately) not open as a door would be open,
- You do not necessarily use your foot when you *kick the bucket*.[1]

In addition to idiomatic expressions, many other constructions in language present some particularities which allow us to see them as MWEs. In order to recognise them, one can apply simple linguistic tests. For example, we can ask: is it possible to replace one word in the expression for a synonym? If we take the compound *full moon*, for instance, it would be quite awkward if someone said *?entire moon*, *?whole moon*, *?total moon* or *?complete moon*. Similar replacements are also not possible for expressions like *full circle*, *whole wheat bread* and *whole milk*. Although the meaning of the alternative forms can be easily understood and would seem natural for a person learning English, a native speaker would argue that "you do not say it like this". This makes MWEs quite hard for foreign language learners who lack experience of language use even though they master general lexical and syntactic rules. MWEs confer naturalness and fluency to the discourse, and are unconsciously used as markers that help spotting non-native speech in dialogue contexts.

Another test for detecting MWEs is word for word translation into another language (see Table 1.1). If the translation sounds weird, unnatural or even ungrammatical, the original expression is probably a MWE. For example, the expression *prince charming* is translated into Portuguese as *príncipe encantado*, that is, *enchanted prince*. Alternatives like *príncipe charmoso (good-looking prince)* and *príncipe encantador (gentle prince)* seem unnatural and funny. Similarly, the *finish line* is translated as the *arrival line* in Portuguese (*linha de chegada*) and in French (*ligne d'arrivée*), while the *home stretch* or *home straight* becomes the *final straight* in Portuguese (*reta final*) and the *last straight line* in French (*dernière ligne droite*). Sometimes, a MWE in one language can be translated as a simple word in other languages. For instance, *give up* translates as *renoncer* in French and as

---

[1] Actually, many of these expressions are ambiguous, and also accept literal interpretations. For example, *by the way* can denote a place, like in *she waits by the way*. We will discuss this in Sect. 2.2.

Table 1.1 Examples of English-French (en-fr) MT errors due to MWE processing

en source	We only go out **once in a blue moon**
fr MT	Nous allons seulement **une fois dans une lune bleue**
fr reference	Nous sortons **tous les 36 du mois**
en source	The **dry run** went on smoothly
fr MT	Le **fonctionnement à sec** est allé en douceur
fr reference	La **répétition** s'est bien passée
en source	The children **ate** my cookies **up**
fr MT	Les enfants **ont mangé** mes biscuits **jusqu'à**
fr reference	Les enfants **ont mangé tous** mes biscuits
en source	The boy **is in** his mother's **black books**
fr MT	Le garçon **est dans les livres noirs** de sa mère
fr reference	Le garçon **n'est pas dans les petits papiers** de sa mère
en source	MWEs are a **pain in the neck** for computers
fr MT	MWEs sont une **douleur dans le cou** pour les ordinateurs
fr reference	Les EPL sont comme une **épine dans le pied** pour les ordinateurs
en source	MWEs are a **tough nut to crack**
fr MT	MWEs sont un **dur à cuire**
fr reference	Les EPL sont **un vrai casse-tête**
en source	I never get on **cable cars**
fr MT	Je ne suis jamais **sur les voitures de câble**
fr reference	Je ne monte jamais dans les **téléphériques**
en source	He rarely **gets drunk** at work
fr MT	Il **se fait** rarement **bu** au travail
fr reference	Il **est** rarement **ivre** au travail
en source	The **workshop proceedings** are online
fr MT	Les **travaux de l'atelier** sont en ligne
fr reference	Les **actes de l'atelier** sont en ligne
en source	We can **count** Poland **in**
fr MT	Nous pouvons **compter** Pologne
fr reference	Nous pouvons **compter sur** la Pologne

desistir in Portuguese, and *thank you* translates as *merci* in French and as *obrigado* in Portuguese. Such asymmetric MWEs will be discussed in Chap. 7.

Some MWEs have the singularity of breaching general grammar rules. For instance, time adverbs like *now* and *often* cannot, in theory, be quantified. However, it is possible to say *every now and then* and *every so often* meaning *occasionally*. Analogously, the preposition *on* (when it is not acting as a particle in a phrasal verb) requires a complement, but expressions like *from now on* and *and so on* do not respect this constraint. Also, the expression *truth be told* corresponds to a very unorthodox use of English syntax, but the equivalent "correct" expressions *the truth has to be told* or *the truth should be told* would not have the same meaning.

Many common names are also examples of MWEs. For instance, the tool used to suck the air and catch the dirt on the floor is a *vacuum cleaner*, a key that opens all doors is a *master key*, an automatic recorder that answers the phone when you are not there is a *voice mail* or an *answering machine*, a shoe that has a protuberance under the ankle is a *high heel shoe*, a character at the end of an interrogative sentence is a *question mark*. Sometimes, the words in the expression are collapsed and form a single word. This is the systematic behaviour in German (and other Germanic languages), but it happens sometimes in English as well (*firearm, honeymoon, sleepwalk, lighthouse*).[2] The computational treatment of MWEs in which words are concatenated is also a challenging problem in NLP applications. However, since they form a single typographic word, they are not the focus of this book.

Some actions require verbal MWEs in order to be expressed. Examples of such expressions include *make sense, take advantage of someone, have something to do with something, get involved, take for granted, have the last word, put in place*. Sometimes it is hard or impossible to find a single-word equivalent, while some expressions do have (almost) equivalent single-word paraphrases. The use of the simple or multiword form might depend on the context or simply on the speaker's intuition. Examples of expressions that can be paraphrased are *give a wave = to wave, take a walk = to walk, take a shower = to shower* and *let down = disappoint*. MWEs can also behave as adverbial or adjectival complements, or even as grammatical locutions like multiword conjunctions and prepositions. We will discuss MWE types and characteristics in Chap. 2.

1.1.2 Why Do They Matter?

MWEs are frequent in everyday language. Native speakers rarely realise it, but colloquial speech is full of formulaic expressions such as *good morning, my bad, too bad, never mind* and *bye bye*. For instance, almost all the examples of the previous section were taken from a 30-min episode of an American TV show, and there were many more that were not included here. Researchers in theoretical and computational linguistics evaluated the recurrence of MWEs in a more systematic way. Linguistic studies provide examples and figures proving how frequently MWEs occur in text collections across different languages and domains (Biber et al. 1999). It is often assumed that a native speakers' lexicon contains as many MWEs as simple words (Jackendoff 1997). Empirical results and computational lexicons often corroborate this hypothesis, showing that MWEs occur frequently in many language registers, from written to oral, from general to domain-specific, etc. In the English Wordnet, for example, out of its 117,827 nouns, 60,292 (51.4 %) are multiword;

---

[2]There are no clear rules as to whether an English compound should be spelled as a single word, with a hyphen or as two words (Procter 1995). For instance, both *data set* and *dataset* are acceptable forms. An overview of noun compound processing is provided in Szpakowicz et al. (2013).

and out of its 11,558 verbs, 2,829 (25.5 %) are multiword (Ramisch et al. 2013b). Thus, any computational system dealing with human language must take MWEs into account.

Instead of trying to demonstrate the recurrence of MWEs, we chose to present another argument, hopefully more convincing, of the importance of MWEs in natural language processing. That is, we analyse the potential and real impact of MWE treatment in a list of NLP tasks and applications. The following list presents some NLP tasks and applications that will generate ungrammatical or unnatural output if they do not handle MWEs correctly.

- **Computer-aided lexicography.** Lexicographers are professionals who design and build lexical resources such as printed and machine-readable dictionaries and thesauri. Building a lexical resource is a very onerous task that demands expert knowledge and takes a lot of time. If writing a dictionary for single words is costly, dictionaries containing MWEs are even more complex and require more effort. However, as MWEs are often the source of difficulties for both humans and machines to process a sentence, it is very important that lexical resources include them. One of the seminal papers in the MWE field is the work by Church and Hanks (1990). They use a lexicographic environment as their evaluation scenario, comparing manual and intuitive dictionary compilation with the automatic association ratio they propose. They show that tools used to support lexicographic work should also help identify MWEs and extract their meaning and syntactic behaviour from texts. We explore this application further in Chap. 7.
- **Optical character recognition (OCR).** If an OCR system recognises with equal probabilities the words *farm* and *form* in *federal farm/form credit*, it can choose the first option, because it is most likely that it occurs as part of a MWE (Church and Hanks 1990). Currently, this is performed using n-gram language models, but n-grams fail to model highly flexible expressions like *take patient risk factors and convenience into account*. Therefore, MWEs could help improve OCR technology, overcoming length limitations of n-gram language models.
- **Morphological and syntactic analysis.** Recent work in parsing and POS tagging indicates that MWEs can help remove syntactic ambiguities. For instance, the French expressions *faire une marche à pied* (lit. *make a walk by foot*) and *faire un verre à pied* (lit. *make a glass by foot*) look syntactically identical. However, in the first case the adverbial complement is attached to the verb *faire* while, in the second example, the complement is attached to the noun *verre*, as it corresponds to the MWE *verre à pied (wine glass)*. The integration of MWEs into POS taggers and parsers has been the subject of many publications is discussed in Sect. 3.3.4.1.
- **Information retrieval (IR).** When a user queries a web search engine like Google for *rock star*, he/she is probably not looking for websites containing geological descriptions of *rocks*, nor astronomy websites about *stars*, nor descriptions of *star-shaped rocks*. Even though traditional vectorial IR models are able to model the fact that both words must occur in relevant documents, they will

probably be unable to distinguish between literal and idiomatic interpretations of an expression. In other words, the presence of the exact query words in a document does not mean that it is relevant, and vice-versa. Therefore, if MWEs like *rock star* are indexed as lexical and semantic units, the accuracy and usefulness of the system will probably improve. This hypothesis has been verified by several publications discussed in Sect. 3.3.4.3

- **Foreign language learning.** MWEs are hard for non-native speakers learning a foreign language. Dictionaries and other lexical resources containing MWE entries can be very useful to avoid common mistakes. Most printed and electronic dictionaries include a certain number of MWE entries, either as headwords or in examples and explanations. There are dedicated publications which focus on specific MWE types, like the Cambridge Idioms Dictionary (Walter 2006) and the COLLINS-COBUILD Dictionary of Phrasal Verbs (Sinclair 1989) in English, or the bilingual dictionary of Portuguese-Italian idioms (Termignoni 2009). MWEs also play an important role in the design of computer environments for foreign language *e*-learning like Duolingo.[3] Language certificate exam platforms like ETS Internet-based TOEFL test can use automatic MWE processing to spot errors and evaluate fluidity of non-native text (Klebanov et al. 2013). MWE-aware spell checkers and grammatical correctors can also help language learners to produce more natural sentences (Ferraro et al. 2014).

- **Computational semantics.** Many NLP applications require some degree of semantic interpretation. Examples include automatic summarisation, text simplification, word sense disambiguation and induction, text mining, textual entailment and inference, automatic ontology construction, semantic role labelling and information extraction. These applications must take semantic compositionality into account, and as a consequence must also model non-compositional MWEs. For instance, a textual entailment system must know that *once in a blue moon* means *rarely* in order to decide whether the sentence *they go to the movies once in a blue moon* entails *they rarely go to the movies*. Whether an application uses a semantic resource like Wordnet or Framenet, or corpus-derived information like in distributional approaches, ignoring MWEs will certainly degrade the quality of semantic processing. Moreover, MWEs tend to be less polysemous than the composition of the senses of the individual words in it. Finlayson and Kulkarni (2011) exemplify that the word *world* has 9 senses in Wordnet, *record* has 14, but *world record* has only 1. We discuss the importance of MWEs for WSD and for other semantic tasks in Sect. 3.3.4.2. Additionally, we discuss in Sect. 6.2.1.1 the importance of MWEs for a related task, that is, the annotation of semantic roles.

- **Machine translation (MT).** MWEs have been a concern of MT system designers from the very beginning. Often, MWEs cannot be translated word for word, and should be represented as units in the translation model. Expert systems usually include dictionaries of phrases and expressions, that are looked up before

---

[3]http://duolingo.com

performing compositional transfer.[4] Statistical MT systems[5] tend to represent expressions as bilingual word sequences or trees, automatically learned from parallel corpora. To date, MWEs remain a challenging problem for automatic translation, independently of the MT paradigm (Mitkov et al. 2013). We discuss the interaction between MT and MWEs in Sect. 3.3.4.4, and present some experimental results in Sect. 7.2.

Despite their importance, MWEs are often neglected in the development of NLP applications. In 1993, Smadja pointed out that, in automatic MWE acquisition, "...the collocations [MWEs] retrieved have not been used for any specific computational task" (Smadja 1993, p. 150). Most of the recent and current academic research in the community still focuses on identification and extraction tasks instead of focusing on the integration of automatically acquired or manually compiled MWE resources into applications (Kordoni et al. 2011, 2013, 2014; Ramisch et al. 2013b). This is one of our motivations to develop a generic platform for MWE acquisition which allows the integration of the extracted lexicons into applications.

1.1.3 What Happens If We Ignore Them?

Taking MWEs into account is important to confer naturalness to the output of NLP systems. An MT system, for instance, needs to be aware of idiomatic expressions like *it is raining cats and dogs* to avoid literal translations. The equivalent expressions in French would be *il pleut des cordes* (lit. *it rains ropes*), in German *es regnet junge Hunde* (lit. *it rains young dogs*), in Portuguese *chove canivetes* (lit. *it rains Swiss knives*), and so on.[6] Likewise, a parser needs to deal with verb-particle constructions like *take off from Paris*, noun compounds like *give food for thought*, and light verb constructions like *take a walk along the river*, in order to avoid prepositional phrase attachment errors.

Google's popular MT system was used to translate the example sentences of Table 1.1 from English into French.[7] For the system, a MWE (boldface) is any group of words which, when not translated as a unit, can generate translation errors. Possible problems include ungrammatical or unnatural constructions, awkward literal translations of idioms and collocations, and problems of lexical choice and word order. While sometimes the resulting sentences can still be understood, in other cases they may lead to confusion and misunderstanding. As Seretan (2013) points out, a literal translation of *we would like you to pay us a visit* could

---

[4]Expert MT systems are also sometimes called *rule-based* MT systems.

[5]Also sometimes called *empirical* MT systems.

[6]A list of similar expressions in other languages is available at http://en.wikipedia.org/wiki/Raining_animals

[7]Extracted from the extended list of translation examples, see Appendix A.

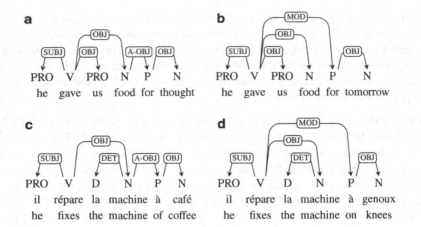

Fig. 1.1 Example sentences in which MWEs can introduce prepositional phrase attachment errors during parsing

be wrongly interpreted and provoke a diplomatic incident, should the receiver understand that he/she will have to spend money. These anecdotal examples clearly demonstrate how awkward the resulting sentences produced by an MT system are when compared to the reference expected translations produced by humans. Nonetheless, MWEs are as hard a nut to crack for automatic translation as for human translators.

Another NLP application in which incorrect MWE processing can lead to errors is syntactic analysis (parsing). Consider for instance the sentences in Fig. 1.1. In sentence (a), *food for thought* is an expression, and the prepositional phrase *for thought* must be attached to the noun *food*. Sentence (b) is identical in terms of sequence of parts of speech, but *for tomorrow* is not part of a MWE and modifies the verb *gave*. Similarly, the French examples also share the same parts of speech, but sentence (c) contains a noun compound, *machine à café (coffee machine)*, while sentence (d) contains an adverbial locution, *à genoux* (on one's Knees). Information about MWEs in the sentence can be obtained by looking them up in a lexicon (Seretan 2011) or by modelling them as features (Constant et al. 2013; Green et al. 2011; Mirroshandel et al 2012), and can help disambiguating the parse trees. On the other hand, failing to identify them will probably reduce the parser's accuracy. In MT and in parsing, as well as in numerous other NLP applications, when the words composing a MWE are treated as separate units, the system will probably produce erroneous output.

We can summarise the importance of MWEs for NLP as follows:

- Important information can be lost if MWEs are not treated;
- MWEs confer naturalness to a system's output; and
- They are frequent and pervasive in language, and are very likely to occur in texts to be processed.

Taking MWEs into account can be quite complicated for traditional NLP applications. The usual or conventional way of saying things, that is, the natural tendency that words have of attracting each other, is the key phenomenon behind MWE. However, this phenomenon lies in a fuzzy zone between lexicon and syntax, involving both lexical and compositional semantic aspects, thus constituting a real challenge for NLP systems. In Sect. 2.3.2, we will discuss some idiosyncrasies of MWEs that make them a wild animal to tame. This is the perfect scenario for a paradox: it is at the same time difficult and necessary to deal with MWEs in applications that involve some degree of semantic interpretation of natural language. As a consequence, the computational treatment of MWEs is considered as a major challenge in NLP and has been the focus of much research effort, as many problems remain to be solved.

1.2   A New Framework for MWE Treatment

The goal of this book is twofold: it provides a general introduction to MWE processing and it presents a new computational framework for dealing with them. With respect to related work presented in Chap. 3, our framework has several conceptual differences. In this section, we outline some of these differences, which constitute original contributions.

1.2.1   Hypotheses

The construction of lexical resources is an onerous task. Thus, one of the goals of NLP research is to propose techniques and tools that aid in the automatic creation and exploitation of monolingual and multilingual resources, helping linguists and domain experts to speed up lexicographic work (Preiss et al. 2007; Messiant et al. 2008; Gala and Zock 2013). Nonetheless, when it comes to MWEs, the availability of such tools is still quite limited, both in terms of effectiveness and of applicability to languages, contrasting with the ubiquitous and pervasive nature of MWEs. Therefore, there is a need for developing, consolidating and evaluating techniques for the automatic acquisition of MWEs from corpora.

The adequate treatment of MWEs in NLP applications is an open and challenging problem. Therefore, our framework tries to answer the following questions:

- How can we *acquire* MWEs automatically from texts?
- How can we *evaluate whether a given method for MWE acquisition is useful?*
- What is the best way to *represent* MWEs in machine-readable resources?
- How can we *integrate MWEs into applications?*

We address the problem of MWE treatment in NLP applications, ranging from their automatic acquisition in raw text to their integration into two real-life applications: computer-aided lexicography and statistical MT. Our evaluation experiments focus on the two most frequent broad classes of MWEs: noun compounds and verbal expressions. We develop a conceptual model for the pipeline of MWE treatment, as well as a concrete software framework that validates the proposed methodology, the mwetoolkit. We have evaluate this model thoroughly and systematically. The hypotheses that guide our work are:

- Mono- and multilingual (parallel and comparable) corpora are rich information sources for automatic lexical acquisition.
- A combination of techniques can be used as a basis for automatic MWE extraction, and will perform better than each of them.
- It should be possible to extract MWEs automatically in resource-poor languages, not only in English and a few "main" languages.
- The evaluation of MWE acquisition is a research topic on its own, and designing an evaluation scenario is as important as designing an acquisition method.
- The adequate integration of MWE treatment can improve the performance of NLP applications in terms of linguistic quality, helping to generate more natural results and remove ambiguities.
- Different NLP applications and integration strategies will yield different performance improvements.

1.2.2 Goals

We believe that MWE research has finally reached its maturity, becoming a consolidated research field. Therefore, the time has come to move forward from acquisition methods to their integration into NLP applications, for higher linguistic quality (more natural and fluent results). Our three main goals are:

1. We would like to develop generic and portable techniques for automatic MWE acquisition from corpora.
2. We would like to evaluate these techniques extrinsically, that is, by measuring their usefulness in real NLP applications.
3. We would like to investigate these tasks in bi- and multilingual contexts, studying how different parameters of the acquisition context, such as language, domain, type of expression and data sources, influence the quality of automatically acquired MWEs.

The motivation behind the first goal is that, currently, many punctual techniques and tools exist that focus on a small, *well defined* task. We believe that the time has come to systematise and unify these experimental approaches into a single and generic methodological framework. This framework has a proof-of-concept companion software tool, implementing all steps in the MWE acquisition pipeline (e.g., candidate generation, counting, filtering and evaluation), thus replacing other tools that only perform part of the processing. Available software and open evaluation campaigns are pointed out by Steedman (2008) as two factors that can help determine the maturity of a research field.

The second goal is motivated by our revision of the state of the art. The evaluation of automatic MWE acquisition techniques is a challenge on its own. Evaluation results depend on several factors like MWE type, corpus size, domain, existing lexical resources, among others. On the one hand, we would like to perform a theoretical analysis of the evaluation of MWE acquisition, making explicit the axes that define an acquisition context, the evaluation measures, and the factors determining the generalisation of results. On the other hand, we would like to perform a systematic thorough evaluation of our proposed methodological framework in the context of real applications. We believe that intrinsic evaluation of acquisition results per se, as the final result of a process, can be interesting to compare several techniques and parameters. However, only extrinsic application-based evaluation can effectively prove the usefulness of MWE acquisition.

This brings us to the third goal of our research: multilingual contexts. Multilingualism is an important characteristic of the World Wide Web, which contains a very large amount of information expressed in natural language. Therefore, NLP systems dealing with web texts must be naturally language independent and scalable. In this book, our goal is to develop techniques for the acquisition of MWEs from corpora in many languages. This will allow us, in the future, to extract multilingual MWE correspondences and integrate them into multilingual systems, in particular machine translation.

1.2.3   Guiding Principles

In order to achieve these goals, we follow some guiding principles that characterise and justify our conceptual choices in Chap. 5.

1.2.3.1   Hybrid Acquisition

To date, there is little agreement on methods for acquiring MWEs. There has been much discussion about whether there is a single optimal method for acquiring any MWE type, a combination of methods, or if different methods work better for a given MWE type than for others. Therefore, one of our goals is to investigate the largest possible range of methods to automatically acquire MWEs from corpora, dissecting the influence of the different types of resources employed on the quality of the results. Our philosophy is that we do not want to elect *the* best technique for MWE acquisition, but to investigate a plethora of them, thus developing a naturally hybrid methodological framework which mixes several state-of-the-art techniques.

1.2.3.2 Integrated Processing

Most of recent research on MWE treatment focused on their automatic identification and extraction from textual corpora. Some authors focus on the candidate extraction process from parsed text (Seretan 2008), others on the automatic filtering and ranking through association measures (Evert 2004; Pecina 2010). Nonetheless, few publications provide a whole picture of the MWE treatment pipeline. One of our objectives is to model the MWE acquisition as an integrated process, with modular tasks, each task having several techniques and parameters that can be optimised according to the target MWE types.

1.2.3.3 Generality

Our method should not depend on a fixed length of MWE. Similarly, it should not depend on any adjacency assumption, as the words composing an expression might be several words away from each other in the corpus. The only constraint generally imposed is that word association should not cross sentence boundaries. This constraint could, in theory, be lifted, but it seems to make sense as MWEs do not split over more than one sentence. We consider fixed word order, that is, differently from Church and Hanks (1990) and Smadja (1993), we consider w_1w_2 as being different from w_2w_1, to distinguish cases like *to conform* from *conform to*. When acquiring non fixed collocations like *drastically drop*, it might be interesting to relax the order constraint.

1.2.3.4 Portability

Because the methods we develop are generic, they should be applicable to virtually any language, MWE type and domain, not strictly depending on a given formalism or on the availability of analysis tools.[8] It should be possible to apply our methodology on a very large range of acquisition contexts. For a given language, if analysis tools like POS taggers, lemmatisers and/or parsers are available, their use will probably yield better results than those obtained by running our methods on raw corpus data. Nonetheless, our software and methods were designed to be applicable even when no automatic analysis tool is available at all.

---

[8]However, we do not deal with languages whose writing systems do not use spaces to separate words.

1.2.3.5 Customisation and Scalability

One of the main features of our methodology is that it should be highly customisable. It is not designed as a push-button tool, that is, someone who is not familiar with the domain will not be able to use it without some prior training. As a counterpart, we would like to allow for a large number of parameters to be tuned, and modules could be chained in several different ways. For instance, as opposed to similar tools, it should not be necessary to work only with 2-grams, but working with arbitrarily long n-grams must possible. This does have some implications in terms of the association scores that can be calculated, but we leave this decision for the user: it is not taken a priori during the design of the methodology. This customisation allied with efficient methods to deal with large amounts of data is one of the differences of our framework with respect to similar proposals.

1.2.3.6 Evaluation of MWE Acquisition

Published results comparing MWE acquisition techniques usually evaluate them on small controlled data sets using objective measures such as precision, recall and mean average precision (Schone and Jurafsky 2001; Pearce 2002; Evert and Krenn 2005). On the one hand, the results of *intrinsic evaluation* are often vague or inconclusive. Although they shed some light on the optimal parameters for the given scenario, they are hard to generalise and cannot be directly applied to other configurations. On the other hand, *extrinsic evaluation* consists of inserting acquired MWEs into NLP applications and evaluating the impact of this new data on the overall system performance. For instance, it is easier to ask a human annotator to evaluate the acceptability of a translation than to ask whether a given sequence of words constitutes a MWE. Thus, another original contribution of our research is application-oriented extrinsic evaluation of MWE acquisition on two study cases: computer-aided lexicography and statistical MT. Our goal is to investigate (1) how much MWEs impact on the performance and (2) what are the best ways of integrating them in the complex pipeline of the target application. In addition to evaluation results themselves, we would like to come up with a typology for MWE acquisition evaluation that classifies the evaluation context according to four orthogonal axes: acquisition goals, nature of measures, available resources and type of MWE (see Sect. 4.1.1).

1.2.3.7 Available Software

In academic research, one often needs to re-implement techniques described in an article, mostly because it was either not implemented in a consistent software piece or because the software was not made available. Therefore, one of our goals is to provide a usable and downloadable tool for MWE acquisition, analysis and evaluation. This tool, called mwetoolkit, is a practical and concrete contribution of our work. To the best of our knowledge, there are few similar tools available. These will be compared to our tool in Sect. 5.3. The mwetoolkit covers a larger part of the MWE treatment pipeline, is extensible and open-source, and thus offers advantages over similar software.

1.2.3.8 Available Lexical Resources

As a by-product of our evaluation, we generate lexical resources that can support future NLP research. For instance, the lexical resources resulting from the work described in Chap. 6 are available on the MWE community website.[9] They are, namely, a lexicon of nominal MWEs in Greek and a lexicon of complex predicates in Brazilian Portuguese. In addition, further resources have been developed using our framework, like a version of the English Childes corpus annotated with phrasal verbs (Villavicencio et al. 2012) and a set of parallel English-French sentences annotated with phrasal verbs (Ramisch et al. 2013a). The list of lexical resources built with the help of our framework keeps growing as these lines are being written. Since such resources are freely available, they can be extended, enriched and applied to develop NLP applications, foreign language *e*-learning systems, and can more generally be used as resources for ground research in MWE acquisition (Grégoire et al. 2008).

1.3   Chapters Outline

This book is structured into eight chapters. Chapters 1–3 are intended as a generic introduction to MWEs, discussing fundamental linguistic and computational concepts, methods, state of the art. Chapters 4 and 5 present a methodological framework for automatic MWE acquisition and its evaluation. Chapters 6 and 7 present two experiments that employ the proposed methodology in applicative contexts. Chapter 8 discusses some future directions of our work with respect to what we identify as challenging open problems in MWE processing. The reader should be able to quickly navigate through the chapters and locate parts most interesting to her/him.

In this first introductory chapter, we have presented the motivations of our work, its goals and contributions. Chapter 2 provides the common ground for our research. It starts with a historical review of the MWE field, exploring theoretical and computational perspectives in both academic and industrial research. MWE definitions found in the literature vary from very generic ones to definitions covering a single aspect of the phenomenon. Therefore, we adopt a generic, application-oriented definition, that can be instantiated according to the context. MWEs are a recurrent and heterogeneous phenomenon, presenting varying degrees of syntactic

---

[9]http://multiword.sf.net

and semantic fixedness. Thus, we present and discuss these characteristics and suggest a typology based both on their morphosyntactic categories and on the difficulty to treat them in computational applications.

In the field of computational linguistics, MWEs have gained increasing popularity in the last decades. There is a vast body of published work witnessing this progression. Chapter 3 is dedicated to drawing a state of the art of automatic MWE processing techniques. For the sake of completeness, we first introduce some elementary concepts, like notions of linguistic analysis, word frequency distributions, n-grams and association measures. Users familiar with such concepts might want to skip this first section of the chapter. The remainder of the chapter is divided into two sections: first, we discuss several proposed techniques for MWE acquisition, and second, we briefly describe other NLP tasks involving MWE treatment, namely interpretation, disambiguation, representation and applications.

The goal of Chap. 4 is to emphasise the difficult and challenging nature of the evaluation of MWE acquisition. We introduce a new classification that describes the evaluation context through four orthogonal axes. The measures such as precision and recall, as well as the annotation guidelines provided to the human judges, are described in detail. Evaluation results depend on several factors such as corpus size, corpus nature, level of preprocessing, type of MWE, language, domain and existing resources. Thus, results are often difficult to interpret and generalise. This fact motivates the use of extrinsic rather than intrinsic evaluation, as described later in Chaps. 6 and 7.

This book presents a new methodological framework and a corresponding software tool called `mwetoolkit`, aimed at automatic acquisition of MWEs from corpora. Its modules are presented and discussed in Chap. 5, which can be complemented by the software documentation found on the website.[10] In addition to a detailed description of the modules and of how they can be combined, we present a pedagogical experiment in which we go step by step, extracting MWEs from a toy corpus. There are some similar freely available tools, and we compare the `mwetoolkit` with them in terms of linguistic quality, use of computational resources and flexibility.

Extrinsic evaluations of the proposed methodology are performed in Chaps. 6 and 7. In the former, we evaluate it in the context of computer-aided lexicography, showing how it helps in the creation of several lexical resources. These lexical resources are a dictionary of nominal MWEs in Greek and two dictionaries of complex predicates in Brazilian Portuguese, one aimed at semantic role labelling (CP-SRL) and the other aimed at automatic sentiment analysis (CP-SENT).

We start Chap. 7 with a brief review of statistical machine translation. Again, users familiar with this subject can skip this first section. The next section provides a discussion of current approaches to MWEs in existing MT systems. Then, we show our experiments on the evaluation and integration of verbal expressions into an English–French SMT system. We chose this language pair in order to study the

---

[10]http://mwetoolkit.sf.net

asymmetries that arise when MWEs in one language (phrasal verbs in English) are translated as simple words (single verbs in French). At the end of this more practical chapter, we discuss further directions for MWE integration into MT.

The reader will find in Chap. 8 the conclusions which summarise the work presented in the book. The promising results obtained in our experiments allow us to discuss the future directions and long-term goals of our research. We finish by discussing some of the current challenges and open problems in the area of MWE processing.

Significant changes were made during the adaptation of the original thesis manuscript into this book. First, as the topic of this book is a very active research area, we updated the references and description of the state of the art. Second, corrections and improvements were made, specially in the first chapters, in order to provide more complete textbook material on multiword expressions. Third, we included additional examples, like those in Sect. 1.1, and extra experimental results, specially in Chap. 7. Fourth, we updated Chap. 5 to reflect the last improvements and optimisations in the mwetoolkit. Part of the work presented in this book has been previously published in scientific conferences, workshops and journals. These are indicated and included in the references. Co-authors are acknowledged in the preface.

1.4   Summary

Multiword expressions are a hard and open problem in natural language processing, due to their complex nature. The question of what counts as a MWE is a polemic one. Put simply, MWEs are habitual recurrent word combinations of everyday language (Firth 1957). Probably the most prototypical types of MWEs are idiomatic expressions like *loan shark, stand on someone's feet, cut someone a break, buy someone some time, save someone's breath, French kiss,* and *open mind.* In addition to idiomatic expressions, other constructions can be seen as MWEs, like noun compounds (*vacuum cleaner, voice mail, high heel shoe*) and verbal expressions (*make sense, take advantage, take a shower, take for granted*).

Native speakers rarely realise it, but colloquial speech is full of formulaic expressions such as *good morning, my bad, too bad* and *bye bye.* It is often assumed that a native speakers' lexicon contains as many MWEs as simple words (Jackendoff 1997). Any computational system dealing with human language must take MWEs into account. In numerous NLP applications, when the words composing a MWE are treated as separate units, this can induce the system to produce erroneous output. Taking MWEs into account can be complicated for traditional NLP applications, as MWEs lie in a fuzzy zone between the lexicon and the syntax of a language. The availability of tools and resources containing MWEs is still limited, contrasting with the ubiquitous and pervasive nature of MWEs. As a consequence, there is a need for developing, consolidating and evaluating techniques for the automatic acquisition of MWEs from corpora.

This book addresses the problem of MWE treatment in NLP applications, ranging from automatic acquisition to integration into two real-life applications. In addition to providing textbook material on MWEs in the first chapters, we will present a new conceptual model for the pipeline of MWE treatment, as well as a concrete software framework that validates the proposed methodology. We can summarise its goals and guiding principles as follows:

1. To propose and combine generic and portable techniques for automatic MWE acquisition from corpora.
2. To evaluate these techniques extrinsically, that is, by measuring their usefulness in NLP applications.
3. To investigate these tasks in multilingual contexts, studying how different parameters of the acquisition context influence the quality of automatically acquired MWEs.

References

Biber D, Johansson S, Leech G, Conrad S, Finegan E (1999) Longman grammar of spoken and written English, 1st edn. Pearson Education, Harlow, 1204p

Church K, Hanks P (1990) Word association norms mutual information, and lexicography. Comput Linguist 16(1):22–29

Constant M, Roux JL, Sigogne A (2013) Combining compound recognition and PCFG-LA parsing with word lattices and conditional random fields. ACM Trans Speech Lang Process Spec Issue Multiword Expr Theory Pract Use Part 2 (TSLP) 10(3):1–24

Evert S (2004) The statistics of word cooccurrences: word pairs and collocations. PhD thesis, Institut für maschinelle Sprachverarbeitung, University of Stuttgart, Stuttgart, 353p

Evert S, Krenn B (2005) Using small random samples for the manual evaluation of statistical association measures. Comput Speech Lang Spec Issue MWEs 19(4):450–466

Ferraro G, Nazar R, Ramos MA, Wanner L (2014) Towards advanced collocation error correction in Spanish learner corpora. Lang Resour Eval Spec Issue Resour Lang Learn 48(1):45–64. doi:10.1007/s10579-013-9242-3, http://dx.doi.org/10.1007/s10579-013-9242-3

Finlayson M, Kulkarni N (2011) Detecting multi-word expressions improves word sense disambiguation. In: Kordoni V, Ramisch C, Villavicencio A (eds) Proceedings of the ALC workshop on multiword expressions: from parsing and generation to the real world (MWE 2011), Portland. Association for Computational Linguistics, pp 20–24. http://www.aclweb.org/anthology/W/W11/W11-0805

Firth JR (1957) Papers in linguistics 1934-1951. Oxford University Press, Oxford, 233p

Gala N, Zock M (eds) (2013) Ressources Lexicales : Contenu, construction, utilisation, évaluation. No. 30 in Lingvisticæ Investigationes Supplementa, John Benjamins Publishing Company, Amsterdam/Philadelphia, 364p

Green S, de Marneffe MC, Bauer J, Manning CD (2011) Multiword expression identification with tree substitution grammars: a parsing tour de force with French. In: Barzilay R, Johnson M (eds) Proceedings of the 2011 conference on empirical methods in natural language processing (EMNLP 2011), Edinburgh. Association for Computational Linguistics, pp 725–735. http://www.aclweb.org/anthology/D11-1067

Grégoire N, Evert S, Krenn B (eds) (2008) Proceedings of the LREC workshop towards a shared task for multiword expressions (MWE 2008), Marrakech, 57p. http://www.lrec-conf.org/proceedings/lrec2008/workshops/W20_Proceedings.pdf

Jackendoff R (1997) Twistin' the night away. Language 73:534–559

Klebanov BB, Burstein J, Madnani N (2013) Sentiment profiles of multiword expressions in test-taker essays: the case of noun-noun compounds. ACM Trans Speech Lang Process Spec Issue Multiword Expr Theory Practice Use Part 2 (TSLP) 10(3):1–15

Kordoni V, Ramisch C, Villavicencio A (eds) (2011) Proceedings of the ACL workshop on multiword expressions: from parsing and generation to the real world (MWE 2011), Portland. Association for Computational Linguistics, 144p. http://www.aclweb.org/anthology/W/W11/W11-08

Kordoni V, Ramisch C, Villavicencio A (eds) (2013) Proceedings of the 9th workshop on multiword expressions (MWE 2013), Atlanta. Association for Computational Linguistics, 144p. http://www.aclweb.org/anthology/W13-10

Kordoni V, Savary A, Egg M, Wehrli E, Evert S (eds) (2014) Proceedings of the 10th workshop on multiword expressions (MWE 2014), Gothenburg. Association for Computational Linguistics, 133p. http://www.aclweb.org/anthology/W14-08

Messiant C, Poibeau T, Korhonen A (2008) Lexschem: a large subcategorization lexicon for French verbs. In: Proceedings of the sixth international conference on language resources and evaluation (LREC 2008), Marrakech. European Language Resources Association, pp 533–538

Mirroshandel SA, Nasr A, Roux JL (2012) Semi-supervised dependency parsing using lexical affinities. In: Proceedings of the 50th annual meeting of the association for computational linguistics (volume 1: long papers), Jeju Island. Association for Computational Linguistics, pp 777–785. http://www.aclweb.org/anthology/P12-1082

Mitkov R, Monti J, Pastor GC, Seretan V (eds) (2013) Proceedings of the MT summit 2013 workshop on multi-word units in machine translation and translation technology (MUMTTT 2013), Nice. European Association for Machine Translation, 71p. http://www.mtsummit2013.info/workshop4.asp

Pearce D (2002) A comparative evaluation of collocation extraction techniques. In: Proceedings of the third international conference on language resources and evaluation (LREC 2002), Las Palmas. European Language Resources Association, pp 1530–1536

Pecina P (2010) Lexical association measures and collocation extraction. Lang Resour Eval Spec Issue Multiword Expr Hard Going Plain Sail 44(1–2):137–158. doi:10.1007/s10579-009-9101-4, http://www.springerlink.com/content/DRH83N312U658331

Preiss J, Briscoe T, Korhonen A (2007) A system for large-scale acquisition of verbal, nominal and adjectival subcategorization frames from corpora. In: Proceedings of the 45th annual meeting of the association for computational linguistics (ACL 2007), Prague. Association for Computational Linguistics, pp 912–919

Procter P (ed) (1995) Cambridge international dictionary of English. Cambridge University Press, Cambridge

Ramisch C, Besacier L, Kobzar O (2013a) How hard is it to automatically translate phrasal verbs from English to French? In: Mitkov R, Monti J, Pastor GC, Seretan V (eds) Proceedings of the MT summit 2013 workshop on multi-word units in machine translation and translation technology (MUMTTT 2013), Nice, pp 53–61. http://www.mtsummit2013.info/workshop4.asp

Ramisch C, Villavicencio A, Kordoni V (2013b) Introduction to the special issue on multiword expressions: from theory to practice and use. ACM Trans Speech Lang Process Spec Issue Multiword Expr Theory Pract Use Part 1 (TSLP) 10(2):1–10

Schone P, Jurafsky D (2001) Is knowledge-free induction of multiword unit dictionary headwords a solved problem? In: Lee L, Harman D (eds) Proceedings of the 2001 conference on empirical methods in natural language processing (EMNLP 2001), Pittsburgh. Association for Computational Linguistics, pp 100–108

Seretan V (2008) Collocation extraction based on syntactic parsing. PhD thesis, University of Geneva, Geneva, 249p

Seretan V (2011) Syntax-based collocation extraction, text, speech and language technology, vol 44, 1st edn. Springer, Dordrecht, 212p

Seretan V (2013) On translating syntactically-flexible expressions. In: Mitkov R, Monti J, Pastor GC, Seretan V (eds) Proceedings of the MT summit 2013 workshop on multi-word units in machine translation and translation technology (MUMTTT 2013), Nice, pp 11–11

Sinclair J (ed) (1989) Collins COBUILD dictionary of phrasal verbs. Collins COBUILD, London, 512p

Smadja FA (1993) Retrieving collocations from text: Xtract. Comput Linguist 19(1):143–177

Steedman M (2008) On becoming a discipline. Comput Linguist 34(1):137–144

Szpakowicz S, Bond F, Nakov P, Kim SN (2013) On the semantics of noun compounds. Nat Lang Eng Spec Issue Noun Compd 19(3):289–290. doi:10.1017/S1351324913000090, http://journals.cambridge.org/article_S1351324913000090

Termignoni S (2009) Mil expressões idiomáticas e coloqualismos Italiano-Português. Editora da PUCRS, Porto Alegre, 172p

Villavicencio A, Idiart M, Ramisch C, Araujo VD, Yankama B, Berwick R (2012) Get out but don't fall down: verb-particle constructions in child language. In: Berwick R, Korhonen A, Poibeau T, Villavicencio A (eds) Proceedings of the EACL 2012 workshop on computational models of language acquisition and loss, Avignon. Association for Computational Linguistics, pp 43–50

Walter E (ed) (2006) Cambridge idioms dictionary, 2nd edn. Cambridge University Press, Cambridge, 519p

Part I
Multiword Expressions: A Tough Nut to Crack

Chapter 2
Definitions and Characteristics

In this chapter, we discuss definitions and properties of MWEs and we present a brief introduction to the research field of automatic MWE treatment. Although we include pointers toward linguistic and psycholinguistic studies, most of the related work cited in this chapter has a strong computational background.

As motivated in Chap. 1, the computational treatment of MWEs is a tough problem. However, it does not constitute a new problem neither in linguistics nor in computational linguistics. Therefore, Sect. 2.4 starts with a brief overview of the history of the field, discussing some seminal papers and works that built on them.

Section 2.2 provides a set of popular definitions for the term "multiword expression", which will engender the definition adopted by us. We close this section on a clarification note about the similarities and differences between MWEs, idioms, phraseology, collocations and terms.

In Sect. 2.3, we describe some linguistic properties of MWEs, including many examples based on linguistic intuition and coming from corpora. We complement this discussion with a presentation of existing taxonomies for MWE types and a suggestion of a new classification which groups similar constructions in terms of their morphosyntactic category and difficulty to process automatically.

Finally, Sect. 2.4 discusses current trends and provides a snapshot of the MWE research landscape. This brief presentation paves the ground for a more detailed state of the art on MWE treatment, which is the subject of Chap. 3.

2.1 A Brief History

The study of MWEs is almost as old as linguistics itself. Traditional generative linguistic studies presented an idealised point of view in which language phenomena can be formally classified into *lexical* or *syntactic* levels, as in formal languages. The *lexical level* considers words as separate units, independently of their neighbour

© Springer International Publishing Switzerland 2015
C. Ramisch, *Multiword Expressions Acquisition*, Theory and Applications
of Natural Language Processing, DOI 10.1007/978-3-319-09207-2_2

words. It deals with questions such as morphology, inflection (e.g., number, gender, verb tense), word formation (prefixes, suffixes) and lexical semantics (the meanings of a word). The main object of lexical studies is the lexicon, that is, the set of lexical units used in a language, and its description, which constitutes a dictionary. The *syntactic level* deals with word order in natural language utterances. Grammars are used to formalise the rules that govern the position of words and phrases, and how they can be combined. Syntax studies investigate, for instance, the place of epithet adjectives with respect to their corresponding noun, and the order of verb, subject and object in languages.

However, when trying to classify linguistic phenomena into either lexical or syntactic, one realises that some of them, and in particular MWEs, lie in between these two levels. Therefore, linguistic and computational approaches to grammar need to include MWE representations in their models. In what follows, we present some of the linguistic and computational work that gave origin to the current research field of MWEs.

2.1.1 Theoretical Linguistics

In the traditional generative grammatical framework, the representation of idioms poses a challenge. For example, the English idiom *first off* is an adverbial locution synonym to *firstly*, that is, before anything else. The information about the morphosyntactic category and meaning of each of these two words taken individually, *first* and *off*, is contained in the lexicon. However, by combining them, it is impossible to guess the syntactic category and the meaning of the idiom as a whole. Moreover, general syntax rules of English formally forbid to combine an adjective/adverb with a preposition in order to form an adverbial phrase. This would make us consider such idioms as a single lexical unit containing a space. However, other constructions such as *spill the beans* also have idiomatic meaning, but they conform to general syntactic rules (for example, the verb can be inflected). Should one consider all possible inflections as separate lexical units, thus filling the lexicon with redundancy? Should one represent it in the grammar as separate entries, thus supposing that the idiom allows free modification according to general syntactic rules?

Such grammar engineering questions show that there are limitations in the structural approach to language à la Chomsky and Tesnière. One of the seminal papers of the *construction grammar* trend is the work of Fillmore et al. (1988). They illustrate and discuss in detail the weaknesses of the idealised atomistic approach to grammar, arguing that:

> As useful and powerful as the atomistic schema is for the description of linguistic competence, it doesn't allow the grammarian to account for absolutely everything in its terms. [...] the descriptive linguist needs to append to this maximally general machinery certain kinds of special knowledge—knowledge that will account for speakers' ability to construct and understand phrases and expressions in their language which are not covered

by the grammar, the lexicon and the principles of compositional semantics, as these are familiarly conceived. Such a list of exceptional phenomena contains things which are larger than words, which are like words in that they have to be learned separately as individual whole facts about pieces of the language, [...] (Fillmore et al. 1988, p. 504)

Construction grammar suggests that there must be an appendix to the set of lexical units and syntactic rules of a language's model. This appendix is a repository containing a large amount of *idiomatic* entries and their specific syntactic, semantic and pragmatic characteristics. Idioms become thus part of the core of the grammar: a language can be fully described by its idioms and their properties. These idioms correspond to what we call MWEs in this book.

In *corpus linguistics*, MWEs play a central role. According to Sinclair (1991), language production is guided by two principles: the *open-choice principle* and the *idiom principle*. While the former explains productivity, as speakers can combine many possible lexical units to express some information, the latter constrains this choice in the sense that some of these units are prefabricated. Thus, while some constructions allow free variation, others cannot have their members modified to some extent (like *strong tea* vs *?powerful tea*).

Another linguistic theory that gives much importance to MWEs is the *meaning-text theory* (MTT). This theory proposes a rigorous description of the lexicon in the form of an explanatory combinatorial dictionary (Mel'čuk et al. 1984, 1988, 1992, 1999). Mel'čuk et al. (1995, p. 17) state that "exaggerating a little, we could even say that the set of lexies [the lexicon] *is* the language."[1]

According to Mel'čuk and Polguère (1987), a dictionary entry contains three zones: (i) the semantic zone, (ii) the syntactic zone, and (iii) the lexical combinatorics zone. MWEs are present at two points of the computational MTT model: as *phrasemes* and as lexico-semantic functions (LSF) in the *lexical combinatorics zone*. The head of an entry in the explanatory combinatorial dictionary is a "lexie", that is, a lexeme or a phraseme used with a specific meaning. This second type of entry, the phraseme, represents a fixed expression that needs to be described as a separate lexical unit, in spite of the fact that it is composed of more than one word. Phrasemes are more rigid MWEs that only allow very low or no morphosyntactic flexibility. The second type of MWE present in the explanatory combinatorial dictionary is in the lexical combinatorics zone. The latter contains a set of LSFs describing the interactions of the described lexical unit with other lexical units. A lexico-semantic function can be, for instance, the diminution of a word: in order to say that the *rain* is not intense, one uses the adjectives *light* or *thin*, thus **AntiMagn**(*rain*) = {*light, thin*}. The content of the lexical combinatorics zone in the explanatory combinatorial dictionary is what linguists usually describe as *collocations*, that is, habitual or conventional words that are used together with

---

[1]En exagérant quelque peu, on pourrait même dire que l'ensemble des lexies [le lexique] *est* la langue.

the target lexical unit.[2] Mel'čuk et al. (1995, p. 46) explain the difference between phrasemes and collocations as follows:

> The ECD [Explanatory Combinatorial Dictionary] does not describe all phrasemes in the same way. The *complete phrasemes* [...] and *quasi-phrasemes* [...], that is, the phrasemes that cannot be completely described based on at least one of their constituents, form independent entries — like the lexemes. The *semi-phrasemes* (= *collocations* [...]) are described under the entry of one of their constituents — through what we call lexical functions.[3]

Psycholinguistic and cognitive linguistics have also shown interest in MWEs. Research in language acquisition proposes cognitively plausible models for the acquisition of MWE knowledge from exposure to language. Thus, there has been work on learning verb-particle constructions (Villavicencio et al. 2012), noun compounds (Devereux and Costello 2007), light verb constructions (Nematzadeh et al. 2012) and multiword terms (Lavagnino and Park 2010) based on corpora evidence and language learning models. In particular, these models try to validate computational models for MWE acquisition by checking their correlation with experiments that use similar models for human language acquisition (Joyce and Srdanović 2008; Rapp 2008).

For an extensive account of MWEs in different linguistic theories, we recommend the reading of Seretan (2011, p. 20–27), where a quite complete discussion about theoretical linguistic aspects of MWEs can be found.

2.1.2 Computational Linguistics

In computational linguistics, interest in MWEs arose from the availability of very large corpora and of computers capable of analysing them, by the end of the 1980s and beginning of the 1990s. One of the main goals of these first attempts to process MWEs using machines was to build systems for computer-assisted lexicography and terminography of multiword units. Among the seminal papers of the field, one of the most often cited ones is Choueka (1988), who proposed a method for collocation extraction based on *n*-gram statistics. His method extracted sequences of two to six adjacent words, sorting them by number of occurrences. Although simple, this

---

[2]See Sect. 2.2 for a clarification on the difference between MWE and collocation.

[3]Le DEC [Dictionnaire Explicatif Combinatoire] ne décrit pas tous les phrasèmes de la même façon. Les *phrasèmes complets* [...] et les *quasi-phrasèmes* [...], c'est-à-dire les phrasèmes qui ne peuvent pas être complètement décrits en fonction d'au moins un de leurs constituants, forment des entrées indépendantes — tout comme les lexèmes. Les *semi-phrasèmes* (= les *collocations* [...]) sont décrits sous l'entrée d'un de leurs constituants — par ce qu'on appelle les fonctions lexicales.

technique retrieved several interesting expressions and was one of the first attempts to process a very large corpus of 11 million words.

Another ground-breaking work is that of Smadja (1993). He proposed Xtract, a tool for collocation extraction based on some simple POS filters and on mean and standard deviation of word distance. His approach had the advantage of handling non-contiguous constructions. His work was strongly based on the notion of collocation as outstanding co-occurrence. The reported precision on specialised texts was around 80 %.

Church and Hanks (1990) suggested the use of a more sophisticated association measure based on mutual information. They provided theoretical justification for it and then tested it on relatively large corpora for the extraction of terminological and collocational units. Later, Dagan and Church (1994) proposed a terminographic environment called Termight, which used this association score. Termight performed bilingual extraction and provided tools to easily classify candidate terms, find bilingual correspondences, define nested terms and investigate occurrences through a concordancer.

Also in the context of terminographic extraction, Justeson and Katz (1995) proposed a simple approach based on a small set of POS patterns and frequency thresholds. They obtained surprisingly good results given the simplicity of the technique. A pedagogical example of the application of this technique on a corpus is given by Manning and Schütze (1999, p. 156).

The indiscriminate use of association measures was criticised by Dunning (1993). He argued that the assumption underlying most measures is that words are distributed normally, but corpus evidence does not support this hypothesis. Therefore, he proposed a 2-gram measure called *likelihood ratio*. It estimates directly how more likely a 2-gram is than expected by chance. In addition to being theoretically sound, Dunning's score is also easily interpretable. Nowadays, measures based on likelihood ratio (e.g., the log-likelihood score) are still largely employed in several MWE extraction contexts.

Lin (1998b) introduced the use of syntactic dependencies in order to extract candidate collocations restricted to a specific category. In order to filter relevant collocations, he used a measure based on Church and Hank's pointwise mutual information, but adapted it to take syntactic relations into account (Lin 1998a). Later, he proposed the use of a measure based on Dunning's log-likelihood ratio instead (Lin 1999).

At the beginning of the 2000s, the Stanford MWE project[4] has revived interest of the NLP community in this topic. One of the most cited publications of the MWE project is the famous "pain-in-the-neck" paper by Sag et al. (2002). It provided an overview of MWE characteristics and types and then presented some methods for dealing with them in the context of grammar engineering. The Stanford MWE project is also at the origin of the MWE workshop series, which will be presented in Sect. 2.4. The "boom" of publications that followed is covered in Chap. 3.

---

[4]http://mwe.stanford.edu/

2.2 Defining MWEs

MWEs are hard to define. Yet, it is crucial to define them precisely, because evaluation of automatic MWE acquisition depends on the MWE definition adopted. Annotators need to know what they are looking for, otherwise they cannot perform a binary choice of telling whether a word combination constitutes a genuine MWE or just a random word combination. For example, the meaning of the English expression *take a shower* seems fairly compositional. In other words, the meaning of the whole (*take a shower*) is similar to the meaning of the verb (*take*) combined with the meaning of the noun phrase (*a shower*). Therefore, using semantic compositionality as a criterion, this expression would *not be considered as a MWE*.

However, when translated into Italian, a word-for-word translation is impossible as the correct corresponding Italian expression would be *fare la doccia* (lit. *make the shower*) instead of the literal translation *?prendere una doccia*. Therefore, for an MT system, it would be important to *consider this expression as a MWE*. In this section, we present and discuss the coverage of some classical definitions of MWE, concluding on the definition adopted in this work.

2.2.1 What Is a Word?

Before we start to explore the jungle of multi*word* expression definitions, we must define what we consider to be a *word*. Behind this apparently simple question, there are deep theoretical questions and there is little agreement on the answer. For instance, Mel'čuk et al. (1995, p. 15) say that "we know the restive character of the word *word*, which, to date, has escaped the attempts to circumscribe it with precision although much has been written about this subject throughout the decades."[5]

As pointed out by Manning and Schütze (1999, p. 125), "the question of what counts as a word is a vexed one in linguistics, and often linguists end up suggesting that there are words at various levels". They suggest to simply yet operationally define graphic words as "contiguous alphanumeric characters with spaces on either side". However, this definition poses several problems in English for tokens involving hyphens (*language-independent approach*), punctuation (*google.com, US$ 1,299.99*), contractions (*do not* as *'don't*). In languages other than English, this definition is not suitable. For example, the writing systems of many Asian languages, like Chinese and Japanese, do not use whitespace between words at all. Noun compounds in many languages, like German, Swedish and sometimes in English, tend to be concatenated together as a single word (*snowman, wallpaper*). Other morphologically rich languages like Turkish and Finnish tend to form new words by appending lexical units rather than using spaces. In short, defining words

---

[5]on connaît tout aussi bien le caractère rétif du mot *mot*, qui, jusqu'à présent, a échappé aux tentatives de le circonscrire avec précision et a fait couler beaucoup d'encre pendant des décennies.

in terms of whitespace as a separator depends on morphology, writing systems and conventions, and is not always suitable.

We adopt the definition by Evert (2004), who considers a "word as an entirely generic term which may refer to any kind of lexical item, depending on the underlying theory or intended application." We should justify that the term "multiword" is very popular, and it is therefore used throughout this book. Nonetheless, strictly speaking, we should refer to "multilexeme" expressions, as we prefer to define them as composed of multiple *lexemes*, rather than of multiple *words*.

Lexemes, in turn, are lexical items (or units) who constitute the basic blocks of a language's lexicon. They are the minimal linguistic units that convey a meaning. Therefore, morphological affixes like the final *-s* in English plural nouns or the final *-ing* in gerund verbs are lexical units which are not lexemes themselves, and morphologically inflected units do not constitute new lexemes with respect to their canonical forms (lemmas). On the other hand, lexical items like nouns, verbs and prepositions are lexemes as they do convey one (or several) meanings. A useful test to decide whether a given lexical item is a lexeme is to ask whether it should be listed as a headword in a dictionary.

2.2.2 What Is a MWE?

The notion of MWE has its origin in Firth's famous quotation "you shall know a word by the company it keeps". He affirms that "collocations of a given word are statements of the habitual and customary places of that word" (Firth 1957, p. 181).

Analogously, Smadja (1993) considers collocations as "arbitrary and recurrent word combinations". The definition adopted by Choueka (1988) focuses on non-compositionality; for him, a collocation is "a syntactic and semantic unit whose exact and unambiguous meaning or connotation cannot be derived directly from the meaning or connotation of its components".

For Fillmore et al. (1988, p. 504), non-compositionality is also the main property of MWEs, as "an idiomatic expression or construction is something a language user could fail to know while knowing everything else in the language", that is, that cannot be modelled using general lexical knowledge, grammatical rules and compositional semantics. Sag et al. (2002) generalise this same property to roughly define MWEs as "idiosyncratic interpretations that cross word boundaries (or spaces)".

In some publications, the authors do not define MWEs, but instead enumerate examples. For instance, the special issue on MWEs of the Language Resources and Evaluation journal (Rayson et al. 2010) starts as follows:

MWEs range over linguistic constructions such as idioms (*a frog in the throat, kill some time*), fixed phrases (*per se, by and large, rock'n roll*), noun compounds (*telephone booth, cable car*), compound verbs (*give a presentation, go by [a name]*), etc.

This enumeration may be well suited, specially because this is not a closed class and new interpretations of linguistic phenomena may create "new" types of MWEs, like the discourse relation markers suggested by Joshi (2010).

The list of MWE definitions provided here is far from being complete. A broad inventory of definitions is provided in appendix B of Seretan (2008, p. 182–184). All of them make sense, and are valid in a given context. However, the definition of MWE adopted will influence the evaluation results, as it will be used to write annotation guidelines and/or to select reference lists (see Sect. 4.1.1). Even if choosing only one definition is tricky, it is absolutely necessary.

Our definition of MWE is based on the one proposed by (Baldwin and Kim 2010):

Multiword expressions are lexical items that: (a) can be decomposed into multiple lexemes; and (b) display lexical, syntactic, semantic, pragmatic and/or statistical idiomaticity.

The first interesting aspect of this definition is that MWEs are defined in terms of lexemes, and not in terms of words. This allows the inclusion of lexical items like joint noun compounds (e.g. *database*, *notebook*, *whitespace*) regardless of orthographic conventions like the use of whitespace and hyphens. It clarifies many of the problems discussed in Sect. 2.2.1.

The second interesting aspect is related to the notion of *idiomaticity*. In linguistics, this term generally denotes some particularity of a language or dialect with respect to a given standard. However, we employ this term in a more generic sense. For us, it means any idiosyncratic behaviour that deviates from standard composition rules, resulting in unpredictable combinations. For instance, at the semantic level, idiomaticity happens when the meaning of the parts (*dry + run*) do not add up to the meaning of the expression (*dry run*). Semantically idiomatic MWEs are often referred to as *idioms*.

While semantic idiomaticity is probably the most emphasised characteristic of MWEs, Baldwin and Kim (2010) underline several other levels in which idiomaticity can occur. For example, a MWE like *ad hoc* is composed by lexical items that do not occur as standalone headwords in a lexicon (*ad* and *hoc*). Hence, we can talk about *lexical idiomaticity*. *Syntactic idiomaticity*, on the other hand, occurs when we combine lexical items in ways that seem to breach syntactic rules, like in *first off* and *kingdom come*. This is also known as extra-grammaticality (see Sect. 2.3) In short, we see every linguistic analysis level as a continuum ranging from completely compositional (predictable) to highly idiomatic (unpredictable) behaviour. Lexeme combinations in which at least one linguistic level tends toward the idiomatic end of the range are MWEs. This property is further discussed in Sect. 2.3.1.

While the definition by Baldwin and Kim (2010) is linguistically precise, it does not say anything about systems processing MWEs. Therefore, we would also like to discuss the definition by Calzolari et al. (2002), who define MWEs as:

[...] different but related phenomena [...]. At the level of greatest generality, all of these phenomena can be described as a sequence of words[6] that acts as a single unit at some level of linguistic analysis.

This generic and intentionally vague definition can be narrowed down according to the application needs. For example, for the MT system used in the examples shown in Table 1.1, a MWE is any sequence of words which, when not translated as a unit, generates errors or unnatural output.

Another concrete example: when translating technical documentation of the technology domain, should filenames and paths containing spaces be considered as MWEs? In theory, no, as they are not true "words" in general language. However, before running an MT system, a preprocessing step must identify such cases in order to keep them untranslated and/or post-process them after translation. They are sort of "easy" MWEs because simple patterns based on regular expressions can detect them (e.g., most email clients detect URLs in the messages you write). From the point of view of this work, at some level of processing these items need to be treated as a unit. Therefore, they can be considered as MWEs.

To summarise, our definition of MWEs is a combination of the two previous definitions:

Definition 2.1 (Multiword expression). MWEs are lexical items that:

1. Are decomposable into multiple lexemes,
2. Present idiomatic behaviour at some level of linguistic analysis and, as a consequence,
3. Must be treated as a unit at some level of computational processing.

The level at which a combination of lexemes needs to be treated as a unit varies, according to the system's architecture and specially according to the kind of idiomaticity presented by the MWE. In a real sentence analysis system, for instance, fixed expressions such as *ad hoc* and *by and large* will probably constitute lexical entries on their own, while more flexible constructions like *take off* and *bus stop* will be dealt with as a unit during syntactic parsing and more non-compositional constructions like *kick the bucket* are likely to be treated during semantic processing.

2.2.3 A Note on Terminology

At this point, a clarification on the nomenclature adopted is required. In the preceding definitions, we used the terms *collocation*, *idiom* and *multiword expression*. In the literature, these terms are commonly and sometimes interchangeably employed, with no unique definition as both theoretical and computational linguists did not

---

[6]Although this definition refers to *sequences of words*, thus assuming that MWEs are contiguous, we prefer to seem them as word *combinations* or *groups* for greater generality.

reach a consensus to date. Actually, there are slight differences between them, from our point of view.

The term *idiom* is generally employed in the construction grammar tradition[7] to denote a combination of words with non-compositional semantics. In other words, an idiom is a combination whose meaning cannot be predicted by applying general rules to combine the meaning of the individual words (Fillmore et al. 1988). The degree of non-compositionality of an idiom may vary in a continuum from almost transparent idioms to completely opaque ones.

The notion of *collocation*, however, does not depend as much on semantic compositionality as it does on co-occurrence. Combinations such as *heavy rain*, *strong coffee* and *drop drastically* are prototypical examples of collocations. In many linguistic theories and, in particular, in meaning-text theory,[8] the term *collocation* expresses a combination of words usually appearing together in a given language (Mel'čuk et al. 1995). Collocations correspond to the usual way of expressing something in a language. Formally, for a target *base* word, there is a set of usual *collocates* that modify and disambiguate it (Yarowsky 2001).

Another related notion is *phraseology*. Phraseological or formulaic units are closely related to collocations. Phraseology is frequently mentioned in the context of terminological and specialised language studies, like scientific and technical texts (Krieger and Finatto 2004). They do not necessarily have a well defined linguistic status, and may be composed of large text chunks that occur frequently in a given sublanguage. An example of long phraseological unit in the stock exchange domain is the template sentence *The Dow Jones average of 30 industrials fell NUMBER points to NUMBER* (Smadja 1993).

It is worth noting that, while the term *collocation* has been used for a long time in linguistics and also in the beginning of the 1990s in computational linguistics, the term *multiword expression* has gained popularity in the beginning of the 2000s after the seminal "pain in the neck" article by Sag et al. (2002) and the Stanford MWE project.[9] Thus, the term *multiword expression* (or *multiword unit*) is more popular in computational linguistics. It represents a generalisation in the sense that it covers linguistic phenomena that cross the borders between words without being compositional combinations (Sag et al. 2002). As in Sag et al. (2002), we will assume that "the term collocation [refers] to any statistically significant co-occurrence, including all forms of MWE". That is, the notion of collocation is corpus-dependent and encompasses the notion of MWE. However, there are collocations (e.g., *doctor—nurse*) that are not MWEs because they breach the property that a MWE "has to be listed in a lexicon" (Evert 2004, p. 17). The term MWE seems to be the most generic one and matches the goals of the present work, therefore this will be the term employed from now on. However, in the quotations above, we kept the original denominations for the sake of coherency with the source.

---

[7]See Sect. 2.4.

[8]See Sect. 2.4.

[9]http://mwe.stanford.edu/

A definition related to MWEs in the context of domain-specific texts is that of *term* (Cabré 1992):

Definition 2.2 (Term). A terminology is a specialised lexicon corresponding to the set of words that characterise a specialised language of a domain. A term is the basic lexical unit of a terminology.

MWEs and terms have some similar aspects: both have non-conventional semantics and both are a challenge for NLP systems. Manning and Schütze (1999, p. 152) point out that:

> There is considerable overlap between the concept of collocation and notions like *term*, *technical term* and *terminological phrase*. As these names suggest, the latter three are commonly used when collocations are extracted from a technical domain (in a process called terminology extraction). The reader should be warned, though, that the word *term* has a different meaning in information retrieval. There, it refers to both words and phrases. So it subsumes the more narrow meaning that we will use.

From the point of view of the present work, there are several differences between MWEs and terms, not only epistemologically, but also pragmatically. First, terms may be either simple (single-word) or multiword units like nominal and verbal locutions, whereas MWEs are inherently composed of two or more lexemes. Second, MWEs occur in both technical/scientific language and in general-purpose everyday language while terms occur only in the former. Even though the sharp distinction between general and specialised communication has been questioned, the difference is important here because the available computational methods to deal with MWEs in general-purpose texts are potentially different from methods to handle specialised corpora and terminology. *Multiword terms* (MWT) lie in the intersection between terms and MWEs (SanJuan et al. 2005; Frantzi et al. 2000; Ramisch 2009):

Definition 2.3 (Multiword term). A multiword term is a specialised lexical unit composed of two or more lexemes, and whose properties cannot be directly inferred by a non-expert from its parts because they depend on the specialised domain and on the concept it describes.

Notice that this definition is essentially different from what terminologists consider to be a *phraseological expression* like in *to initiate a remote digital loopback test*. Phraseological expressions are much more related to specialised collocations than to our conception of MWT. Specialised phraseology deals with more complex constructions that often involve more than one domain-specific concept, and are often seen as intermediary entities between terms and institutionalised sentences. We, on the other hand, consider a MWT as a multiword lexical representation of an abstract term, but sharing with the latter the same properties of monosemy and limited variability. In other words, a MWT, as well as a single-word term, is a lexical manifestation of a specialised concept.

2.3   Characteristics and Characterisations

As for almost everything else—and as a consequence of the fact that there is no
unique definition for the concept of MWE—there is also no unique taxonomy to
organise them into classes presenting similar characteristics. However, the literature
reports several attempts to typify MWEs based mostly on their syntactic and
semantic idiosyncrasies. In this section, we first present some characteristics of
MWEs (Sects. 2.3.1 and 2.3.2). Then, we summarise several proposals of hierarchical classification for MWE types (Sect. 2.3.3). Finally, we present our own rough
classes used in this work (Sect. 2.3.4). Our typology is based on the morphosyntactic
role of the whole expression in a sentence and on the degree of difficulty to treat
them in NLP systems. Wherever possible, we explicit the link between "our" classes
and the cited classification propositions.

2.3.1   The Compositionality Continuum

Describing human language with a generic theoretical model is undoubtedly an
open question. However, most linguists will agree that it is possible to define some
analysis levels which describe different types of linguistic phenomena. For instance,
word formation and inflection are phenomena that can be described at the *lexical*
level. Word order and grammar rules are dealt with during *syntactic* processing.
Everything related to meaning is a matter for *semantics*, and so on.

At each level of linguistic processing, it is possible to infer general rules from
observed data. This is what non-native speakers and children do all the time when
they learn a language. For instance, if we take the English words *car*, *dog* and *tree*,
their plurals are *cars*, *dogs* and *trees*. Thus, we may infer that the general rule for
plural in English is adding a final *-s* suffix. When these rules deal with more than
one lexeme, we talk about *compositionality*. In other words, compositionality is
the power of predicting the characteristics (semantics, syntax, etc.) of a group of
lexemes based on the application of standard composition rules on the individual
lexemes.

However, human languages are not as structured and "well behaved" as artificial
languages. Even though there are rules, many exceptions exist, and a certain
degree of freedom is allowed. For instance, the semantic compositionality rule for
adjective-noun combinations would say that the meaning of the noun is modified by
adding a property or state described by the adjective, like a *yellow dress* is a *dress*
whose colour property is *yellow*. However, the same is not true for *dry run*. A *dry
run* is not a *run* with the property of being *dry*, but it actually means a rehearsal or
test. When a group of lexemes must use a specific, idiomatic rule to be processed,
we talk about *idiomaticity*. Table 2.1 shows some examples of constructions and the
corresponding idiomaticities.

Table 2.1 Examples of expressions and their respective idiomaticity levels. Inspired on a similar table by Baldwin and Kim (2010)

	lexical	syntactic	semantic	pragmatic	statistical
bye bye	+	+		+	+
ad hoc	+	+			+
give up		+	+		+
rely on		+			+
rocket science			+		+
washing machine			+		+
give a try			+		+
and so on		+	+		+
every now and then		+	+		+
drastically drop					+
yellow dress					
give a present					
several options					

From a cognitive point of view, the creation of MWEs seems counter-intuitive. It would be simpler to learn the general composition rules without caring about exceptions and idiomatic cases, for humans as well as for computers. However, if we see language as a communication tool, it is plausible to assume that humans would like to optimise information transfer by creating shortcuts. Thus, expressions that are frequently employed to describe a given situation will tend to appear more and more often, and collocations will be created. Furthermore, language is full of metaphors, projections of expressions from one context to another, like in expressions like *stand on someone's feet* and *set the bar high*. At some point of language evolution, metaphors become frozen, and sometimes it is even impossible to recover the original sense, generating idioms (Cruse 1986). In other words, humans are always inventing creative ways of saying more with less words.

It is important to keep in mind that, while Table 2.1 depicts idiomaticity as a binary feature, it would actually be more accurate to describe the *degree* of idiomaticity in a continuum, ranging from totally compositional and predictable combinations like *yellow dress* to frozen idiomatic constructions like *dry run*. Using a metaphor from computer interface design, it would be preferable to use sliders instead of checkboxes if we should describe a MWE's idiomaticity. Like in fuzzy logic, expressions would respect compositionality rules to some degree. Figure 2.1 shows a pedagogical computer interface for expression tuning, in which it is possible to artificially generate MWE examples by adjusting the idiomaticity at several levels. If all slides are towards the low end, then an ordinary combination of words like *yellow dress* is generated. However, when at least one of the sliders is moved toward the high idiomaticity end, we get a MWE like *dry run* as a result.

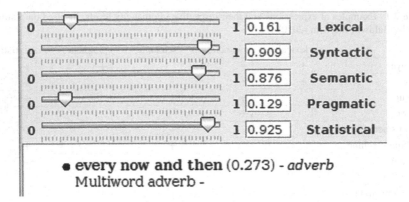

Fig. 2.1 Imaginary sliders that describe the idiomaticity degree of a MWE at various levels

2.3.2 Derived MWE Properties

Based on intuition and on corpus observation, researchers describe some common properties of MWEs in general, which we summarise below. It is important to keep in mind that these are not binary yes/no flags, but values in a continuum going from completely flexible, ordinary word combinations to totally prototypical and/or fixed expressions. Thus, any particular expression will present the properties described below to a variable extent and will probably not manifest a high degree for all of them simultaneously.

1. **Arbitrariness**. This is probably the most challenging property of MWEs. Their arbitrary character is well illustrated by Smadja (1993, p. 143–144), who listed eight different and valid ways of referring to the Dow Jones index, from which only four are acceptable.[10] This happens because sometimes a perfectly valid construction both syntactically and semantically is not acceptable simply because people do not talk that way. That is also why MWEs are hard for second language learners, who know the lexicon and grammar of the language but lack knowledge about language use.
2. **Institutionalisation**. MWEs are recurrent, as they correspond to conventional ways of saying things. Fillmore et al. (1988) argue that the inventory of constructions in a language is too large to be considered as an appendix or as a list of exceptions. Jackendoff (1997) estimates that they correspond to half of the entries of a speaker's lexicon. Sag et al. (2002) point out that this may be an underestimate if we take domain-specific MWEs into account. Indeed, some researchers assume that the proportion of multiword terms in a specialised

---

[10]One can say *The Dow Jones average of 30 industrials*, *The Dow average*, *The Dow industrials* or *The Dow Jones industrial*, but never ?*The Jones industrials*, ?*The industrial Dow*, ?*The Dow of 30 industrials* nor ?*The Dow industrial*.

lexicon is around 70 % (Krieger and Finatto 2004). Empirical measurements showed that this ratio is between 50 and 80 % in a corpus of scientific biomedical abstracts (Ramisch 2009). As pointed out in Sect. 1.1, there are 60,292 out of 117,827 (51.4 %) multiword nouns and 2,829 out of 11,558 (25.5 %) multiword verbs in English Wordnet. This is only the tip of the iceberg as some classes of MWEs, like support verb constructions, are not covered in Wordnet (Ramisch et al. 2013). Church (2013) discusses the size of the MWE lexicon from the point of view of computer applications, arguing that it is probably not a good idea to try to include *all* MWEs of a language in a lexicon. Institutionalisation is directly related to collocational behaviour, and motivates using frequency information (and all the related statistical tools) in order to automatically identify MWEs in corpora.

3. **Limited semantic variability**. MWEs do not undergo the same semantic compositionality rules as ordinary word combinations. This is often expressed in terms of the following sub-properties:

   (a) **Non-compositionality**. The meaning of the whole expression often cannot be directly inferred from the meaning of the parts composing it. Therefore, there is a lack of compositionality that ranges in a continuum from completely compositional MWEs (*bus stop*) to completely opaque ones (*kick the bucket* as *to die*). The MTT models a MWE as being composed of two parts: a base which carries the core meaning (e.g., *rain* in *heavy rain*) and a collocate that modifies the sense of the base (*heavy*). While this model captures semi-fixed expressions, it fails to generalise when the meaning of the MWE is closer to the edges of the compositionality spectrum. For instance, it is hard to designate a base and a collocate for completely idiomatic expressions (e.g., *big deal*) and for expressions where both elements seem to be equally relevant to the meaning of the expression (e.g., *cable car*).

   (b) **Non-substitutability**. Because MWEs are non-compositional, it is not possible to replace part of a MWE by a related (synonym/equivalent) word or construction. This motivates the notion of *anti-collocations* (Pearce 2001), which are awkward or unusual word combinations (e.g., *strong coffee* vs *?powerful coffee*). Syntactic and semantic variations are used in several techniques aimed at the automatic identification and classification of MWEs (Pearce 2001; Fazly and Stevenson 2007; Ramisch et al. 2008).

   (c) **No word-for-word translation**. This is a consequence of the above properties. However, it constitutes a useful test to decide whether a construction should be considered as a MWE or not, as we exemplified in Sect. 1.1.3. This motivates the application-oriented evaluation of Chap. 7. Ideally, the knowledge about MWEs should be available in both, source and target languages, within an MT system (Smadja 1993). However, knowing MWEs at the source side already can improve the quality of MT (Carpuat and Diab 2010), and sometimes it is better to transliterate them instead of translating them (Pal et al. 2010). Translational (non-)equivalences can also be used to detect MWEs when parallel data is available (de Medeiros Caseli et al. 2010; Attia et al. 2010), as discussed in Sect. 3.2.2.

(d) **Domain-specificity/idiomaticity**. Smadja (1993) emphasises that MWEs are related to a specific sublanguage. Thus, for the layman not familiar with it, it is hard to identify them. A sublanguage may be a specialised scientific or technical domain (e.g., epistemology, chemistry, cars, fashion), a regional or dialectal variation (e.g., Brazilian vs European Portuguese), or a text genre (e.g., poetry vs textbooks).

4. **Limited syntactic variability (or non-modifiability)**. Standard grammatical rules do not apply to some MWEs, and this can be demonstrated by the following sub-properties:

(a) **Extragrammaticality**. Fillmore et al. (1988) introduce this property, arguing that such expressions are unpredictable and seem "weird" for somebody (e.g., a second language learner) who only knows general lexical and morphosyntactic rules. Examples of extragrammatical MWEs include, in English, *kingdom come*, *by and large*; in Portuguese, *dar para trás* (lit. *give toward behind*, *fail a commitment*), *um Deus nos acuda* (lit. *a God help us*, *a mess*), *minha nossa!* (lit. *my our!*, *oh my God!*); and in French, *faire avec* (lit. *make with*, *accommodate*), *sens dessus dessous* (lit. *without above under*, *nonsense*), *de par le monde* (lit. *of by the world*, *somewhere in the world*).

(b) **Lexicalisation**. MWEs are, to some extent, autonomous lexical units. Somehow, the knowledge that a set of graphical words "belongs together" in a single lexical unit must be available to NLP applications. Because "MWEs can be regarded as lying at the interface between grammar and lexicon" (Calzolari et al. 2002), parsing engineers often need to choose where each MWE belongs. It is not enough to list them all in the lexicon, because this would result in undergeneration. Conversely, listing them all in the grammar as free combinations would make a parser overgenerate. In other words, they have a variable degree of lexicalisation, and identifying this degree of lexicalisation for each MWE (class) is important for NLP analysis and generation tasks. This property relates to what Smadja (1993) calls "cohesive lexical clusters" and to the assumption of Evert (2004), who argues that MWEs need to be represented as a lexical unit.

5. **Heterogeneity**. It is not a coincidence that MWEs are hard to define, as the term encompasses a large amount of distinct phenomena. This complexity makes them hard to deal with by NLP applications, which cannot use a unified approach and usually need to rely on some type-based approach using one of the multiple MWE classifications available.

2.3.3   Existing MWE Typologies

2.3.3.1   Constructionist Typology

Fillmore et al. (1988) suggest a typology based on the predictability of a construction with respect to standard syntactic rules (and somehow related to semantic compositionality). They define three classes among the four possibilities of unfamiliar/familiar pieces unfamiliarly/familiarly combined.

- **Unfamiliar pieces unfamiliarly combined**: this class contains idiomatic constructions that are extremely unpredictable. This may concern, for instance, words that only appear in a specific idiom (*ad hoc*, *with might and main*) or very specialised syntactic configurations that do not occur anywhere else in language (*the more, the merrier*, and more generally expressions of the type *the X-er, the Y-er*).
- **Familiar pieces unfamiliarly combined**: these constructions require special syntactic and semantic rules for their interpretation. Examples are *all of a sudden*, *stay at home* and constructions of the type *first cousin two times removed*.
- **Familiar pieces familiarly combined**: constructions in this class do not present any particular syntactic idiosyncrasy and their members are combined using standard grammatical rules. However, they have an idiomatic interpretation like in *pull someone's leg* and *tickle the ivories*.

2.3.3.2   MTT Typology

Another classification is suggested by Mel'čuk et al. (1995), who use as a criterion the relevance of a given expression as an entry in a dictionary. According to them, complete phrasemes and quasi-phrasemes must be full entries in the dictionary while semi-phrasemes are represented as LSFs in the lexical co-occurrence zone of the entries corresponding to the base words. Their goal is to optimise the access to information based on the most probable circumstance in which a speaker would require it. Their classification can be easily expressed in terms of semantic compositionality, and contains the following classes: complete phrasemes, semi-phrasemes and quasi-phrasemes.

- **Complete phraseme**: fully idiomatic expression, that is, the meaning of the expression has no intersection with the meaning of any of its components, for instance, *kick the bucket* and *Achilles' heel*. In other words, the expression is fully non-compositional.
- **Semi-phraseme**: expressions in which the meaning of at least one of the components is present in the meaning of the whole expression, but the global meaning still does not correspond to the systematic composition of all individual meanings. This is the case of most collocations that can be expressed in terms of a base word (the one which contributes its meaning to the expression) and the

collocate word (which modifies or adds some new interpretation to the meaning of the base word). Examples include *take a nap* and *break up*. Such expressions can be expressed in terms of LSFs in the explanatory combinatorial dictionary. They correspond to the set of familiar pieces familiarly arranged in Fillmore's classification.

- **Quasi-phrasemes**: expressions in which all the words keep their original meanings but an extra element of meaning is added by the fact that they occur in an expression. So for instance a *bus stop* is actually a place where the bus stops, but not any place. If the bus stops at the traffic light, nobody can get on and off the bus, so this will not be considered as a bus stop. Analogously, not every light that helps controlling the traffic is a *traffic light*.

2.3.3.3 "Pain-in-the-Neck" Typology

A slightly more sophisticated classification scheme is proposed by Sag et al. (2002). They separate institutionalised from lexicalised expressions and further classify the latter into three sub-types according to their degree of syntactic flexibility:

- **Institutionalised phrases**: are sets of words which co-occur often but have no syntactic idiosyncrasy, and whose semantics are fairly compositional. As they undergo full syntactic variability, they cannot be represented using a words-with-spaces approach. This class corresponds to the notion of collocation denominated in the previous schemes as semi-phrasemes and familiar pieces familiarly combined.
- **Lexicalised phrases**: present some idiosyncratic syntactic or semantic characteristics. This class can be further divided into three sub-classes according to their degree of flexibility: fixed, semi-fixed and syntactically flexible expressions.

  - **Fixed expressions**: they are expressions that do not allow any morphosyntactic modification. This includes expressions containing words that do not occur in isolation (*ad hoc*, *vice versa*) and extragrammatical expressions such as *kindom come* and *in short*. These expressions are immutable, not allowing any morphological inflection (**in shorter*), syntactic modification (**coming kingdom*) and internal insertion (**in very short*). This corresponds to the set of unfamiliar pieces unfamiliarly combined and would be included in the class of complete phrasemes.
  - **Semi-fixed expressions**: they have strict syntactic and semantic interpretation but undergo morphological inflection. This class contains notably noun compounds (*cable car*) and proper names (*San Francisco*), as well as non-decomposable idioms (*kick the bucket*, *shoot the breeze*). The latter are idiomatic expressions with completely opaque semantic interpretation. That is, it is impossible to decompose the semantics of the whole into pieces assigned to parts of the expression.
  - **Syntactically flexible expressions**: they allow a much larger range of syntactic variation than the former, still presenting idiosyncratic semantics.

Examples include phrasal verbs (*take off, give up*), light verb constructions (*take a picture, make a mistake*) and decomposable idioms, that is, idioms in which it is possible to assign parts of a possibly non-standard meaning to parts of the expression (*spill the beans* can be analysed as *spill = reveal, the beans = the secret*).

2.3.3.4 Xtract Typology

Probably, the typology most similar to the one we propose in this work in terms of selection criteria is that of Smadja (1993). His classification is oriented toward automatic terminology recognition. His classes are inspired by the types of filters which he applies during MWE acquisition.[11]

- **Predicative relations**: they correspond to a word modifying or adding some new meaning to the semantics of a base word, like *make a presentation* and *drop drastically*. According to the author, this class corresponds to the LSFs of Mel'čuk et al. (1995). Therefore, it presents a large overlap with what, in the previous classifications, is denominated as semi-phrasemes, institutionalised phrases and familiar pieces familiarly combined.
- **Rigid noun phrases**: they are nominal expressions such as noun compounds (*stock market*) and proper nouns (*the Dow Jones index*). Smadja characterises these expressions as allowing little or no flexibility (fixed and semi-fixed expressions), and often being used to describe a concept in a specialised domain (see *multiword term* in Sect. 2.2.3). These constructions are full lexical entries, as semantically equivalent formulations are not possible or would not designate the same concept.
- **Phrasal templates**: they are whole phrases prototypical in specialised texts. This class covers what terminologists often call phraseological expression, that is, some usual way of saying something in a domain. Phraseological expressions can be as long as a whole sentence and often look like a template containing gaps for variable parts, for example, *The average finished the week with a net loss of* NUMBER.

2.3.4 A Simplified Typology

In this work, we use a simplistic typology based firstly on the morphosyntactic role of the whole expression in a sentence (Sect. 2.3.4.1), and secondly on its difficulty to be dealt with using computational methods (Sect. 2.3.4.2). We provide

---

[11]This classification is largely incomplete. It does not cover the whole set of MWEs defined in our work.

some examples of smaller classes, like noun compounds and phrasal verbs, that are included in the more coarse classes proposed below.

2.3.4.1 Morphosyntactic Classes

In our typology, expressions that act as or are heads of noun phrases are broadly classified as nominal expressions (Sect. 2.3.4.1); expressions containing a verb and other lexical items attached to it (adverbs, objects, complements) are considered verbal expressions (Sect. 2.3.4.1); likewise for adverbial and adjectival expressions (Sect. 2.3.4.1). Idioms, an important class of MWEs, are not mentioned explicitly because they have varied syntactic classes: they can be nominal (big deal), verbal (spill the beans), adjectival (second hand), etc. Complex conjunctions, preposition and formulaic phrases and collocations are not covered by this typology either.

By no means do we argue that the classification proposed here is better or more general than the existing ones. However, the existing schemes are quite complex and/or intentionally vague. Thus, for the sake of practicality, we suggest a simplified taxonomy. Even though it is far from being exhaustive, it is quite simple and yet rigorous enough to describe the MWEs dealt with in our experiments and in particular in NLP applications.

Nominal Expressions

Nominal expressions are word combinations acting as nouns, that is, as noun phrases or heads of noun phrases, in a sentence. This class covers the following sub-types: nominal compounds, proper names and multiword terms.

- **Nominal compounds**: they are sequences formed by head nouns and other elements appended to it, like other nouns (*traffic light*, *soup pot cover*), adjectives (*Russian roulette*, *bulletproof vest*) and adjectival locutions introduced by prepositions (*degree of freedom*, *part of speech*). Nominal compounds generally denote a specific concept for which there is no equivalent single-word formulation. When the nominal compound is composed exclusively of nouns, it is called a *noun compound* (Nakov 2013). Work on English tends to distinguish noun compounds (*wine glass*, *liver cell line*) from nominal compounds including other parts of speech (*dry run*, *food for thought*). In other languages, however, this distinction may not make sense. In some cases, the words of the compound are concatenated together, like the English compounds *database* and *snowball* and all German noun compounds.
- **Proper names**: they are very similar to nominal compounds except that they usually denote a very specific named entity of the world such as a name of a city (e.g., *Porto Alegre*), institution (e.g., *United Nations*) or person (e.g., *Alan Turing*). In some languages, they are distinguished from regular nouns using capitalised

initials. According to Manning and Schütze (1999, p. 186), "[proper names] are usually included in the category of collocations in computational work although they are quite different from lexical collocations". The question of whether proper names should be considered as MWEs is an open one because (a) not all proper names are MWEs (e.g., *Paris*, *Google*) and (b) computational methods used for the automatic identification of proper names are different from methods to identify regular nominal compounds. We will assume that identification of proper names is the concern of another NLP area called named entity recognition, which has its own methods and goals, thus falling out of the scope of our work.

- **Multiword terms**: they are also nominal compounds with the specificity of being used in a specialised domain to denote a specific concept (see Sect. 2.2.3). Similarly to proper names, multiword terms are the main object of study in automatic term recognition, which is a research area on its own in computational linguistics, not being covered by our work.

Verbal Expressions

Verbal expressions are those in which a verb is the head of the expression and other elements are appended to it. According to the class of the appended elements, they can be further sub-classified as phrasal verbs and light verb constructions.

- **Phrasal verbs**: they are constructions in which a preposition or adverb plays the role of a particle adding some meaning to the meaning of the base verb. This includes basically two types of constructions: (a) transitive prepositional verbs that are compositional but require a specific preposition introducing the object, like *rely on* and *agree with*, and (b) more opaque verb-particle constructions where the particle is actually attached to the verb, forming a cohesive lexical-semantic unit, like *give up* and *take off*. They are frequent in Germanic languages like English and German but rare in Latin languages like Portuguese and French. A detailed characterisation of phrasal verbs is provided in Sect. 7.2.1.
- **Light verb constructions**: they are also sometimes called support verb constructions, and correspond to a semantically "light" verb used with a noun that conveys most of the meaning of the expression. Thus, when one *takes a shower*, most of the semantics comes from the noun *shower* and not from the highly polysemous verb *take*. The complement of the verb is often a deverbal nominalisation derived from a simple verb[12] which is synonym of the light verb construction, like *to shower = take a shower* and *to present = make a presentation*.[13] As the choice of the light verb is rigid and unpredictable in this kind of construction, a simple test to verify whether it is a genuine light verb construction consists of trying

---

[12]Sometimes, the opposite may occur, that is, the simple denominal verb may come from the corresponding noun in the construction, for instance, *give an example = exemplify*.

[13]*To present* may also mean *make a gift*, and the use of the analytic expression using the same support verb helps disambiguating.

to replace the verb, yielding unnatural expressions (e.g., ?*make a shower*, ?*get a shower*). A detailed characterisation of complex predicates including light verb constructions is provided in Sect. 6.2.1.

Adverbial and Adjectival Expressions

Expressions acting as adverbs or adjectives in sentences belong to a separate class. Examples in English are *upside down*, *second hand*, *on fire*, *at stake*, and *in the buff*. These expressions are also quite frequent in other languages such as in French (*à poil*, *à la bourre*, *dans l'absolu*, *la tête en bas*) and Portuguese (*sem mais nem menos*, *de braços abertos*, *mais ou menos*, *de cabeça para baixo*).

2.3.4.2 Difficulty Classes

In addition to these three main types, we also define three orthogonal types that are more related to the computational methods used to treat MWEs. Fixed expressions can be dealt with using relatively simple techniques, while idiomatic expressions are very hard to recognise and require the use of external semantic resources. The last class contains what we call "true" collocations because they correspond to the notion of words that co-occur more often than expected by chance.

- **Fixed expressions**: they correspond to the fixed expressions of Sag et al. (2002), that is, it is possible to deal with them using the words-with-spaces approach. Such expressions often play the role of functional words (*in short*, *with respect to*), contain foreign words (*ad infinitum*, *déjà vu*) or breach standard grammatical rules (*by and large*, *kingdom come*).
- **Idioms**: idiomatic MWEs have completely non-compositional semantics, that is, the literal interpretation of its members is completely unrelated to the meaning of the expression. Therefore, they are very hard to automatically identify in texts without the help of semantic resources. Examples include expressions from the three morphosyntactic classes above like nominal expressions (*dead end*, *dry run*, *bird brain*), verbal expressions (*put in place*, *shoot the breeze*) and adjectival expressions (*on the same wavelength*, *all ears*).
- **"True" collocations**: MWEs corresponding to the notion of institutionalised phrases are fully compositional expressions both syntactically and semantically, but co-occurring more often than expected by chance. This class corresponds to Firth's definition of MWEs as " habitual and customary places of that word" and can be modelled using Mel'čuk's notion of LSF.

2.4   A Snapshot of the Research Field

MWEs are a hot topic and an exciting research field of computational linguistics. Research has made significant progress in recent years, and this is reflected on the large number of papers that focus on data-driven automatic acquisition of multiword units from corpora. A considerable body of techniques, resources and tools to perform automatic extraction of expressions from text are nowadays available. This is an evidence of the growing importance of MWE processing within the NLP community (see Sect. 3.2.1).

The MWE research community is organised and shares some common resources. The first and most important place to exchange ideas on MWE research is the annual workshop on MWEs. It is a series of workshops that have been held since 2001 in conjunction with major computational linguistics conferences (Bond et al. 2003; Tanaka et al. 2004; Rayson et al. 2006; Moirón et al. 2006; Grégoire et al. 2007, 2008; Anastasiou et al. 2009; Laporte et al. 2010; Kordoni et al. 2011, 2013, 2014). The recent editions of the workshop show that there is a shift from research on identification and extraction methods work toward more application-oriented research. The evaluation of MWE processing techniques and multilingual aspects are also current issues in the field. For example, there has been some published work and also a specific workshop at MT Summit on the automatic translation of several types of MWEs (Mitkov et al. 2013).

From 2012 on, the MWEs are also an area of the *SEM conference, which gathers several sub-fields of NLP around a common theme: natural language semantics.[14] In addition to the specialised workshops, main computational linguistics conferences such as COLING, ACL and LREC regularly feature papers on MWEs. For example, the best paper award of COLING 2010 went to a paper about compositionality measures for multiword units (Bu et al. 2010).

Courses and tutorials on MWEs are also part of conference and summer school programs like ACL 2013 and RANLP 2013. The SemEval campaign also features some tasks related to MWE processing, like noun compound classification (Hendrickx et al. 2010), noun compound intepretation (Butnariu et al. 2010) and keyphrase extraction (Kim et al. 2010). There are also many research projects on MWEs, like the European network PARSEME: a COST action whose goal is to propose better models for parsing MWEs.[15]

Most of the information concerning past editions of the MWE workshop series can be found at the MWE SIGLEX Section website.[16] The site also hosts a repository with several annotated data sets and a list of software capable of dealing with MWEs. The community also uses as communication tool a mailing list to which anyone can subscribe.

---

[14]http://clic2.cimec.unitn.it/starsem2013/

[15]http://typo.uni-konstanz.de/parseme/

[16]http://multiword.sourceforge.net/

Finally, as a complement to workshops and conferences, special issues on MWEs have been published by leading journals in computational linguistics: the journal of Computer Speech and Language (Villavicencio et al. 2005), the journal of Language Resources and Evaluation (Rayson et al. 2010), the Natural Language Engineering journal (Szpakowicz et al. 2013) and the ACM Transactions on Speech and Language Processing (Ramisch et al. 2013). The special issues generally gather publications describing consolidated research projects around MWEs. Thus, they provide a broad overview and present the most relevant research results coming from different authors and research groups working on the subject.

In short, researchers from several fields view MWEs as a key bottleneck in current NLP technology. And yet, there are still important and urgent open matters to be solved, as we will see throughout this book.

2.5   Summary

The study of MWEs is almost as old as linguistics itself. When trying to classify linguistic phenomena into either lexical or syntactic, one quickly realises that some of them, and in particular MWEs, lie in between these two levels. Therefore, there are limitations in the structural approach to language. One of the seminal papers of the *construction grammar* trend is the work of Fillmore et al. (1988). They illustrate and discuss in detail the weaknesses of this idealised atomistic approach to grammar. In construction grammar, idioms are part of the core of the grammar: a language can be fully described by its idioms and their properties. These idioms correspond to what we call MWEs. Another linguistic theory that gives much importance to MWEs is the *meaning-text theory* (MTT). MWEs are present at two points of the computational MTT model: as *phrasemes* and as lexico-semantic functions in the *lexical combinatorics zone*.

MWEs are hard to define, as there is little agreement on the definition of the word *word* itself. The notion of MWE has its origin in Firth's famous quotation "you shall know a word by the company it keeps". He affirms that "collocations of a given word are statements of the habitual and customary places of that word" (Firth 1957, p. 181). Smadja (1993) considers collocations as "arbitrary and recurrent word combinations", while for Choueka (1988), a collocation is "a syntactic and semantic unit whose exact and unambiguous meaning or connotation cannot be derived directly from the meaning or connotation of its components". Sag et al. (2002) generalise this same property to vaguely define MWEs as "idiosyncratic interpretations that cross word boundaries (or spaces)".

We adopt a definition based on the one by Baldwin and Kim (2010). For us, MWEs are lexical items that are decomposable into multiple lexemes and present idiomatic behaviour at some level of linguistic analysis. As a consequence, they must be treated as a unit at some level of computational processing. This generic and intentionally vague definition can be narrowed down according to the application needs. For example, for an MT system, a MWE is any combination of words which, when not translated as a unit, generates unnatural output. The level at which a combination of words needs to be treated as a unit varies according to the type of system and expression.

The literature describes some common properties of MWEs in general: arbitrariness, institutionalisation, limited semantic variability (non-compositionality, non-substitutability, no word-for-word translation, domain-specificity/idiomaticity), limited syntactic variability (extragrammaticality, lexicalisation), and heterogeneity. These are not binary yes/no flags, but values in a compositionality continuum going from completely flexible, ordinary word combinations to totally prototypical and/or fixed expressions.

There exist several typologies to classify MWEs, based on different views on grammatical theories: constructionism, meaning-text theory, grammar engineering, and automatic MWE acquisition. In this work, we propose a typology based firstly on the morphosyntactic role of the whole expression in a sentence, and secondly on its difficulty to be dealt with using computational methods. The first typology classifies MWEs into nominal, verbal and adverbial/adjectival expressions. Nominal expressions cover noun compounds (*Russian roulette*), proper names (*Porto Alegre*), and multiword terms (*DNA-binding domain*). Verbal expressions include phrasal verbs (*give up*) and light verb constructions (*take a shower*). Adverbial and adjectival expressions include examples such as *upside down* in English, *à poil* in French, and *sem mais nem menos* in Portuguese. In addition to these types, we define three orthogonal types that are more related to the computational methods used to treat MWEs: (i) fixed expressions like *in short*, (ii) idiomatic expressions like *dry run*, *put in place* and *on the same wavelength*, and (iii) "true" collocations, corresponding to fully compositional expressions co-occurring more often than expected by chance. This typology is quite simple and yet rigorous enough to describe the MWEs dealt with in our experiments.

References

Anastasiou D, Hashimoto C, Nakov P, Kim SN (eds) (2009) Proceedings of the ACL workshop on multiword expressions: identification, interpretation, disambiguation, applications (MWE 2009), Singapore. Association for Computational Linguistics/Suntec, 70p. http://aclweb.org/anthology-new/W/W09/W09-29

Attia M, Toral A, Tounsi L, Pecina P, van Genabith J (2010) Automatic extraction of Arabic multiword expressions. In: Laporte É, Nakov P, Ramisch C, Villavicencio A (eds) Proceedings of the COLING workshop on multiword expressions: from theory to applications (MWE 2010), Beijing. Association for Computational Linguistics, pp 18–26

Baldwin T, Kim SN (2010) Multiword expressions. In: Indurkhya N, Damerau FJ (eds) Handbook of natural language processing, 2nd edn. CRC/Taylor and Francis Group, Boca Raton, pp 267–292

Bond F, Korhonen A, McCarthy D, Villavicencio A (eds) (2003) Proceedings of the ACL workshop on multiword expressions: analysis, acquisition and treatment (MWE 2003), Sapporo. Association for Computational Linguistics, 104p. http://aclweb.org/anthology-new/W/W03/W03-1800

Bu F, Zhu X, Li M (2010) Measuring the non-compositionality of multiword expressions. In: Huang CR, Jurafsky D (eds) Proceedings of the 23rd international conference on computational linguistics (COLING 2010), Beijing. The Coling 2010 Organizing Committee, pp 116–124. http://www.aclweb.org/anthology/C10-1014

Butnariu C, Kim SN, Nakov P, Séaghdha DO, Szpakowicz S, Veale T (2010) Semeval-2 task 9: the interpretation of noun compounds using paraphrasing verbs and prepositions. In: Erk K, Strapparava C (eds) Proceedings of the 5th international workshop on semantic evaluation (SemEval 2010), Uppsala. Association for Computational Linguistics, pp 39–44. http://www.aclweb.org/anthology/S10-1007

Cabré MT (1992) La terminologia. La teoria, els mètodes, les aplicacions. Empúries, Barcelona, 527p

Calzolari N, Fillmore C, Grishman R, Ide N, Lenci A, Macleod C, Zampolli A (2002) Towards best practice for multiword expressions in computational lexicons. In: Proceedings of the third international conference on language resources and evaluation (LREC 2002), Las Palmas. European Language Resources Association, pp 1934–1940

Carpuat M, Diab M (2010) Task-based evaluation of multiword expressions: a pilot study in statistical machine translation. In: Proceedings of human language technology: the 2010 annual conference of the North American chapter of the Association for Computational Linguistics (NAACL 2003), Los Angeles. Association for Computational Linguistics, pp 242–245. http://www.aclweb.org/anthology/N10-1029

Choueka Y (1988) Looking for needles in a haystack or locating interesting collocational expressions in large textual databases. In: Fluhr C, Walker DE (eds) Proceedings of the 2nd international conference on computer-assisted information retrieval (Recherche d'Information et ses Applications – RIA 1988), Cambridge. CID, pp 609–624

Church K (2013) How many multiword expressions do people know? ACM Trans Speech language processing Spec Issue Multiword Expr Theory Pract Use Part 1 (TSLP) 10(2):1–13

Church K, Hanks P (1990) Word association norms mutual information, and lexicography. Comput Linguist 16(1):22–29

Cruse DA (1986) Lexical semantics. Cambridge University Press, Cambridge, 310p

Dagan I, Church K (1994) Termight: identifying and translating technical terminology. In: Proceedings of the 4th applied natural language processing conference (ANLP 1994), Stuttgart. Association for Computational Linguistics, pp 34–40. doi:10.3115/974358.974367, http://www.aclweb.org/anthology/A94-1006

de Medeiros Caseli H, Ramisch C, das Graças Volpe Nunes M, Villavicencio A (2010) Alignment-based extraction of multiword expressions. Lang Resour Eval Spec Issue Multiword Expr Hard Going or Plain Sailing 44(1–2):59–77. doi:10.1007/s10579-009-9097-9, http://www.springerlink.com/content/H7313427H78865MG

Devereux B, Costello F (2007) Learning to interpret novel noun-noun compounds: evidence from a category learning experiment. In: Buttery P, Villavicencio A, Korhonen A (eds) Proceedings of the ACL 2007 workshop on cognitive aspects of computational language acquisition, Prague. Association for Computational Linguistics, pp 89–96. http://www.aclweb.org/anthology/W/W07/W07-0612

Dunning T (1993) Accurate methods for the statistics of surprise and coincidence. Comput Linguist 19(1):61–74

Evert S (2004) The statistics of word cooccurrences: word pairs and collocations. PhD thesis, Institut für maschinelle Sprachverarbeitung, University of Stuttgart, Stuttgart, 353p

Fazly A, Stevenson S (2007) Distinguishing subtypes of multiword expressions using linguistically-motivated statistical measures. In: Grégoire N, Evert S, Kim SN (eds) Proceedings of the ACL workshop on a broader perspective on multiword expressions (MWE 2007), Prague. Association for Computational Linguistics, pp 9–16. http://www.aclweb.org/anthology/W/W07/W07-1102

Fillmore CJ, Kay P, O'Connor MC (1988) Regularity and idiomaticity in grammatical constructions: the case of let alone. Language 64:501–538. http://www.jstor.org/stable/414531

Firth JR (1957) Papers in linguistics 1934-1951. Oxford University Press, Oxford, 233p

Frantzi K, Ananiadou S, Mima H (2000) Automatic recognition of multiword terms: the C-value/NC-value method. Int J Digit Libr 3(2):115–130

Grégoire N, Evert S, Kim SN (eds) (2007) Proceedings of the ACL workshop on a broader perspective on multiword expressions (MWE 2007), Prague. Association for Computational Linguistics, 80p. http://aclweb.org/anthology-new/W/W07/W07-11

Grégoire N, Evert S, Krenn B (eds) (2008) Proceedings of the LREC workshop towards a shared task for multiword expressions (MWE 2008), Marrakech, 57p. http://www.lrec-conf.org/proceedings/lrec2008/workshops/W20_Proceedings.pdf

Hendrickx I, Kim SN, Kozareva Z, Nakov P, Séaghdha DO, Padó S, Pennacchiotti M, Romano L, Szpakowicz S (2010) Semeval-2010 task 8: multi-way classification of semantic relations between pairs of nominals. In: Erk K, Strapparava C (eds) Proceedings of the 5th international workshop on semantic evaluation (SemEval 2010), Uppsala. Association for Computational Linguistics, pp 33–38. http://www.aclweb.org/anthology/S10-1006

Jackendoff R (1997) Twistin' the night away. Language 73:534–559

Joshi A (2010) Multi-word expressions as discourse relation markers (DRMs). In: Laporte É, Nakov P, Ramisch C, Villavicencio A (eds) Proceedings of the COLING workshop on multiword expressions: from theory to applications (MWE 2010), Beijing. Association for Computational Linguistics, p 89

Joyce T, Srdanović I (2008) Comparing lexical relationships observed within Japanese collocation data and Japanese word association norms. In: Zock M, Huang CR (eds) Proceedings of the COLING 2008 workshop on cognitive aspects of the lexicon (COGALEX 2008), Manchester. The Coling 2008 Organizing Committee, pp 1–8. http://www.aclweb.org/anthology/W08-1901

Justeson JS, Katz SM (1995) Technical terminology: some linguistic properties and an algorithm for identification in text. Nat Lang Eng 1(1):9–27

Kim SN, Medelyan O, Kan MY, Baldwin T (2010) Semeval-2010 task 5: automatic keyphrase extraction from scientific articles. In: Erk K, Strapparava C (eds) Proceedings of the 5th international workshop on semantic evaluation (SemEval 2010), Uppsala. Association for Computational Linguistics, pp 21–26. http://www.aclweb.org/anthology/S10-1004

Kordoni V, Ramisch C, Villavicencio A (eds) (2011) Proceedings of the ACL workshop on multiword expressions: from parsing and generation to the real world (MWE 2011), Portland. Association for Computational Linguistics, 144p. http://www.aclweb.org/anthology/W/W11/W11-08

Kordoni V, Ramisch C, Villavicencio A (eds) (2013) Proceedings of the 9th workshop on multiword expressions (MWE 2013), Atlanta. Association for Computational Linguistics, 144p. http://www.aclweb.org/anthology/W13-10

Kordoni V, Savary A, Egg M, Wehrli E, Evert S (eds) (2014) Proceedings of the 10th workshop on multiword expressions (MWE 2014), Gothenburg. Association for Computational Linguistics, 133p. http://www.aclweb.org/anthology/W14-08

Krieger M, Finatto MJB (2004) Introdução à Terminologia: teoria & prática. Editora Contexto, São Paulo, 223p

Laporte É, Nakov P, Ramisch C, Villavicencio A (eds) (2010) Proceedings of the COLING workshop on multiword expressions: from theory to applications (MWE 2010), Beijing. Association for Computational Linguistics, 89p. http://aclweb.org/anthology-new/W/W10/W10-37

Lavagnino E, Park J (2010) Conceptual structure of automatically extracted multi-word terms from domain specific corpora: a case study for Italian. In: Zock M, Rapp R (eds) Proceedings of the 2nd workshop on cognitive aspects of the lexicon (COGALEX 2010), Beijing. The Coling 2010 Organizing Committee, pp 48–55. http://www.aclweb.org/anthology/W10-3408

Lin D (1998a) Automatic retrieval and clustering of similar words. In: Proceedings of the 36th annual meeting of the Association for Computational Linguistics and 17th international conference on computational linguistics, Montreal, vol 2. Association for Computational Linguistics, pp 768–774. doi:10.3115/980691.980696, http://www.aclweb.org/anthology/P98-2127

Lin D (1998b) Extracting collocations from text corpora. In: First workshop on computational terminology, Montreal, pp 57–63

Lin D (1999) Automatic identification of non-compositional phrases. In: Proceedings of the 37th annual meeting of the Association for Computational Linguistics (ACL 1999), College Park. Association for Computational Linguistics, pp 317–324

Manning CD, Schütze H (1999) Foundations of statistical natural language processing. MIT, Cambridge, 620p

Mel'čuk I, Polguère A (1987) A formal lexicon in the meaning-text theory or (how to do lexica with words). Comput Linguist 13(3–4):261–275

Mel'čuk I, Arbatchewsky-Jumarie N, Elnitsky L, Iordanskaja L, Lessard A (1984) Dictionnaire explicatif et combinatoire du français contemporain. Recherches lexico-sémantiques I. Les presses de l'Université de Montréal, Montréal, 172p

Mel'čuk I, Arbatchewsky-Jumarie N, Dagenais L, Elnitsky L, Iordanskaja L, Lefebvre MN, Mantha S (1988) Dictionnaire explicatif et combinatoire du français contemporain. Recherches lexico-sémantiques II. Les presses de l'Université de Montréal, Montréal, 332p

Mel'čuk I, Arbatchewsky-Jumarie N, Iordanskaja L, Mantha S (1992) Dictionnaire explicatif et combinatoire du français contemporain. Recherches lexico-sémantiques III. Les presses de l'Université de Montréal, Montréal, 323p

Mel'čuk I, Clas A, Polguère A (1995) Introduction à la lexicologie explicative et combinatoire. Editions Duculot, Louvain la Neuve, 256p

Mel'čuk I, Arbatchewsky-Jumarie N, Clas A, Mantha S, Polguère A (1999) Dictionnaire explicatif et combinatoire du français contemporain. Recherches lexico-sémantiques IV. Les presses de l'Université de Montréal, Montréal, 347p

Mitkov R, Monti J, Pastor GC, Seretan V (eds) (2013) Proceedings of the MT summit 2013 workshop on multi-word units in machine translation and translation technology (MUMTTT 2013), Nice.

Moirón BV, Villavicencio A, McCarthy D, Evert S, Stevenson S (eds) (2006) Proceedings of the COLING/ACL workshop on multiword expressions: identifying and exploiting underlying properties (MWE 2006), Sidney. Association for Computational Linguistics, 61p. http://aclweb. org/anthology-new/W/W06/W06-12

Nakov P (2013) On the interpretation of noun compounds: syntax, semantics, and entailment. Nat Lang Eng Spec Issue Noun Compd 19(3):291–330. doi10.1017/S1351324913000065, http:// journals.cambridge.org/article_S1351324913000065

Nematzadeh A, Fazly A, Stevenson S (2012, to appear) Child acquisition of multiword verbs: a computational investigation. In: Poibeau T, Villavicencio A, Korhonen A, Alishahi A (eds) Cognitive aspects of computational language acquisition, Springer, Heidelberg

Pal S, Naskar SK, Pecina P, Bandyopadhyay S, Way A (2010) Handling named entities and compound verbs in phrase-based statistical machine translation. In: Laporte É, Nakov P, Ramisch C, Villavicencio A (eds) Proceedings of the COLING workshop on multiword expressions: from theory to applications (MWE 2010), Beijing. Association for Computational Linguistics, pp 45–53

Pearce D (2001) Synonymy in collocation extraction. In: WordNet and other lexical resources: applications, extensions and customizations (NAACL 2001 workshop), Pittsburgh, pp 41–46

Ramisch C (2009) Multiword terminology extraction for domain-specific documents. Master's thesis, École Nationale Supérieure d'Informatique et de Mathématiques Appliquées, Grenoble, 79p

Ramisch C, Villavicencio A, Moura L, Idiart M (2008) Picking them up and figuring them out: verb-particle constructions, noise and idiomaticity. In: Clark A, Toutanova K (eds) Proceedings of the twelfth conference on natural language learning (CoNLL 2008), Manchester. The Coling 2008 Organizing Committee, pp 49–56. http://www.aclweb.org/anthology/W08-2107

Ramisch C, Villavicencio A, Kordoni V (2013) Introduction to the special issue on multiword expressions: from theory to practice and use. ACM Trans Speech Lang Process Spec Issue Multiword Expr Theory Pract Use Part 1 (TSLP) 10(2):1–10

Rapp R (2008) The computation of associative responses to multiword stimuli. In: Zock M, Huang CR (eds) Proceedings of the COLING 2008 workshop on cognitive aspects of the lexicon (COGALEX 2008), Manchester. The Coling 2008 Organizing Committee, pp 102–109. http://www.aclweb.org/anthology/W08-1914

Rayson P, Sharoff S, Adolphs S (eds) (2006) Proceedings of the EACL workshop on multiword expressions in multilingual context (EACL-MWE 2006), Trento. Association for Computational Linguistics, 79p. http://aclweb.org/anthology-new/W/W06/W06-2400

Rayson P, Piao S, Sharoff S, Evert S, Villada Moirón B (2010) Multiword expressions hard going or plain sailing? Lang Resour Eval Spec Issue Multiword Expr Hard Going Plain Sailing 44(1–2):1–5 Springer

Sag I, Baldwin T, Bond F, Copestake A, Flickinger D (2002) Multiword expressions: a pain in the neck for NLP. In: Proceedings of the 3rd international conference on intelligent text processing and computational linguistics (CICLing-2002), Mexico-City. Lecture notes in computer science, vol 2276/2010. Springer, pp 1–15

SanJuan E, Dowdall J, Ibekwe-SanJuan F, Rinaldi F (2005) A symbolic approach to automatic multiword term structuring. Comput Speech Lang Spec Issue MWEs 19(4):524–542

Seretan V (2008) Collocation extraction based on syntactic parsing. PhD thesis, University of Geneva, Geneva, 249p

Seretan V (2011) Syntax-based collocation extraction. Text, speech and language technology, vol 44, 1st edn. Springer, Dordrecht, 212p

Sinclair J (1991) Corpus, concordance, collocation. Describing English language, Oxford University Press, Oxford, 179p

Smadja FA (1993) Retrieving collocations from text: Xtract. Comput Linguist 19(1):143–177

Szpakowicz S, Bond F, Nakov P, Kim SN (2013) On the semantics of noun compounds. In: Nat Lang Eng Spec Issue Noun Compd 19(3):289–290. Cambridge University Press, Cambridge

Tanaka T, Villavicencio A, Bond F, Korhonen A (eds) (2004) Proceedings of the ACL workshop on multiword expressions: integrating processing (MWE 2004), Barcelona. Association for Computational Linguistics, 103p. http://aclweb.org/anthology-new/W/W04/W04-0400

Villavicencio A, Bond F, Korhonen A, McCarthy D (2005) Introduction to the special issue on multiword expressions having a crack at a hard nut. Computer speech Lang Spec Issue MWEs 19(4):365–377 Elsevier

Villavicencio A, Idiart M, Ramisch C, Araujo VD, Yankama B, Berwick R (2012) Get out but don't fall down: verb-particle constructions in child language. In: Berwick R, Korhonen A, Poibeau T, Villavicencio A (eds) Proceedings of the EACL 2012 workshop on computational models of language acquisition and loss, Avignon. Association for Computational Linguistics, pp 43–50

Yarowsky D (2001) One sense per collocation. In: Proceedings of the first international conference on human language technology research (HLT 2001), San Diego. Morgan Kaufmann Publishers, pp 266–271

Chapter 3
State of the Art in MWE Processing

In the previous chapter, we provided the historical and theoretical foundations for the study of multiword expressions. The set of definitions, characteristics and types described give an idea of the difficulty of the computational tasks involving MWEs. The goal of the present chapter is to draw an overview of the state of the art in computational methods for MWE treatment, focusing on acquisition. State-of-the-art techniques to deal with MWEs are the starting point of the methodology proposed in Chap. 5. Information contained in the present chapter allows better comparison and contextualisation of the present work in the computational linguistics panorama.

In Sect. 3.1, we start with a brief review of some practical *elementary notions*, defining concepts like *n*-grams, frequencies and association measures. These are the tools used by the techniques for automatic *MWE acquisition* described in Sect. 3.2. Although the largest part of research effort in the community has been devoted to acquisition, other tasks such as interpretation, disambiguation and representation are also relevant. Mainly in the last decade, work on these tasks started to emerge, and this is presented in Sect. 3.3.

3.1 Elementary Notions

In this section, we review standard NLP concepts useful in the present work. We focus on general notions that appear recurrently throughout the book, while more detailed explanations of concepts specific to a certain experiment are provided later, whenever they are required.[1]

---

[1]The goal of this section is not to provide a substantial introduction to empirical methods in computational linguistics. Instead, we remind and try to disambiguate as much as possible the definitions of concepts that are already familiar to the reader to some extent. If this is not the case, we recommend Jurafsky and Martin (2008) as a consolidated and wide introduction to NLP and

© Springer International Publishing Switzerland 2015
C. Ramisch, *Multiword Expressions Acquisition*, Theory and Applications
of Natural Language Processing, DOI 10.1007/978-3-319-09207-2_3

We define a *corpus* as a body of texts used in empirical language studies (Manning and Schütze 1999, p. 6). One usually wants for corpora to be representative of the target language, where the meaning of *representative* depends on the context (e.g., application, domain, genre, sublanguage). In our experiments, we use only written corpora like the collection of speech transcripts from the European parliament (Koehn 2005), the 100-million words British National Corpus (Burnard 2007) and the collection of news from the Brazilian *Folha de São Paulo* newspaper. Half a dozen of sentences in French are not a big enough corpus of general French language, as well as a million sentences of computer science articles in English are not representative if the target application will deal with botany texts or with texts in Portuguese.

A corpus may contain data in one language (monolingual) or in several languages (multilingual); when the sentences in one language are translations of sentences in another language, we consider it as a sentence-aligned *parallel corpus*. We will also use the term *general-purpose* corpus to refer to corpora that contain a wide variety of texts corresponding to most common language use over a given time span, while a *specialised* corpus contains texts of a specific knowledge domain or sub-language, like botany, computer science or sailing. We consider a *word token* to be an occurrence of a word in a corpus while a *word type* is a unique occurrence of a word as a lexeme in a dictionary, thesaurus or other lexical resource. The set of unique word types in a corpus constitutes its *vocabulary*.

In Sect. 3.1.1, we introduce linguistic notions such as part of speech and dependency syntax. We provide an overview of the statistical distribution of words in a corpus in Sect. 3.1.2. Section 3.1.3 is about *n*-grams, presenting the basics of *n*-gram probability estimation. In Sect. 3.1.4, we present lexical association measures frequently employed in the automatic acquisition of MWEs.

3.1.1 Linguistic Processing: Analysis

Linguistic analysis is the process of creating more abstract representations from raw text. It is generally seen as a set of steps, each of which must solve ambiguities inherent to language. More sophisticated systems may not solve ambiguities, but represent multiple solutions in the form of weighted lattices (Nasr et al. 2011). However, for concision purposes, we present here a simplified example in the form of a sequence of analysis steps which can be applied on corpora for MWE acquisition.

A corpus may be structured as a set of documents, each document being composed of several paragraphs, which in turn are sequences of sentences. While the higher level divisions are optional and task-dependent, most of the current NLP

Manning and Schütze (1999) for a more specific introduction to empirical methods. Our text is inspired by these two standard reference textbooks.

systems require the text to be split into sentences prior to processing. Splitting the sentences in running text can be accomplished through language-dependent regular expressions on anchor punctuation signs (such as periods and question marks) and lists of common exceptions like abbreviations (*Ph.D.*), acronyms (*Y.M.C.A.*) numbers (*1,399.99*), proper names (*Yahoo!*), filenames and web addresses (*www. google.com*). These can also be modelled through learning sequence tagging models from corpora (Mikheev 2002). Although apparently simple, sentence splitting is challenging in highly structured texts like scientific articles containing many tables, itemised lists and mathematical formulas. Ambiguities about possible splitting points must be dealt with by the system.

Further decomposition takes us from sentences to words. The definition of *word* is discussed in Sect. 2.2.1. In practice, for languages whose writing system uses spaces to separate words, one needs to split from adjacent words punctuation such as commas, periods, apostrophes, dashes and contractions (e.g., the English possessive marker *'s*). It may also be necessary to split contractions such as *du = de + le* in French and *no = em + o* in Portuguese.[2] Other morphological phenomena like prefixes, suffixes and agglutination can also be dealt with at this point. The process of word splitting is called *tokenisation*, and is generally accomplished using regular expressions or trained statistical sequence models. For example, consider the sentence:

Example 3.1. "Tomorrow, I'll be paying a visit to Mary's parents."

After tokenisation, it becomes[3]:

Example 3.2. "␣Tomorrow␣,␣I␣'ll␣be␣paying␣a␣visit␣to␣Mary␣'s␣parents␣.␣"

A word in the corpus occurs in its inflected form, also called the *surface form*. A surface form like *parents* is the plural of the base form *parent*, the verb form *paying* is the gerundive of *pay*, and so on. The morphology of languages models word formation (derivation, compounding) and modification (inflection). The latter often encodes information such as gender, number, tense, mood, voice, person, aspect and case of words. Moreover, distinctive capitalisation marking the beginning of a sentence, for example, needs to be normalised so that *Tomorrow* and *tomorrow* are considered as being the same word.[4] The base form from which an inflected word is derived is called *lemma*. The process of assigning lemmas to words is called *lemmatisation*.

---

[2]Contraction identification usually requires context-aware analysis. For instance, in French, the contraction *des = de + les* is homonym to the partitive/indefinite article *des*.

[3]We use the character ␣ only to emphasise the spaces between words.

[4]However, it is not enough to lowercase the whole text as case information may be important, for instance, in domain-specific texts (chemical element *NaCl*), acronyms (*NASA*, *CIA*) and to distinguish named entities (*Bill Gates*, *March*) from common words (*pay the bill*, *open the gates*, *the soldiers march*).

Generally, lemmatisation is performed simultaneously or immediately after another process called *part-of-speech tagging*. The latter is the assignment of part-of-speech (POS) tags to each word. POS tags represent the grammatical function of words in a sentence, like nouns, verbs and adverbs. They are useful, for example, to distinguish closed-class words or *function words* like prepositions, pronouns and determiners, from open-class words or *content words* like verbs, nouns, adverbs and adjectives. The software performing POS tagging and, usually, lemmatisation, is the *POS tagger*. The set of all POS tags that can be assigned to words in a corpus or tool is the *tagset*. In some of our experiments, we use a POS tagger called TreeTagger (Schmid 1994), described in Appendix B. When the English version of the TreeTagger is applied to the sentence of Example 3.1, the system performs sentence splitting, tokenisation, lemmatisation and POS tagging, resulting in[5]:

Example 3.3. " tomorrow[NN], I[PP] will[MD] be[VB] pay[VBG] a[DT] visit[NN] to[TO] Mary[NNP] 's[POS] parent[NNS]."

The process of going from surface forms to more abstract representations like POS and lemmas is called *analysis*. In order to perform a deeper analysis, one can group POS-tagged words into chunks like noun phrases, and represent chunks as part of a *syntax tree*. There are several formalisms to represent syntactic structures in theory and in practice. We adopted *dependency syntax*. In dependency syntax, all nodes of the syntax tree are the words themselves and the arrows are the dependency relations, tagged with the corresponding relation type (e.g., direct object, subject, determination). A software capable of generating such trees from sentences is a *dependency parser*. For English, we use the RASP parser (Briscoe et al. 2006), described in Appendix B. RASP generates the following surface dependency tree[6] for the example sentence[7]:

Example 3.4.

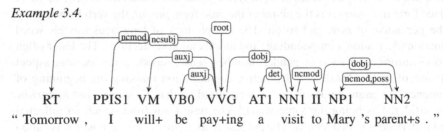

RT   PPIS1 VM   VB0   VVG   AT1 NN1 II NP1   NN2
" Tomorrow ,   I   will+ be   pay+ing a   visit to Mary 's parent+s . "

---

[5]The tagset used by the TreeTagger in English is available at ftp://ftp.cis.upenn.edu/pub/treebank/doc/tagguide.ps.gz and reproduced in Appendix D.4.

[6]Actually, RASP does not generate dependency relations directly, but it infers *grammatical relations* using equivalence rules applied to a traditional constituent parsing tree. Relations are mostly acyclic and exceptions can be dealt with on a case by case basis.

[7]Documentation about RASP's tagset and grammatical relations is available at http://www.cl.cam.ac.uk/techreports/UCAM-CL-TR-662.pdf and in Appendix C of Jurafsky and Martin (2008). Moreover, the tags used by RASP for POS and syntax are reproduced in Appendices D.2 and D.3.

Notice that, for the dependency parser, some nodes like punctuation are ignored, as they are considered irrelevant for syntax.[8] Also, the tagset and the lemmas used by the RASP parser for morphosyntactic analysis are much more fine-grained than those of the TreeTagger. Finding equivalences and adapting the granularity of POS tags is a practical problem in NLP and often demands writing dedicated conversion scripts.

Many other parsers and formalisms exist for English and for other languages, and related work on MWE acquisition explores some of them, as we will discuss in Sect. 3.2.1. Nonetheless, we will limit our discussion to dependency parsing because it is the formalism used in our experiments. The advantage of the dependency formalism is that the resulting tree can be represented on a word basis, that is, for every word we assign two labels: the other word of the sentence on which it depends and the type of the relation. This has practical implications in the data structures used to represent parsed corpora, as we will discuss in Chap. 5. Moreover, more meaningful relations such as subject and object tend to appear closer to the root while auxiliaries and determiners appear as leafs, as shown in Example 3.4.

3.1.2 Word Frequency Distributions

In order to design statistical methods for dealing with corpora, one needs to understand how words and word counts behave in text. We will use as a toy example a fragment of 20,000 English sentences randomly chosen from the British National Corpus, henceforth BNC-frg. Table 3.1 summarises the number of tokens and types in the toy corpus. It can be considered as a sample of English language, and therefore the size N of the sample is the number of tokens, that is, around 414K tokens (surface forms). The vocabulary V is a set containing around 37.6K distinct word types.[9]

Let us define a function $c(w) : V \rightarrow \mathbb{N}$ which associates to each word type w in a vocabulary its number of occurrences in a corpus. When more than one corpus is considered simultaneously, the function is subscripted with the name of the corpus in which the token was counted, for instance, $c_{\text{BNC-frg}}(Mary) = 18$.

Table 3.1 Statistics of BNC-frg—sample of 20,000 random sentences taken from the BNC

# of sentences	20,000
# of tokens	414,602
# of types	37,649

---

[8]This is a simplification, as described by Briscoe et al. (2006).

[9]The *type/token ration*, that is, the number of types with respect to the number of tokens in a text, has been used as a measure of the richness of the vocabulary. This measure depends on the corpus size (Baayen 2001). In BNC-frg, the type/token ratio is of 0.091.

Table 3.2 Counts of the 30 most frequent tokens in BNC-frg

r	c(w)	w	r	c(w)	w	r	c(w)	w
1	20,765	the	11	3,248	for	21	2,173	you
2	19,031	,	12	3,064	it	22	2,146	'
3	16,022	.	13	2,996	was	23	2,029	'
4	11,923	of	14	2,899	's	24	1,899	by
5	9,830	to	15	2,816	I	25	1,800	are
6	9,771	and	16	2,550	on	26	1,782	at
7	7,346	a	17	2,535	be	27	1,727	have
8	6,758	in	18	2,405	with	28	1,668	not
9	4,351	that	19	2,356	as	29	1,532	from
10	4,029	is	20	2,255	The	30	1,496	he

Fig. 3.1 Rank plot of the vocabulary of BNC-frg, with counts in descending order

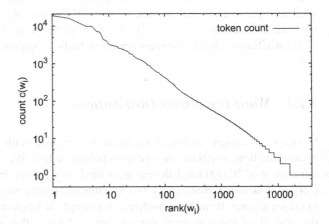

The values of $c(\cdot)$ for the 30 most frequent tokens of BNC-frg are listed in Table 3.2. The most frequent words in any corpus are generally function words like prepositions, determiners, pronouns and punctuation signs. Notice that, as our corpus was not analysed using the tools described in Sect. 3.1.1, the words *the* and *The* are considered as two distinct tokens. Also, because of an encoding problem, there are two different apostrophe characters.

In Sect. 3.1.3, our goal is to estimate the probability of an arbitrary token or sequence of tokens. Therefore, it is useful to study the empirical distribution of the values of function $c(\cdot)$. Unlike the heights of humans or the grades of students in a class, the word counts in a corpus are not normally distributed around the mean. Instead, they are distributed according to a *power law*, also known as *Zipfian distribution*. Many other events in the world are distributed according to power laws (Newman 2005).

In order to illustrate the Zipfian distribution, we will use the rank plot of Fig. 3.1. A rank plot is a graphic where the word counts are sorted in descending order and assigned to their rank positions r, like those in the first column of Table 3.2. Formally, the rank r of a given word w can be defined as the value of a bijective function $rank(w) : V \rightarrow [1..|V|]$ which assigns a distinct integer to each word respecting the constraint $(\forall w_1, w_2 \in V)[rank(w_1) \leq rank(w_2) \iff c(w_1) \geq c(w_2)]$. Notice that, in the presence of ties, the *rank* function is not uniquely defined. Any valid function respecting the aforementioned constraint could be used. Therefore, we assume that lexicographic order is used to assign the ranks of words with identical numbers of occurrences, uniquely defining the *rank* function.

The rank plot of Fig. 3.1 is in logarithmic scale, otherwise it would be impossible to visualise the counts. The main characteristic of power laws is that there is a very large number of rare events. In BNC-frg, for example, there are 21,423 word types occurring only once in the corpus,[10] that is, almost 57 % of the vocabulary. On the opposite end of the range, frequent words correspond to a tiny portion of the vocabulary. The graphic shows that the number of words decreases exponentially in the ranked vocabulary. In other words, Zipf's law states that the number of occurrences of a type in the corpus is inversely proportional to its position in the rank.

A derived property is that the size of the vocabulary increases logarithmically with the size of the corpus. This is exemplified by plotting the number of types in a corpus as its size, that is, the number of tokens, increases, on shown in Figure 3.2. While the number of tokens increases linearly, the number of types increases fast at the beginning and much slower afterwards. This happens because, as the sample increases, many common words tend to be repeated while new words become harder to find. One could assume that, if an infinitely large corpus (the sample) was available, the size of the vocabulary would stop growing at some point, converging to the total number of words used in that language (the population).

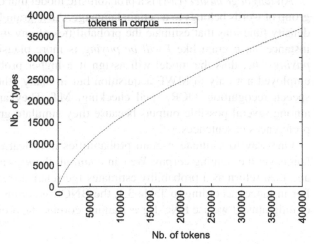

Fig. 3.2 Tokens in the corpus versus types in the vocabulary

---

[10] A word occurring once in the corpus is called a *hapax*, from the Greek *hapax legomena*.

The statistics of a corpus depend on its size, language, genre, domain and sublanguage. Nonetheless, the logarithmic relation between the number of word tokens and the number of different word types holds as well as Zipf's law. This means that, in general, around half of the words in a corpus occur only once. Distributions like these are called *large number of rare events* (LNRE). When the underlying model is a LNRE distribution, specific statistical tools able to deal with sparse data must be employed. Besides, one needs to be careful because standard assumptions for a sample drawn from a population normally distributed do not apply to corpora. Operations like parameter estimation, hypothesis testing and the like need to be adapted when working with LNRE distributions. This has an impact on the types of lexical association measures that can be used for unsupervised MWE acquisition (Sect. 3.1.4). For further details, one may refer to Baayen (2001).

3.1.3 N-Grams, Language Models and Suffix Arrays

When we consider word sequences, each token in the corpus is represented as w_i, where the subscript i stands for its position with respect to other tokens. For instance, a sequence of n consecutive tokens in the corpus can be represented as $w_1 w_2 \ldots w_{n-1} w_n$. Such contiguous sequences are called n-grams.[11] We use the abbreviated notation w_i^j to represent an n-gram formed by $j - i + 1$ words w_i through w_j. By extension, the function $c(\cdot)$ can be applied to n-grams and returns the number of times they occur in a corpus. For example, $c_{\text{BNC-frg}}(I \; will \; be) = 5$ because this 3-gram occurs 5 times in the corpus BNC-frg.

An *language model* (LM) is a probabilistic model that estimates to what extent a group of words belongs to a certain language. An n-gram LM is a set of probability density functions that estimate the probabilities of any n-gram in a language. For instance, an n-gram like *I will be paying* is more plausible in English than *will paying I be*, thus the model will assign it a higher probability. LMs are widely employed not only in MWE acquisition but in many other NLP applications like speech recognition, OCR, spell checking, MT. They are often used to choose among several possible outputs because they simulate grammatical and semantic preferences in sentences.

One way to estimate n-gram probabilities is to learn them from a sample of language: the training corpus. We can count all the n-grams in the training corpus and then return as a probability estimates the relative frequencies of the n-grams. For instance, according to Table 3.1, the BNC-frg corpus contains 414,602 tokens or unigrams. If we use BNC-frg as training corpus, the probability estimate p of the

---

[11]Discontiguous sequences are sometimes referred to as *flexigrams*, that is, n-grams with gaps.

unigram *Mary* is $p(Mary) \approx \dfrac{18}{414{,}602}$ and the probability estimate of the 3-gram *I will be* is $p(I\ will\ be) \approx \dfrac{c(I\ will\ be)}{N} = \dfrac{5}{414{,}602}$.

Although a good idea in theory, it is not feasible to store all the counts for each distinct *n*-gram of arbitrary length (1 to N) in a large corpus, as the number of *n*-grams grows quickly. For instance, BNC-frg contains 37,651 unigrams, 210,183 2-grams, 346,450 3-grams and so on. In order to solve this practical problem, we first apply the probability chain rule, that is, for an arbitrary *n*-gram:

$$p(w_1^n) = p(w_1) \times p(w_2|w_1) \times p(w_3|w_1^2) \ldots p(w_n|w_1^{n-1}) = p(w_1) \times \prod_{k=2}^{n} p(w_k|w_1^{k-1})$$

$$(3.1)$$

We further simplify calculations by applying the Markov assumption in order to approximate the conditional probability of a token given a short history instead of using the whole preceding sequence. That is, given $m > 1$ as the fixed maximum size of *n*-gram that we can store, we ignore all words preceding w_{k-m+1}. The *order m* of the model typically ranges from 2 to 5 according to the target application. This simplification assumes that the presence of a word only depends on a short number of words to the left of it, completely ignoring the right context.

$$p(w_k|w_1^{k-1}) \approx p(w_k|w_{k-m+1}^{k-1}) \qquad (3.2)$$

For instance, let us consider a model of order $m = 2$, built using the BNC-frg corpus as training data. Given this model, we want to estimate the probability of the 4-gram *I will be visiting*. Thus, $p(I\ will\ be\ visiting) = p(I) \times p(will|I) \times p(be|\ will) \times p(visiting|be) = \frac{c(I)}{N} \times \frac{c(I\ will)}{c(I)} \times \frac{c(will\ be)}{c(will)} \times \frac{c(be\ visiting)}{c(be)} = \frac{2{,}816}{414{,}602} \times \frac{34}{2{,}816} \times \frac{312}{1{,}093} \times \frac{1}{2{,}535} = 0.000000009$.

This model uses the principle of *maximum likelihood estimation* (MLE), that is, it assumes that the sample *is* the population. In other words, the chosen model parameters are those that maximise the likelihood of the observed sample. The problem with MLE is that it does not take into account *n*-grams that were not observed in the corpus as a side effect of sampling a very large event space. In other words, no matter how large a training corpus is, a large number of perfectly valid *n*-grams will surely be missing from the model, thus yielding zero probability for the whole product. In order to solve this problem, current LM tools implement sophisticated *smoothing* techniques. The idea of smoothing is to assign some probability mass to unseen events, discounting it from the probabilities of seen *n*-grams (Chen and Goodman 1999; Good 1953; Kneser and Ney 1995). Furthermore, it is also possible to use *backoff* in order to estimate the probabilities of larger unseen *n*-grams by combining the probabilities of smaller *n*-grams contained in them. Because such techniques are rarely employed in empirical MWE acquisition from corpora, we

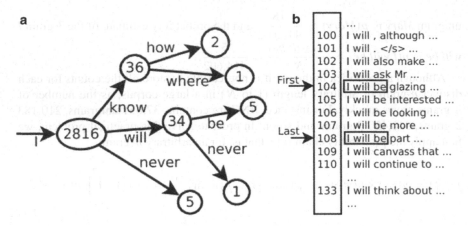

Fig. 3.3 (a) Example of suffix tree. (b) Example of suffix array

will not discuss their details here. One of the rare works concerning smoothing for MWE acquisition is that of Lapata (2002).

When dealing with very large corpora, it is crucial to have efficient access to n-gram counts in order to estimate their probabilities. The intuition behind quick access to n-gram counts in a corpus is to organise the n-grams in a data structure that allows fast search (that is, direct access or binary search). N-gram models with a fixed order m can be represented using structures based on suffix trees. A *suffix tree* is a representation in which each edge is labelled with a word and each node contains a count. Concatenating the words on the edges of a path from the root to a node n_i generates an n-gram whose count is stored in n_i. For example, in Fig. 3.3a, the path *I will be* leads to a node containing the value of c(I will be) $= 5$. In order to optimise the access to the child nodes, it is possible to build hash tables for constant access or ordered lists for binary search.

While suffix trees are appropriate for LMs with fixed order, counting arbitrarily long n-grams requires another kind of data structure. A *suffix array* is an efficient structure to represent n-grams of arbitrary size (Manber and Myers 1990; Yamamoto and Church 2001). The corpus is viewed as an array of N words w_1 to w_N. Each word w_i is the beginning of a corpus suffix of size $N - i + 1$, for instance, $w_{N-2}w_{N-1}w_N$ is a suffix of size 3. The trick is that the list containing all the N suffixes is sorted in lexicographic order. Therefore, one can perform binary search in order to locate the first and the last positions starting with the searched n-gram. For example, in Fig. 3.3b we represent part of a suffix array of BNC-frg. If we want to know how many times the n-gram *I will be* occurs in the corpus, we will perform two binary searches in $O(\log N)$ time to find the first index F and last index L in the array containing a suffix which starts with the searched n-gram. The number of occurrences of the n-gram is then simply $L - F + 1 = 108 - 104 + 1 = 5$. If now we need to obtain the count for *I will*, we repeat the procedure and find $133 - 100 + 1 = 34$.

Table 3.3 Top-15 most frequent n-grams in BNC-frg

r	$c(w_1 w_2)$	$w_1 w_2$	$c(w_1)$	$c(w_2)$	$E(w_1 w_2)$	t-score
1	3,060	of the	11,923	20,765	597.2	44.5
2	1,788	in the	6,758	20,765	338.5	34.3
3	1,139	to the	9,830	20,765	492.3	19.2
4	772	on the	2,550	20,765	127.7	23.2
5	738	and the	9,771	20,765	489.4	9.2
6	733	to be	9,830	2,535	60.1	24.9
7	687	for the	3,248	20,765	162.7	20.0
8	526	at the	1,782	20,765	89.3	19.0
9	525	by the	1,899	20,765	95.1	18.8
10	500	that the	4,351	20,765	217.9	12.6
11	473	of a	11,923	7,346	211.3	12.0
12	457	from the	1,532	20,765	76.7	17.8
13	456	with the	2,405	20,765	120.5	15.7
14	369	it is	3,064	4,029	29.8	17.7
15	362	in a	6,758	7,346	119.7	12.7

In our implementation (see Sect. 5.1.2) each suffix is represented with an integer index pointing to the position in the corpus where it starts, thus optimising memory use. Thus, a suffix array uses a constant amount of memory with respect to N: if every word and every word position in the corpus is encoded as a 4-byte integer, a suffix array uses precisely $4 \times 2 \times N$ bytes, plus the size of the vocabulary, which is generally very small if compared to N.

3.1.4 Lexical Association Measures

The principle of corpus-based MWE acquisition is that words that form an expression will co-occur more often than if they were randomly combined by a coincidence of syntactic rules and semantic preferences. In this context, *lexical association measures* are applied to n-gram counts in order to estimate how much the occurrences of two or more words depend on each other.[12]

A simple method to acquire MWEs from corpora is to use ranked n-gram lists. For example, Table 3.3 lists the 15 most frequent n-grams of BNC-frg. Unfortunately, all of the returned items are uninteresting combinations of function words like determiners *the* and *a*, prepositions and auxiliary verbs. Moreover, the list only contains 2-grams and no 3-grams and larger n-grams. This is a consequence of the fact that the count of a larger n-gram will always be less than or equal to

---

[12]The term *association measure* is standard in MWE acquisition, but it would be more appropriate to talk about association scores instead, since not all the scores discussed here are proper measures.

the count of the n-grams that it contains, thus biasing the acquisition towards short n-grams.

We could solve these problems by separately acquiring n-grams of different lengths, using regular expression patterns to filter out sequences of function words contained in stopword lists or matching unwanted POS tags. This is actually performed in many real-world systems, specially for automatic terminology acquisition, with surprisingly good results (Justeson and Katz 1995; Ramisch 2009). However, if we are to acquire general MWEs (and not only multiword terms), we need a more sophisticated way to tell whether an n-gram is just a random co-occurrence of frequent words or whether it presents some statistical idiomaticity.

A common preprocessing step when dealing with n-gram counts is to eliminate all combinations that occur less than a fixed threshold. This is important because statistics tend not to be reliable in low frequency ranges. As the counts decrease, it is impossible to distinguish statistically significant events from coincidences due to sampling error. Unfortunately, there is no rule or algorithm for determining the value of such threshold except common sense and trial and error. For example, statistics calculated over hapax are surely unreliable while setting the threshold at 100 occurrences will probably result in too little data (if any).

3.1.4.1 Measures Based on Hypothesis Testing

Now, in order to investigate whether an n-gram is a MWE, let us assume that words are combined randomly. That is, the occurrence of words at given positions are independent events. This hypothesis does not hold, otherwise languages would have no grammar. Nonetheless, it provides a powerful way to test the association strength between words. By the definition of statistical independence, if the occurrence of a word w_2 does not depend on the occurrence of the preceding word w_1, then we expect that the joint probability of the 2-gram is the product of the probabilities of the individual events, that is:

$$p(w_1^2) = p(w_1) \times p(w_2) \tag{3.3}$$

For the sake of simplicity, let us use MLE estimators for the probabilities of the individual words through relative frequencies, that is $p(w_i) = \dfrac{c(w_i)}{N}$. Then, for an arbitrary n-gram w_1^n, the expected relative frequency would be the probability:

$$p(w_1^n) = \frac{c(w_1)}{N} \times \frac{c(w_2)}{N} \times \ldots \times \frac{c(w_n)}{N} = \frac{c(w_1) \times c(w_2) \times \ldots \times c(w_n)}{N^n} \tag{3.4}$$

We can scale this probability estimate by the approximate number of n-grams in the corpus ($N - n + 1 \approx N$) to obtain the expected count $E(w_1^n)$:

$$E(w_1^n) = N \times \frac{c(w_1) \times c(w_2) \times \ldots \times c(w_n)}{N^n} = \frac{c(w_1) \times c(w_2) \times \ldots \times c(w_n)}{N^{n-1}} \tag{3.5}$$

Column 6 of Table 3.3 shows the values of $E(w_1^n)$ for the top-30 most frequent 2-grams in BNC-frg. Combinations of frequent words are expected to occur frequently while combinations involving rarer words are expected to occur less. One way to test whether the difference between the expected count $E(\cdot)$ and the observed count $c(\cdot)$ is statistically significant is to use a hypothesis test. Our null hypothesis H_0 is that an n-gram will occur as many times as we expect it to occur, and our alternative hypothesis H_1 is that the observed number of occurrences $c(w_1^n)$ is actually greater than the expected number of occurrences:

$$H_0 : c(w_1^n) = E(w_1^n)$$

$$H_1 : c(w_1^n) > E(w_1^n)$$

Our goal is to reject this null hypothesis using a one-tailed test. If we can reject H_0 at some significance level, this means that the number of occurrences of the n-gram is above what we expected, and we have good chances of finding a MWE. In theory, we should perform an exact test, using the binomial or Poisson test statistics,[13] that model the discrete distribution of n-gram counts (Evert 2004). For instance, a binomomial test statistic uses the binomial distribution to estimate the probability of observing $c(w_1^n)$ or more occurrences of an n-gram given its expected probability $\frac{E(w_1^n)}{N}$:

$$p(X > c(w_1^n)) = \sum_{k=c(w_1^n)}^{N} \binom{N}{k} \left(\frac{E(w_1^n)}{N}\right)^k \left(1 - \frac{E(w_1^n)}{N}\right)^{N-k} \tag{3.6}$$

In practice, however, this test statistic is computationally costly. The number of terms in the sum, $N - c(w_1^n) + 1$ is prohibitive in most cases because N is much larger than $c(w_1^n)$. Moreover, for large values of N, the binomial distribution can be approximated by a normal distribution. As a consequence, it is possible use a z test statistic instead of the exact binomial test statistic: $p(X > c(w_1^n)) = \frac{c(w_1^n) - E(w_1^n)}{E(w_1^n)}$.

A very common test statistic employed in MWE acquisition is *Student's t test* statistic, a heuristic variation of the z test statistic in which the variance of the sample is estimated through its observed count $c(w_1^n)$ rather than from the expected count $E(w_1^n)$. This approximation holds if we consider the corpus as a sequence of randomly generated n-grams and a Bernoulli trial that assigns 1 to the occurrence of w_1^n and 0 otherwise. Then, the probability p of generating 1 is the mean of the sample, $\bar{x} = p = \frac{c(w_1^n)}{N}$. For small values of p, $s^2 = p \times (1 - p) \approx p$, thus the variance of the sample s^2 is equivalent to the mean $\bar{x}$. Finally, the estimated theoretical mean μ is the normalised estimated count $\frac{E(w_1^n)}{N}$, thus yielding the following formulation for the t test statistic:

---

[13]The *test statistic* is a random variable with a known distribution, from which we can obtain the p-value. If the p-value is below a certain significance level, we can reject the null hypothesis.

$$t = \frac{\bar{x} - \mu}{\sqrt{\frac{s^2}{N}}} = \frac{\frac{c(w_1^n)}{N} - \frac{E(w_1^n)}{N}}{\sqrt{\frac{c(w_1^n)}{N^2}}} = \frac{c(w_1^n) - E(w_1^n)}{\sqrt{c(w_1^n)}} \qquad (3.7)$$

As we have seen in Sect. 3.1.2, word counts do not follow a normal distribution, but they can be modelled using a power law distribution, and the same applies to n-grams. As a consequence, from a theoretical perspective, the use of Student's t test statistic here does not make sense as it assumes that the $c(w_1^n)$ follows a normal distribution. Nonetheless, most of the time in MWE acquisition, our goal is to rank candidate n-grams according to their association strength. Thus, the value of the t test statistic is not used to calculate the p-value, but is used directly as a ranking criterion. This ranking criterion is called the t-score, and it is interpreted as follows: a large value means strong word association and thus a potential MWE, a small value means that n-gram is more likely to be a random word combination, thus uninteresting for MWE acquisition. Notice that, for the examples in Table 3.3, the statistic is larger when the combination is composed of rarer words.

3.1.4.2   Measures Based on Pointwise Comparisons

The t-score is an example of lexical *association measure* (AM), that is, a numerical score that estimates the degree of dependence or association strength between the number of occurrences of the n-gram and the number of occurrences of the individual words that compose it. Similarly to n-gram counts, when more than one corpus is involved, we will subscribe the name of the association measure with the name of the corpus from which the counts used to calculate it were obtained, like in t-score$_{\text{BNC-frg}}$. In addition to the t-score, there are many other proposed measures in the literature, not necessarily based on hypothesis testing. Church and Hanks (1990), for instance, suggest to use *pointwise mutual information* (pmi), a notion coming from information theory which estimates the predictability of a word given the preceding words. In other terms, pmi quantifies the discrepancy between the observed count and the expected count:

$$\text{pmi} = \log_2 \frac{c(w_1^n)}{E(w_1^n)} \qquad (3.8)$$

This AM has its maximal value when the two words only occur together, that is $c(w_1) = \ldots = c(w_n) = c(w_1^n)$. One disadvantage of pmi is that there is no lower bound for its value, since $\log 0$ is undefined. Another disadvantage is that this score requires hard frequency thresholds, as it overestimates the importance of rare n-grams. For instance, the maximal value can be obtained for any n-gram with $c(w_1) = \ldots = c(w_n) = c(w_1^n) = 1$.

Another commonly employed AM is Dice's coefficient, a classical score used in information retrieval to calculate the similarity between two sets. The original version of Dice's coefficient divides the size of the intersection between n sets (scaled by n) by the sum of their individual sizes. In the case of n-grams, we adapt this measure to compare the n-gram count (intersection between all words) with the sum of the counts of the individual words contained in it:

$$\text{dice} = \frac{n \times c(w_1^n)}{\sum_{i=1}^{n} c(w_i)} \qquad (3.9)$$

These scores are applicable to arbitrary-length n-grams, but they only take into account the observed number of occurrences $c(w_1^n)$. In spite of their simplicity, they are quite popular in MWE acquisition and in other NLP tasks.

3.1.4.3 Measures Based on Contingency Tables

Nonetheless, more robust and theoretically sound AMs exist for the special case of 2-grams. These measures are based on *contingency tables*, that is, a representation like the one showed in Table 3.4, in which we consider the occurrence of two words as two random variables. We denote as $\neg w_i$ the occurrence of any word different from w_i. Notice that all the cell values are derived from the count of the 2-gram $c(w_1 w_2)$, the individual word counts $c(w_1)$, $c(w_2)$ and the total number of tokens in the corpus N. The values in the last row represent the sum of the values of the inner cells, and analogously for the last column. These are often called *marginal counts* because they are written in the margins of the contingency table. The value of the cell in the last row and column corresponds the number of elements in the sample N, and is equivalent to the sum of the marginal counts in both directions.

For every cell in the contingency table, it is possible to calculate the equivalent expected value if the occurrences of the two words were independent events, as follows:

$$\forall w_i \in \{w_1, \neg w_1\}, \forall w_j \in \{w_2, \neg w_2\}, E(w_i w_j) = \frac{c(w_i) \times c(w_j)}{N} \qquad (3.10)$$

Table 3.4 Contingency table for two random variables: the occurrence of the first word w_1 and the occurrence of the second word w_2, $\neg w_i$ denotes the occurrence of any word except w_i

	w_2	$\neg w_2$	
w_1	$c(w_1 w_2)$	$c(w_1 \neg w_2)$ $= c(w_1) - c(w_1 w_2)$	$c(w_1)$
$\neg w_1$	$c(\neg w_1 w_2)$ $= c(w_2) - c(w_1 w_2)$	$c(\neg w_1 \neg w_2)$ $= N - c(w_1) - c(w_2) + c(w_1 w_2)$	$c(\neg w_1)$ $= N - c(w_1)$
	$c(w_2)$	$c(\neg w_2)$ $= N - c(w_2)$	N

We can employ the X^2 test statistic in order to estimate whether the difference between observed and expected contingency tables is statistically significant, as we did for the count $c(w_1^n)$. The X^2 test statistic is a scaled mean squared error measure between observed and expected cell values. That is, for all values of $w_i \in \{w_1, \neg w_1\}$ and $w_j \in \{w_2, \neg w_2\}$,

$$X^2 = \sum_{w_i, w_j} \frac{[c(w_i w_j) - E(w_i w_j)]^2}{E(w_i w_j)} \tag{3.11}$$

The X^2 test statistic for two random variables has an asymptotic χ^2 distribution with one degree of freedom. Thus, it is possible to obtain the p-value which, if sufficiently small, indicates a significant difference between the tables. However, as for the t test, usually the test statistic is considered by itself as a ranking criterion.

A very popular AM based on contingency tables is the *log-likelihood ratio* (ll). It was proposed for the first time for MWE acquisition by Dunning (1993). This measure is preferable over X^2 because, for small samples with LNRE distributions, it provides more accurate association estimators, as demonstrated through numerical simulation by Dunning (1993). The simplified version of the ll AM is:

$$ll = 2 \times \sum_{w_i, w_j} c(w_i w_j) \times \log \frac{c(w_i w_j)}{E(w_i w_j)} \tag{3.12}$$

This measure has the advantage that, in addition to being theoretically sound, numerically simple and robust to low frequencies, it has a simple interpretation. Its value equals the number of times the 2-gram is more likely under the hypothesis that the words are not independent than the individual counts would suggest. While on the one hand ll is robust and theoretically sound, on the other hand it is only applicable to the case where $n = 2$. Extensions to larger n-grams, although possible, are far from being intuitive (see the documentation of the NSP package, described in Sect. 3.2.3.1, for an example).

3.1.4.4   Other Measures

There are numerous AMs available for MWE acquisition. Pecina (2008) presents a table containing 84 measures among which some are rank-equivalent to each other. Hoang et al. (2009) propose and evaluate the adaptation of traditional AMs for word pairs in which one word is very frequent and the other is rather rare, like it is the case for English phrasal verbs formed by rare verbs (e.g., *nail*) with frequent prepositions and adverbs (e.g., *down*).

Table 3.5 shows the top-15 n-grams acquired from BNC-frg as ranked by some of the AMs presented here. A threshold of at least 3 occurrences was set to reduce noise. The first measure, the t-score, seems to retrieve rather long specialised MWEs like proper names (*Unix System Laboratories Inc*) and terminological

Table 3.5 Top-15 *n*-grams (2–5) extracted from BNC-frg and ranked according to AMs

t-score	pmi	dice	ll
Net earnings per share amounted	of the	CHANCERY DIVISION	of the
reported first quarter net profit	in the	homoclinic orbits	in the
Microsoft Corp 's Windows NT	, and	Los Angeles	, but
(7) mm Hg	to be	Yours sincerely	to be
or fume or other impurity	, but	Greenhouse Effect	I 'm
earnings per share amounted to	on the	Hong Kong	have been
7) mm Hg in	for the	gon na	do n't
dust or fume or other	. '	inter alia	, and
has reported first quarter net	to the	Khmer Rouge	will be
[CHANCERY DIVISION]	at the	Inland Revenue	the the
Inc has reported first quarter	by the	Sri Lanka	per cent
; [1991] 2	from the	Cruz Operation	, ,
N C V O	it is	per cent	has been
Unix System Laboratories Inc	will be	Molecular biology	on the
you 're gon na get	it's	Winston Churchill	the .

phraseology (*reported first quarter net profit*). The list illustrates one of the problems with *n*-gram based methods: the extraction of nested expressions, that is, a shorter expression like *first quarter* contained in a larger one like *first quarter net profit*. Delimiting the borders of a MWE is a current challenge in acquisition tools and methods.

The dice coefficient, on the other hand, retrieves shorter *n*-grams among which we find many MWE types like proper names (*Sri Lanka, Winston Churchill*), noun compounds (*Greenhouse Effect, molecular biology*), formulaic sequences (*Yours sincerely*) and fixed expressions (*per cent, inter alia*). Both t-score and dice tend to retrieve rarer sequences, which only occur three to four times in the corpus.

The other two measures seem to fail in extracting any interesting MWE, as they give much weight to frequent combinations of function words. The ll score retrieves some cases of rare double commas or double *the* determiners. Most of the applications of pmi and ll in the literature are targeted, as these AMs are used to classify possible collocates for a given fixed word, and not to blindly acquire unknown MWEs from a corpus (Dunning 1993; Church and Hanks 1990). The unfortunate reality in AMs for MWE acquisition is that sometimes the most theoretically sound measures perform worse than intuitive heuristics.

This example is an illustration of how AMs work and shows that their results are complementary, suggesting that their combination should be envisaged for broad coverage acquisition. Although there is some published work on fair comparisons among AMs (Pearce 2002; Evert and Krenn 2005; Wermter and Hahn 2006; Schone and Jurafsky 2001), this falls out of the scope of our work and is not the goal of our example. Moreover, the measures have different weaknesses: some overestimate the importance of rare *n*-grams while others are not capable of dealing with frequent items. Thus, different count thresholds should be applied for each AM, specially for such a small corpus as the BNC-frg. In addition, further cleaning of function words and punctuation is an easy step that should be performed in any case.

Besides association measures, there are also other types of statistical measures that can be used as evidence for MWE discovery in corpora. Pecina (2005), for example, discovered that context measures that consider the adjacent words of the n-grams are more adequate to acquire idiomatic expressions. In terminology acquisition, contrastive measures like C-NC and csMWE are employed as a way of verifying the pertinence of the n-gram to the target domain (Frantzi et al. 2000; Bonin et al. 2010a). These measures estimate the difference between the occurrences of an n-gram in a specialised corpus and in a generic corpus (also called the contrastive corpus). They are recommended to identify terms that occur frequently in a specialised corpus but not in general language (see Sect. 5.1.2.4)

For further material on AMs, please refer to Evert (2004), Seretan (2011), and Pecina (2008). A summary of common association measures can also be found on Stefan Evert's website http://www.collocations.de/.

3.2   Methods for Automatic MWE Acquisition

The tasks involved in the computational treatment of MWEs have been structured by the organisers of the 2009 MWE workshop (Anastasiou et al. 2009) as follows.

- **Identification (or acquisition).** Given a text as input, try to locate the interesting multiword units in it.
- **Interpretation.** Given a multiword unit out of context, try to discover its internal structure both in terms of syntactic and semantic relations.
- **Disambiguation.** Given a multiword unit in its context, try to classify it with respect to a closed set of categories. Typically, one tries to distinguish literal from idiomatic uses, but other disambiguation tasks are possible, for instance, distinguishing general-purpose from specialised uses and performing multiword sense disambiguation.
- **Application.** Given a lexicon of MWEs, try to integrate it in another application such as parsing, information retrieval or MT.

Interpretation and disambiguation are similar as both can be modelled as classification tasks. However, they are distinct as the former concerns MWE types whereas the latter deals with MWE tokens as they occur in text. In addition to the four topics above, we consider an additional task which lies between disambiguation and application, representation:

- **Representation.** Given a lexicon containing MWEs (automatically or manually acquired), try to optimise their representation in a given formalism considering their properties and the target application.

As pointed out in the call for papers of the MWE 2009 workshop[14]:

The above topics largely overlap. For example, identification can require disambiguating between literal and idiomatic uses since MWEs are typically required to be non-compositional by definition. Similarly, interpreting three-word noun compounds like *morning flight ticket* and *plastic water bottle* requires disambiguation between a left and a right syntactic structure, while interpreting two-word compounds like *English teacher* requires disambiguating between (a) 'teacher who teaches English' and (b) 'teacher coming from England (who could teach any subject, e.g., math)'.

As a large part of the research developed and presented in this book focuses on the first task, the present section is entirely dedicated to MWE acquisition. We start with a summary of related work on monolingual acquisition in Sect. 3.2.1, and on multilingual acquisition in Sect. 3.2.2. Then, we present a more practical description of tools that perform automatic acquisition, distinguishing between those freely available developed by academic researchers and those which were developed and commercialised by companies.

3.2.1 Monolingual Methods

In this section, we discuss some relevant papers on monolingual MWE acquisition methods. The references discussed here are complemented by the work that has been developed for other MWE tasks (Sect. 3.3).

One of the goals of monolingual MWE acquisition techniques is to help and speed up the creation of lexical resources such as printed or machine-readable dictionaries and thesauri containing multiword entries. We distinguish two types of acquisition tasks:

- *MWE extraction.* The input is a text and the expected output is a list of MWE candidates found in the text. The evaluation can be done on a type basis, as if each expression was an entry of a lexicon, independently of the input corpus. In extraction, it is usual to consider two separate steps: (a) *candidate extraction* and (b) *candidate filtering and/or ranking.* We consider that an *MWE candidate* is a sequence of words which has some of the characteristics described in Sect. 2.3 as measured by some objective measure, but that was not yet validated by a manual or automatic evaluation process.

- In *MWE identification.* The input is a text and the expected output is a mark-up indicating the places where MWEs occur. This may include the use of an existing dictionary or the discovery of new MWEs. What makes MWE identification more difficult than simple regular-expression matching is non-adjacency, morphological inflection and ambiguity of some MWEs that can be used both as compositional and idiomatic sequences (e.g., *look up* as consult

---

[14]http://multiword.sourceforge.net/mwe2009

a dictionary or as staring towards a higher position). In MWE identification, a token-based evaluation is required, taking into account the context in which the expression occurs.

Candidate extraction methods are usually based on some kind of pattern matching, where the patterns range from simple n-grams to structured sequences of part-of-speech tags and syntactic relations. The level of linguistic information employed in candidate extraction depends on various factors such as the language, the type and syntactic variability of the target MWEs and the available analysis tools.

The use of surface forms alone is rare, as generally at least minimal patterns based on stopwords or POS are employed (Gurrutxaga and Alegria 2011). However, there might be cases where flat n-gram extraction is required, for instance, when the target MWEs are generic keyphrases for document description and indexation (Silva and Lopes 2010). The sliding window method consists of considering as MWE candidates pairs that co-occur in a window of at most w words, thus retrieving discontiguous n-grams (Smadja 1993). The extraction of candidates using sliding windows can pose a challenge in terms of computational performance. Indeed, optimised data structures and algorithms must be used because the number of possible combinations, even for relatively small sizes of n, explodes with the size of the corpus (Gil and Dias 2003).

Part of speech sequences are one of the major approaches in candidate extraction because (i) many languages have available push-button POS taggers and (ii) this approach provides good results when the target constructions are relatively rigid in terms of word order, like fixed phrases and nominal MWEs. POS sequences have been used originally in multiword terminology acquisition (Justeson and Katz 1995; Daille 2003), but have also been applied to the extraction of other MWE types, specially noun compounds (Vincze et al. 2011). Even when dealing with more variable constructions such as verbal expressions, POS tag patterns can be used in the absence of syntactic information (Baldwin 2005; Duran et al. 2011). POS patterns can be defined based on various criteria, from linguistic intuition and expert knowledge (Bonin et al. 2010b) to systematic empirical observation of a sample (Duran et al. 2011). Sequences of POS can also be automatically learnt from annotated corpora, using the same methodology as for words, that is, by maximising some AM on the extracted POS n-grams (Dias 2003).

When a parser is available, patterns based on syntactic relations can be used for candidate extraction and/or identification. For example, one may retrieve all candidates that are formed by a noun which is the direct object of a verb (*take/V* $\leftarrow_{\text{DOBJ}}$ *time/N*). According to the accuracy of the parser, simple syntactic patterns can be more precise than POS sequences, specially in the extraction of non-fixed MWEs like "true" collocations (Seretan 2008; Seretan and Wehrli 2009; Seretan 2011). Lexicons containing more or less refined MWE representations can be used to identify MWEs during parsing, with the advantage of disambiguating instances in context (Bejček et al. 2013; Constant et al. 2013). Tree substitution grammars can also be used in order to learn syntactic MWE models from annotated corpora, as in the French version of the Stanford parser (Green et al. 2011). Regardless of the syntactic information and labels, structural regularities in parsing trees can also be used to retrieve MWE candidates using a minimal description length algorithm (Martens and Vandeghinste 2010). Often, these identification techniques require an annotated corpus with MWE markup. While some MWE types may be represented in existing treebanks, in most cases an additional annotation layer must be added (Laporte et al. 2008; Uresova et al. 2013).

In addition to analysed corpora, other monolingual and multilingual resources can be used for MWE acquisition. For instance, by comparing the titles of Wikipedia pages using cross-language links, it is possible to detect multiword titles whose translation in one of the other languages is a single word (Attia et al. 2010). Another way to use the web as a source of information for MWE acquisition is to generate candidates according to generic combination rules and further validate them using web search engine hit counts (Villavicencio et al. 2005). This is explored in our experiments in Sect. 6.2.3.2. The current trend is the integration of several complementary information sources (including linguistic analysis, statistics, the web) in order to maximise the recall of the extraction (de Medeiros Caseli et al. 2009; Attia et al. 2010).

More complex candidate extraction methods, not based on pattern matching, have also been proposed. The LocalMaxs algorithm, for instance, performs extraction based on the maximisation of an AM applied to adjacent word pairs. Thus, it naturally handles nested expressions, extracting maximal sequences that recursively include adjacent words while the overall AM score increases (Silva and Lopes 1999). Similarly, a tightness measure is used in a Chinese IR system for the automatic identification, concatenation and optimised querying of strongly associated word sequences (Xu et al. 2010). Duan et al. (2006) propose a string matching algorithm, inspired by computational biology, to extract sequences that occur recurrently throughout the corpus. Sentences are viewed as DNA sequences and a dynamic programming algorithm is used to match corresponding parts for each sentence pair in the corpus, taking into account gaps that represent variable parts of the expression. These techniques generally do not distinguish candidate extraction from filtering, performing both simultaneously.

As for candidate filtering in MWE extraction, some straightforward procedures are the use of stopword lists and of count thresholds to remove candidates for which statistical information is insufficient. Lexical association measures like those described in Sect. 3.1.4 are also widely employed to rank the candidates and keep only those whose association score is above a certain threshold (Evert and Krenn 2005; Pecina 2005). When several AMs are available, they can be combined using machine learning, possibly considering additional information coming from auxiliary resources. Thus, it is necessary to annotate part of the MWE lists to obtain an annotated extraction dataset (Grégoire et al. 2008). Then, a supervised learning method can be used to build a classifier modelling the optimal weights of all the AMs and extra features (Ramisch et al. 2008; Pecina 2008).

There is a strong predominance of methods based on 2-grams (or more generally on word pairs, not necessarily adjacent) in current techniques for monolingual

MWE acquisition. This is justified because (i) the majority of the interesting and challenging MWEs are formed by two words and (ii) "experiments with longer expressions would require processing of much larger amount of data and [there is a] limited scalability of some methods to [handle] high order n-grams" (Pecina 2005). While this seems like a reasonable justification to keep the methodology simple, it does not correspond to the reality of NLP applications, where many MWEs longer than two words also require proper treatment (Nakov and Hearst 2005; Kim and Nakov 2011).

Monolingual methods have been developed in several languages and are sometimes language independent. The advantage of language-independent methods is that they do not depend on the availability of a specific resource (POS tagger, parser) and can thus be applied to virtually any language, including poorly resourced ones. On the other hand, the use of linguistic information generally improves the precision and the coverage of the acquisition. Finding an adequate trade-off between language independence and quality when designing a method for monolingual acquisition is a challenging problem. However, as MWEs seem to be a universal phenomenon, being present in all human languages, it is important to build methods and evaluate them in multilingual contexts (Seretan and Wehrli 2006).

3.2.2   Bi- and Multilingual Methods

Even though many of the methods described in the previous section can be applied to arbitrary corpora, independently of the language, they are still considered as monolingual methods because the result is a list of MWEs or a marked up text with no cross-lingual correspondences. The extraction of bilingual MWEs is a task in which the resulting list of expressions is bilingual, that is, if a candidate is returned in one language, it contains translation links which relate it to its correspondent candidate(s) in the other language(s). Hence, bi- and multilingual MWE acquisition is different from language-independent MWE acquisition. Existing techniques for bilingual MWE acquisition are frequently based on parallel corpora.

Automatic word alignment can provide lists of MWE candidates by themselves, as described in de Medeiros Caseli et al. (2010). They aligned a Portuguese–English corpus in both directions using GIZA++, and then joined the alignments using the grow-diag-final heuristic. Word sequences of two or more words on the source side aligned to sequences of one or more words on the target side were filtered using several stopword patterns and the resulting candidates were considered as MWEs. The comparison with a simple monolingual n-gram method showed that alignment-based extraction is much more precise, but has very limited recall. This technique has been further validated for the acquisition of Portuguese multiword terms in technical and scientific domains (Ramisch et al. 2010).

Tsvetkov and Wintner (2010) extended this method with two main improvements: (a) they consider all non-bijective 1:1 alignments as candidate sequences and (b) they validate their candidates using an association measure, PMI^n, calculated on a large monolingual corpus. Furthermore, they combine alignment information with other linguistic sources (Tsvetkov and Wintner 2011). They evaluate their method by integrating the automatically extracted bilingual lexicon in a statistical MT system, obtaining small but significant improvements in translation quality.

Bai et al. (2009) present an algorithm capable of mining translations for a given MWE in a parallel aligned corpus. Then, the different translations are ranked according to standard association measures in order to choose the appropriate one. They integrated this extraction method into the statistical MT system Moses for the English–Chinese language pair, obtaining improved translations when compared to a baseline.

The automatic discovery of non-compositional compounds from parallel data has been explored by Melamed (1997). Considering a statistical translation model, he introduced a feature based on mutual information and proposed an iterative algorithm that retrieves an increasing number of compounds. These can in turn be used to improve the quality of the statistical translation system itself.

Conversely, it has been shown that MWEs can improve the quality of automatic word alignment. The English-Hindi language pair presents large word order variation, and it has been shown that MWE-based features that model compositionality can help reduce alignment error rate (Venkatapathy and Joshi 2006). When compared with baseline GIZA++, a system enriched with MWE features obtains significantly lower error rates, from 68.92 to 50.45 %.

The acquisition of bilingual verbal expressions requires not only the availability of parallel corpora, but also of syntactic analysis of both languages. Zarrieß and Kuhn (2009) used syntactically analysed corpora and GIZA++ alignments to extract verb-object pairs from a German–English parallel corpus. They considered a candidate as a true MWE if (i) a verb on the source side was aligned to a verb on the target side, (ii) the noun heading the object of the verb on the source side was tagged as a noun on the target side and (iii) there was a syntactic object relation on the target side between the target verb and the target noun. Their method retrieves 82.1 % of correct translations, and almost 60 % of translations which can be considered as MWEs.

Bouamor et al. (2012) also perform bilingual MWE acquisition using word alignments, but instead of using them as a starting point, they use them a posteriori, after monolingual extraction has been performed on source and target corpora. Therefore, acquiring a bilingual MWE lexicon is seen as an alignment problem between expressions acquired separately in each language.

Instead of relying on large parallel word-aligned corpora, which are not always available for a given language pair, it is possible to use comparable corpora as a source for acquisition. Daille et al. (2004) performed multiword term extraction independently in French and in English using comparable corpora in the environmental domain. Then, using the distances between the context vectors of the acquired terms, they obtained cross-lingual equivalences that were evaluated against a bilingual terminological dictionary. The dictionary reference translation occurred among the top-20 retrieved translations in 47–89 % of the translations, depending on the translation relation type (single word vs multiword).

The acquisition of bilingual MWEs has been explored more often in the context of machine translation. In Sect. 3.3.4.4, we provide an overview of attempts to integrate MWEs into different MT applications. This is further developed in the experiments described in Sect. 7.2.

3.2.3   Existing Tools

The maturity of a research field depends not only on theoretical models and experimental results, but also on concrete tools and available software on the basis of which it is possible to reproduce results, build extensions and perform systematic evaluations. Thus, tools for the automatic acquisition of MWEs are very important for the evolution of this research field. Here, we distinguish two types of tools: those which are freely available for the community (Sect. 3.2.3.1) and those that are either commercial or available in restricted contexts (Sect. 3.2.3.2).

3.2.3.1   Freely Available Tools

To date, the existing research tools follow the main trends in the area, using linguistic analysis and statistical information as clues for finding MWEs in texts. Here, we present a list of freely available tools that can be used mostly for monolingual MWE acquisition.

1. **LocalMaxs**: http://hlt.di.fct.unl.pt/luis/multiwords/
   The "Multiwords" scripts are the reference implementation[15] of the LocalMaxs algorithm. It extracts MWEs by generating all possible n-grams from a sentence and then further filtering them based on the local maxima of a customisable AM's distribution (Silva and Lopes 1999). On the one hand this approach is based purely on word counts and is completely language independent. On the other hand, it is not possible to directly integrate linguistic information in order to target a specific type of construction or to remove noisy ungrammatical candidates.[16] The tool includes a strict version, which prioritises high precision, and a relaxed version, which focuses on high recall. A separate tool is provided to deal with big corpora. A variation of the original algorithm, SENTA, has been proposed to deal with non-contiguous expressions (da Silva et al. 1999). However, it is computationally costly because it is based on the calculation of all possible n-grams in a sentence, which explodes when going from contiguous to

---

[15]Recommended by the author of the algorithm in personal communication.

[16]Although this can be simulated by concatenating words and POS tags together in order to form a token.

non-contiguous n-grams. Furthermore, there is no freely available implementation.

2. **Text::NSP**: http://search.cpan.org/dist/Text-NSP

 The N-gram Statistics Package (NSP) is a standard tool for the statistical analysis of n-grams in text files developed and maintained since 2003 (Pedersen et al. 2011; Banerjee and Pedersen 2003). It provides Perl scripts for counting n-grams in a text file and calculating AMs, where an n-gram is either a sequence of n contiguous words or n words occurring in a window of $w \geq n$ words in a sentence. While most of the measures are only applicable to 2-grams, some of them are also extended to 3- and 4-grams, notably the log-likelihood measure. The set of available AMs includes robust and theoretically sound measures such as Fischer's exact test. The input to the NSP tool is a corpus and a parameter value fixing the size of the target n-grams. The output is a list of types extracted from the corpus along with the counts, which can further be used to calculate the AMs. Although there is no direct support to linguistic information such as POS, it is possible to simulate them to some extent using the same workaround as for LocalMaxs.[16] The tool allows complex expressions in order to express what counts should be calculated in terms of the sub-n-grams contained in a given n-gram.

3. **UCS**: http://www.collocations.de/software.html

 The UCS toolkit provides a large set of sophisticated AMs, in addition to other mathematical procedures like dispersion test, frequency distribution models and evaluation methods. It was developed in Perl and uses the R statistics package. UCS focuses on high accuracy calculations for 2-gram AMs, but, unlike the other approaches, it does not properly perform MWE acquisition. Instead of a corpus, it receives a list of candidates and their respective counts, relying on external tools for corpus preprocessing and candidate extraction. Then, it calculates the measures and ranks the candidates. Therefore, the question about contiguous n-grams or support of linguistic filters is not relevant for UCS.

4. **jMWE**: projects.csail.mit.edu/jmwe

 The jMWE tool (Kulkarni and Finlayson 2011) is aimed at dictionary-based in-context MWE token *identification* in running text, which makes it quite different from *extraction* tools. It is available in the form of a Java library, and expects a corpus as input, possibly annotated with lemmas and parts of speech. In addition, it requires an initial dictionary of valid known MWEs. The system then looks for instances (occurrences) in the corpus of the MWEs included in its internal dictionary. It does not perform any automatic discovery of new expressions, thus the quality of the output heavily depends on the availability of MWE dictionaries. While jMWE is not language independent, it can be configured and straightforwardly adapted to other languages for which a suitable dictionary is available. The system allows quite powerful instance search, similar to multilevel regular expressions. It is possible to deal with non-contiguous expressions and to apply successive filters on the output. jMWE also provides heuristics for disambiguating nested compounds. On the other hand, it is not possible to express constraints based on syntax, nor to apply AMs in order to remove words that co-occur by chance.

5. **Varro**: http://sourceforge.net/projects/varro/
   This tool is not specifically aimed at MWE acquisition, but rather at finding regularities in treebanks (Martens 2010). It implements an optimised version of the *Apriori* algorithm with many adaptations that allow for the efficient and compact representation of tree structures. Statistical scores based on description length gain have been proposed to rank regular subtrees returned by the tool, thus helping in the acquisition of MWEs (Martens and Vandeghinste 2010). In contrast with the preceding tools, the Varro toolkit is not based on word sequences, but it requires syntactically analysed corpora as input. It is thus well suited for the extraction of flexible expressions such as idioms, formulaic phrases, "true" collocations and verbal expressions.

There are also numerous freely available web services and downloadable tools for automatic term extraction. These tools are generally language dependent, having versions for major European languages like English, Spanish, French and Italian. Although multiword terms are included in our definition of MWE, these tools are not appropriate for general-purpose extraction of expressions in everyday language. Examples of such tools are TermoStat,[17] AntConc[18] and TerMine.[19] The Wikipedia page on terminology extraction[20] lists many other freely available tools.

The methodological framework introduced in the present work has also been implemented in a freely available tool, the `mwetoolkit`.[21] This tool is described in detail in Chap. 5.

3.2.3.2 Commercial Tools

There are numerous commercialised systems for automatic terminology extraction from specialised texts. As a great part of terminology is multiword, this kind of software performs MWE acquisition at some point. Déjean et al. (2002), for example, describe a method developed at Xerox that uses morphosyntactic patterns for monolingual term recognition. Afterwards, they perform automatic alignment and extract English–German terminology, reaching an F-measure of around 80 %. This kind of technique has certainly been integrated into their Xerox Terminology Suite (XTS). This software is not commercialised any more, since it has been

---

[17]http://olst.ling.umontreal.ca/~drouinp/termostat_web/

[18]http://www.antlab.sci.waseda.ac.jp/software.html

[19]http://www.nactem.ac.uk/software/termine/

[20]http://en.wikipedia.org/wiki/Terminology_extraction

[21]http://mwetoolkit.sourceforge.net

acquired by the text mining company Temis.[22] Nowadays, it has become part of the Luxid® information extraction package.[23]

Another large company which developed a tool for terminology extraction is Yahoo!. Their term extraction service is freely available for research and personal purposes, limited to 5,000 queries per day per IP address.[24] However, this service is limited to short English texts and is probably based on term dictionaries and gazetteers.

The Fips parser, developed at the University of Geneva, has been used for collocation extraction in several languages (Seretan and Wehrli 2009). Even though it is academic research, the collocation extraction tool FipsCo, based on Fips, is not freely available. The tool is able to extract collocations from monolingual corpora in English, French, Spanish and Italian, and there is a version for Greek (Michou and Seretan 2009). The tool has been used in MT experiments, suggesting that it is able to extract bilingual collocations from word-aligned parallel corpora. Although the system itself is not free, its visualisation tool, FipsCoView,[25] is freely available as a web interface (Seretan and Wehrli 2011).

Translation memory software may use MWEs as basic segments to retrieve. Indeed, MWEs are somehow in-between sentences and words. On the one hand, the retrieval of simple words in a hypothetical translation memory would be of little use. The number of possible translations for a word out of its context is potentially large and additional information is required to choose among the options. Therefore, it would lack precision. On the other hand, the retrieval of whole sentences would be highly precise, but an extremely large translation memory would be required in order to obtain reasonable recall. If the memory of previously translated segments is small, only from time to time (and with some luck) a sentence will be retrieved. Many sentences containing part of the translation would be useful, but will be ignored by a sentence-based exact match system.

One example of system performing bilingual MWE extraction is Similis,[26] previously commercialised by Lingua et Machina and now freely available. According to the official website, "Similis [...] includes a linguistic analysis engine, uses chunk technology to break down segments into intelligent terminological groups (chunks), and automatically generates specific glossaries." The technique implemented in the system is an evolution of the one described in Planas and Furuse (2000). In this article, the authors describe a clever technique for retrieving similar segments in the source language and their correspondences in the target language. Their approach applies a dynamic programming algorithm on a multi-layered structure where sentences are represented as a sequence of surface forms, lemmas and parts

---

[22]http://www.temis.com/

[23]http://www.temis.com/index.php?id=201&selt=1

[24]http://developer.yahoo.com/search/content/V1/termExtraction.html

[25]http://129.194.38.128:81/FipsCoView

[26]http://similis.org/

of speech. The combination of the matchings in these three layers allows for a good balance between precision and recall for the retrieval of bilingual segments.

3.3 Other Tasks Related to MWE Processing

Given that MWE acquisition is our main concern, the whole Sect. 3.2 is dedicated to a detailed review of the state of the art. Here, we overview the state of the art in the other tasks involved in MWE treatment, according to the classification of MWE tasks, namely interpretation (Sect. 3.3.1), disambiguation (Sect. 3.3.2), representation (Sect. 3.3.3) and application (Sect. 3.3.4).

3.3.1 Interpretation

The interpretation and disambiguation of several types of MWEs are the focus of a large body of literature, specially in the computational semantics community. Both can be modelled as classification tasks, so that machine learning algorithms are often employed. Therefore, it is possible to distinguish supervised from unsupervised approaches. In the former, a large effort is usually dedicated to the annotation of a data set that is subsequently used to build classifiers. In the latter, the class attribution is made based on thresholds or rules directly applied to data features. Like for most solutions based on machine learning, supervised methods outperform unsupervised methods. However, unsupervised methods may sometimes perform as well as supervised methods when they are applied on very large corpora like, for instance, web-based corpora (Keller and Lapata 2003).

MWE interpretation can be applied on expressions whose meaning does not change too much according to their occurrence contexts, like compound nouns and some specific types of phrasal verbs and support verb constructions. However, it is not suitable to interpret ambiguous expressions such as phrasal verbs (*look up a word* vs *look up to the sky*) and idioms (*my grandfather kicked the bucket* vs *the cleaning lady accidentally kicked the bucket*). These are explored in MWE disambiguation tasks (see Sect. 3.3.2). Noun compounds (*traffic light, nuclear transcription factor*), on the other hand, are rarely ambiguous and their interpretation has been an active research area. We distinguish two types of noun compound interpretation: syntactic and semantic.

The *syntactic interpretation* has been explored by Nicholson and Baldwin (2006), who distinguish three syntactic relations in noun–noun compounds: subject (*product replacement*), direct object (*stress avoidance*) and prepositional object (*side show* → *show on the side*). For compounds in which the second noun is a nominalisation,[27] they used the inflections of the corresponding verb to generate paraphrases that were looked up in Google. The paraphrases and additional features were fed into a nearest-neighbour classifier, but the results failed to improve over the state of the art.

Three-word or longer noun compounds like *liver cell line* and *liver cell antibody* require syntactic interpretation of the constituent hierarchy. That is, one needs to distinguish left bracketing like in *(liver cell) antibody* from right bracketing like in *liver (cell line)*. Therefore, Nakov and Hearst (2005) compare two models, based on adjacency and on dependency. They use a set of heuristics to generate surface-level paraphrases and then use search engine counts to estimate model probabilities. They obtain sizeable improvements over state of the art on a set of biomedical compounds.

One of the most challenging interpretation problems is the *semantic interpretation* of the relations involved in noun compounds. The goal is to assign to each noun compound one (or several) tags that describe the semantic relation between the two nouns. Nakov and Hearst (2008) try to solve this task using a methodology similar to the one they employed for syntactic interpretation. First, they generate a large number of paraphrases involving verbs related to the semantic classes (e.g., *causes, implies, generates* for relation *CAUSE*) and the relative *that*. Then, they retrieve web counts for the paraphrases and assign the classes with maximal probability according to the corresponding paraphrases. Their method is completely unsupervised. The resource developed in their work, containing noun compounds and corresponding features, is freely available on the MWE community website (Nakov 2008b). Kim and Nakov (2011) revisited the problem, this time using a combination of data bootstrapping and web counts. The main difference is that they generated paraphrases not based on surface forms but on parse trees, thus obtaining more accurate results. A related method is proposed and evaluated by Kim and Baldwin (2013).

Paraphrases can be used not only as means but also as ends. That is, they may be the *actual* representation of semantic classes instead of a set of (somehow arbitrary) abstract tags. The representation of semantic classes for noun–noun relations is discussed in depth by Girju et al. (2005), who compare Lauer's eight prepositional tags with a proposed classification using 35 abstract tags. Moreover, they annotate a corpus sample using both schemes and investigate the correspondences between them. In addition, paraphrases can be used, for instance, in order to artificially generate new data for training MT systems (Nakov 2008a).

Lapata (2002) focuses on the interpretation of noun compounds involving nominalisations. She reformulates noun compound interpretation as a disambiguation task, re-creating missing evidence from corpus. She extracts the counts of the nouns and of the related verb from the BNC, and then uses them as features in a supervised machine learning tool that automatically learns association rules. She

---

[27] A noun derived from a verb, like *replacement* is a nominalisation of the verb *replace*.

also discusses and evaluates several smoothing techniques that help obtaining more realistic counts. Keller and Lapata (2003) used this task as one of their case studies in order to investigate the use of web counts in NLP disambiguation tasks.

Latent semantic analysis has also been employed for the semantic classification of noun–noun compounds (Baldwin et al. 2003). In order to distinguish compositional from idiomatic constructions, the authors compare the context vectors of the compound with the context vectors of the individual nouns composing it. This approach can be generalised and has also been applied and evaluated on other types of MWEs. A similar technique is proposed by Séaghdha and Copestake (2013). However, they use string kernels to build more or less lexicalised semantic representations for the words in the compound. Then, they use standard composition techniques in order to infer the combined semantics of the compound.

A comprehensive and detailed revision of the semantic interpretation of noun compounds can be found in Nakov's Ph.D. thesis (Nakov 2007) and in his later survey article (Nakov 2013). Several techniques used in this task are described in the proceedings of SemEval 2010 and 2013, which feature shared tasks on this topic (Hendrickx et al. 2010; Butnariu et al. 2010). The Special Issue on noun compounds of the Natural Language Engineering journal (Szpakowicz et al. 2013) presents some advances in this area and includes an article that describes in detail the best Semeval system for noun compound interpretation (Nulty and Costello 2010, 2013).

Besides noun compounds, other MWE types also require interpretation. English phrasal verbs are ambiguous and can be used both idiomatically (*look up a word*) and literally (*look up to the sky*). However, if we consider only the most usual sense, it is possible to perform type-based interpretation. Cook and Stevenson (2006) use support vector machines to classify the meaning of the particle *up* in English phrasal verbs. According to the verb, it can have a sense of vertical, completion, goal or reflexive. These are simplified using a 2-way and a 3-way classification. The features used are standard syntactic slots of the verb, particle characteristics such as distance from the verb, and word co-occurrences.

Considering a larger range of constructions, Bannard (2005) investigates the extent to which the components of a phrasal verb contribute their meanings to the interpretation of the whole. He models compositionality through an entailment task, for instance, *split up* $\implies$ *split*? In a comparison between pmi, t-score and a newly proposed measure based on context cosine similarity, the latter correlates better with human judgements.

A similar work is that of McCarthy et al. (2003). They propose several measures involving an automatically acquired distributional thesaurus in order to estimate the idiomaticity of phrasal verbs. Their annotated data set uses a numeric scale from 0 (totally opaque) to 10 (fully compositional). They show that the best association measure, mutual information, is less correlated to human judgements than a proposed measure which calculates the number of neighbours with the same particle as the phrasal verb minus the equivalent number of simple neighbours. A similar annotation scale has been proposed by Roller et al. (2013), who provide a data set with compositionality assessments for German expressions. They show that it is important to perform outlier identification and removal to obtain reliable data. In general, interpretation results based on human annotation of compositionality must always be carefully analysed, since this is a hard task even for humans.

Venkatapathy and Joshi (2006) explore the type compositionality of verb–noun pairs. They describe the creation of an annotated data set with compositionality judgements ranging from 1 to 6. Then, they present seven distinct features to estimate compositionality which are further combined using a support vector machine. They evaluate the features separately and show that the Spearman correlation between the classifier results and human judgements is around 0.448, which is better than all individual features.

Using a variation of the same data, McCarthy et al. (2007) investigate the use of selectional preferences in this task. They propose three different algorithms to obtain this information from parsed corpora: two based on Wordnet and one based on an automatically constructed thesaurus. They show that the best performance is obtained by combining selectional preferences and a subset of Venkatapathy and Joshi's features through a support vector machine.

3.3.2 Disambiguation

Recall that the disambiguation of MWEs is analogous to their interpretation, except that they are considered together with the context in which they appear (sentences). Nicholson and Baldwin (2008) present a data set for noun–noun compound disambiguation where a large set of sentences has been manually annotated with syntactic and semantic information about the compounds contained in it. Girju et al. (2005) investigate methods for their disambiguation. They perform a separate analysis of two- and three-noun compounds, annotating their semantics according to two tagging schemes in a training set of around 3K sentences. In addition to a detailed analysis of the coverage and correspondences between the tagging schemes, they apply several supervised learning techniques. Like for the syntactic disambiguation of three-word compounds, they also employ classifiers. They achieves an accuracy of 83.10 % by using as features (a) the top three WordNet synsets for each noun, (b) derivationally related forms and (c) a flag telling whether the noun is a nominalisation.

Whereas, for MWE interpretation, the majority of publications concerns noun compounds, when it comes to disambiguation a large number of MWE types has been studied. However, English still predominates. One of the rare works on a language different from English concerns the interpretation of German preposition–noun–verb triples (Fritzinger et al. 2010). Constructions like *in Gang kommen* have both a literal interpretation as *to reach the hallway (in den Gang kommen)*, but also idiomatic interpretations as *to be set in motion (in Gang kommen)* and *to get organised (in die Gänge kommen)*. They manually analysed a large set of such constructions retrieved by a parser, classifying them as either literal, compositional or unknown.[28] Then, they investigated the correlation between these classes and morphosyntactic characteristics such as determiners, plural and passivisation.

Light/support verbs in Japanese have also been studied in the past. They include sequences like *donari-ageru* (*shout*) and *odosi-ageru* (*threaten*), that is, formed by two lexical units where the verb is usually highly polysemous like *ageru* (*raise*). Uchiyama et al. (2005) propose two disambiguation methods: a statistical approach using a sense inventory, context and a support vector machine; and a rule-based method where the rules were manually defined based on syntax and on the semantics of the first verb. The rule-based method (94.6 %) outperforms the statistical method (82.6 %) in terms of accuracy, but the latter obtains a surprisingly high performance given its simplicity.

The interpretation of expressions of the type verb–noun has also been explored in English. Cook et al. (2007) explore the idiomaticity of verb–noun pairs, where the noun is the direct object of the verb and may have an idiomatic (*make a face*) or literal (*make a cake*) interpretation. Their basic hypothesis is that idiomatic uses are syntactically more rigid. Thus, they describe a fully unsupervised approach which considers syntactic and context information in order to calculate the similarity with the canonical form of the idiom. In their evaluation, they report results comparable to a supervised approach. The data set used in their experiments is freely available (Cook et al. 2008).

Fazly and Stevenson (2007) propose a more fine-grained classification for light verb–noun constructions. They use a supervised learning strategy based on decision trees in order to perform a 4-way semantic disambiguation. In their scheme, a light verb may be used with its literal meaning (*make a cake*), with its abstract meaning (*make a living*), in light-verb constructions (*make a decision*) or idiomatically (*make a face*). These classes are a mix of syntactic and semantic characteristics and could arguably be improved using more systematic criteria. Even though they perform type-based annotation of their data sets, this work can be considered as disambiguation because the noun is the context used to disambiguate the semantics of a closed set of polysemous light verbs. Considering a random baseline with 25 % accuracy, they obtain an overall accuracy of 58.3 %. F-measure varies according to the classe: abstract constructions are harder to classify (46 %) than light verb constructions (68 %).

3.3.3   Representation

The lexical representation of MWEs was one of the main goals of the MWE project at Stanford, and has for a long time haunted lexicographers in the compilation of lexical resources. Most NLP applications contain at least a small amount of

---

[28]The context unit used for annotation was the sentence. However, due to anaphora, sometimes it was impossible to know the intended meaning without looking at neighbour sentences.

MWE entries, specially closed-class expressions. The Stanford parser, for instance, contains a list of several dozens of 2-word and 3-word conjunctions. However, when it comes to open-class expressions, this coverage is too limited and ways to efficiently represent MWEs in computational lexicons are required. Sag et al. (2002) proposed two approaches: words-with-spaces and compositional. However, between these extremes of the compositionality spectrum, there are some other possibilities, sometimes explored in related work. Laporte and Voyatzi (2008), for instance, describe a dictionary containing 6,800 French adverbial expressions like *de nos jours* (*nowadays*). A set of 15 flat sequences of parts of speech is used to describe the morphosyntactic pattern of each entry using the lexicon–grammar format.

Graliński et al. (2010) present a qualitative and quantitative comparison between two structured representations for Polish MWEs: Multiflex and POLENG. While the former is designed to be generic and language independent, the latter has a more implicit structure aimed at specific applications. The authors focus on nominal compounds and analyse the power of each formalism to incorporate morphological inflection rules such as case, gender and number agreement. They also measure the time taken by one expert and two novice lexicographers to encode new MWEs. Multiflex does not allow the description of non-contiguous units nor units containing slots and it takes much longer for lexicographers to learn and use it. POLENG offers a complementary approach, allowing a faster description of MWEs including non-contiguous ones.

A more corpus-based representation has been proposed for the representation of entries in the Dutch electronic lexicon of MWEs (Grégoire 2007, 2010). She uses an equivalence class method that groups similar expressions according to their syntactic characteristics. In addition to numbers of occurrences and examples, each entry contains a link to a pattern that describes the syntactic behaviour of the expression. This description is quite practical, as the lexicon is aimed for NLP systems such as the Alpino parser and Rosetta MT system.

Izumi et al. (2010) suggest a rule-based method to normalise Japanese functional expressions in order to optimise their representation. They consider two separate problems: the insertion of omitted parts and the removal of satellite parts that do not contribute much to the meaning of the sentence. In a comparison with manually generated paraphrases, they obtain a precision of 77 %. If such normalised representation are adopted in the lexicon, the same paraphrasing rules can be applied to running text in order to align it with expressions contained in the lexicon.

The use of tree-rewriting grammars for describing MWEs is proposed by Schuler and Joshi (2011). They provide arguments and formal proof that this formalism is adequate to represent non-fixed expressions such as *raise X to the Yth power*. The generalisation of their approach to other types of expressions, however, remains to be demonstrated.

Finally, concerning the hierarchical structure among MWEs, SanJuan et al. (2005) explore three strategies (lexical inclusion, Wordnet similarity and clustering) to organise a set of multiword terms manually extracted from the Genia corpus. This kind of representation can be very useful to include extracted expressions in more sophisticated concept nets and ontologies.

When it comes to bilingual and multilingual dictionaries, the problem becomes more complex since it is necessary to represent not only the internal structure of the entries but also cross-language links at global and local levels. To the best of our knowledge, there is little research concerning this problem. Section 3.3.4.4 contains a discussion on the representation of MWEs in MT systems.

In short, due to the modest amount of research in this area and to the complexity of the problem, a model for the efficient lexical representation of MWEs in general remains an open problem.

3.3.4 Applications

A list of potential NLP applications where MWEs are relevant was introduced in Sect. 1.1.2. Here, we provide a summary of these target applications for which concrete results have been obtained. Many results presented here concern pilot studies and techniques as simple as joining contiguous MWE components with an underscore character as a preprocessing step. From all the MWE tasks discussed in this section, application is by far the one with the least amount of published results.

3.3.4.1 Syntactic Analysis

A small set of fixed MWEs like conjunctions are represented in most existing parsers, chunkers and POS taggers. However, the further insertion of additional multiword entries can improve the coverage of the analysis, as more complex MWEs like noun compounds and verbal expressions are valuable information for syntactic disambiguation.

Concerning POS tagging, Constant and Sigogne (2011) present an evaluation on French. They assign special tags to words corresponding to the beginning and to the ending of multiword units. Using a model based on conditional random fields, they learn the MWE-aware tagger from a corpus in which the training data was automatically annotated with entries coming from several lexica containing compounds and proper nouns. This technique obtains 97.7 % accuracy, improving considerably over standard taggers like TreeTagger and TnT. They also compare this strategy with the integration of the same lexicons into a parser trained using a probabilistic context-free grammar with latent annotations (PCFG-LA). Their results show that MWE recognition and parsing quality improve with both approaches (Constant et al. 2013).

Korkontzelos and Manandhar (2010) obtain impressing improvements by enriching a baseline shallow parser with MWEs. Their method simply consists of joining contiguous nominal expressions with an underscore prior to parsing. This makes the system treat them as unknown tokens and assign them a parse based on the context.

They analyse a set of 118 2-word MWEs from WordNet, classifying them by POS sequences and by compositionality. They conclude that, in all cases, the accuracy of the parses was improved, specially for non-compositional adjective–noun pairs, for which the substantial improvements ranged from 15.32 to 19.67 %.

As for deep parsing, Zhang and Kordoni (2006) extended the lexicon of an English HPSG parser with 373 MWE entries represented as words-with-spaces. They obtained a significant increase in the coverage of the grammar, from 4.3 to 18.7 %. Using a compositional representation, Villavicencio et al. (2007) added 21 new MWEs to the same parser, obtaining an increase in the grammar coverage from 7.1 to 22.7 %, without degrading accuracy. However, MWEs do not always improve the performance of the parser, as shown by Hogan et al. (2011). They try to include a set of named entities in their parsing system, replacing them by placeholders. However, they did not obtain significant improvements over the baseline, even when tuning count thresholds.

The use of lexical association measures to model collocational behaviour in dependency parsing has been investigated by Mirroshandel et al. (2012). They enrich the dependency relations in the parsing model, learnt from the treebank, with pairs collected from a very large parsed corpus. Their results show significant improvements in parsing accuracy for specific syntactic relations.

As far as we know, the English and Italian parser Fips is one of the few systems dealing with variable MWEs (Wehrli et al. 2010). Its approach is more sophisticated than words-with-spaces, as it dynamically identifies expressions at the same time as it constructs the parse tree. This technique performs better than post-processing the trees after they are produced. The authors demonstrate that MWEs are not a "pain in the neck" but actually a valuable information to reduce syntactic ambiguity.

3.3.4.2 Word Sense Disambiguation

Given an occurrence of a polysemous word, word sense disambiguation consists of picking up a single sense among those listed in an inventory. For example, the verb *fire* can mean *make somebody lose his/her job*, *pull the trigger of a gun*, or *make something burn*. The sentence in which the verb occurs will determine which of these senses is intended. Although context information is used, MWEs are generally ignored in WSD tasks. As a consequence, not only the correct sense will be ignored but also wrong senses will be inferred for the individual words. For example, in Wordnet, none of the senses of *voice* and of *mail* indicates that *voice mail* means *system that records messages on a telephone when nobody answers*.

As exemplified by Finlayson and Kulkarni (2011), while the word *voice* has 11 senses and the word *mail* has 5, the expression *voice mail* only has 1. They show that, in Wordnet 1.6, the average polysemy of MWEs is of 1.07 synsets, versus 1.53 for simple words. To the best of our knowledge, their work is the first to report a considerable improvement on word sense disambiguation performance due to the detection of MWEs. Despite its simplicity, their method reaches an improvement of 5 F-measure points given lower and upper bounds of 3.3 and 6.1.

Bungum et al. (2013) perform collocation identification prior to translation in order to improve the quality of cross-lingual WSD. They argue that, while the coverage of the method depends on the quality of the collocation dictionaries, it helps improving precision. Thus, the use of even simple MWE resources like monolingual lists can help in a complex task like cross-lingual WSD.

3.3.4.3   Information Retrieval (IR)

Let us consider a simplified IR system, modelling documents as bags of words and not keeping track of co-occurrences. For instance, if a document contains the term *rock star*, it will probably be retrieved as an answer to queries on geology (*rock*) and astronomy (*star*). If this MWE was represented as a unit in the index of the system, the precision of the retrieved documents could increase. Most current IR systems allow more sophisticated queries to be expressed through quotes and wildcards. However, representing only relevant MWEs instead of all possible n-grams in the documents could speed up the searches.

Joining the words of MWEs before indexation is a simple idea that was put in practice by Acosta et al. (2011). They tested the impact of a large set of automatically and manually acquired MWE dictionaries on standard IR test sets from the CLEF campaign. Their results show that there is a gain in mean average precision when MWEs are tokenised as single words.

Choosing the appropriate granularity for units to be indexed can be complicated in languages like Chinese, which do not use spaces to separate words. In this case, a prior phase of segmentation generally takes place before traditional IR indexation. Xu et al. (2010) propose a new measure for the tightness of 4-character sequences, as well as three procedures for word segmentation based on this measure. Then, they compare a standard segmentation tool with their methods in an IR system. They show that two of their segmentation strategies improve mean average precision on a test set.

A related task is topic modelling, a popular approach to joint clustering of documents and terms. The standard document representation in this task is a bag of words. However, as presented by Baldwin (2011), it is possible to consolidate the microlevel document representation with the help of MWEs. He argues that recent experimental results demonstrate that linguistically-richer document representations can enhance topic modelling.

3.3.4.4   Machine Translation

In current MT systems, various practical solutions have been implemented. The expert MT system ITS-2 handles MWEs at two levels (Wehrli 1998). Contiguous compounds are dealt with during lexical analysis and treated as single words in subsequent steps. Idiomatic, non-fixed units are treated by the syntax analysis module, requiring a much more sophisticated description. Once they are correctly identified, however, their transfer is executed in the same way as regular structures. The system implements a more sophisticated approach for non-fixed MWE identification in the syntactic analysis module (Wehrli et al. 2010). When evaluated on a data set of English/Italian→French translations, this strategy improved the quality of 10–16 % of a test set of 100 collocations (manual evaluation).

Haugereid and Bond (2011) enriched the Jaen Japanese–English MT system with MWE rules. Jaen is a semantic transfer MT system based on the HPSG parsers JACY and ERG. The authors use GIZA++ and Anymalign in order to generate phrase tables from parallel corpora, from which they automatically extract the new transfer rules. These rules are then filtered and, when added to the system, improve translation coverage from 19.3 to 20.1% and translation quality from 17.8 to 18.2 % NEVA score – a variant of BLEU). Even though the improvements are quite modest, the authors argue that they can be further improved by learning even more rules.

Morin and Daille (2010) obtain an improvement of 33 % in the French–Japanese translation of MWEs. They implement a morphologically-based compositional method for backing-off when there is not enough data in a dictionary to translate a MWE. For example, *chronic fatigue syndrome* can be decomposed as *[chronic fatigue] [syndrome]*, *[chronic] [fatigue syndrome]* or *[chronic] [fatigue] [syndrome]*.

Grefenstette (1999) addresses the translation of noun compounds from German and Spanish into English. He uses web counts to select translations for compositional noun compounds, and achieves an impressive accuracy of 0.86–0.87. Similarly, Tanaka and Baldwin (2003) compare two shallow translation methods for English–Japanese noun compounds. The first one is a static memory-based method where the compound needs to be present in the dictionary in order to be translated correctly. The second is a dynamic compositional method in which alternative translations are validated using corpus evidence. Their evaluation considers the compounds as test translation units (as opposed to traditional sentence-based evaluation). When they combine the two methods, they achieve 95 % coverage and potentially high translation accuracy. This method is further refined by the use of a support vector machine model to rank all possible translations (Baldwin and Tanaka 2004). The model learns the translation scores based on several features coming from monolingual and bilingual dictionaries and corpora.

The popular phrase-based models of the Moses SMT toolkit represent MWEs as flat contiguous sequences of words (Koehn et al. 2007). Bilingual MWEs are bilingual sequences, called "bi-phrases", and have several probabilities associated to them. Carpuat and Diab (2010) propose two complementary strategies in order to add monolingual MWEs from WordNet into an English–Arabic Moses system. The first strategy is a static single-tokenisation that treats MWEs as words-with-spaces. The second strategy is dynamic, adding to the translation model a count for the number of MWEs in the source part of the bi-phrase. They found that both strategies result in improvement of translation quality, which suggests that Moses bi-phrases alone do not model all MWE information.

Nakov (2008a) propose another approach for minimizing data sparseness in MT, based on the generation of monolingual paraphrases to augment the training corpus. Parse trees are used as the basis for generating paraphrases that are nearly-equivalent semantically (e.g., *ban on beef import* for *beef import ban* and vice versa). The trees are syntactically transformed by a set of heuristics, looking at noun compounds and related constructions. Using Moses' ancestor, Pharaoh, on an English–Spanish task, this technique generates an improvement equivalent to 33–50 % of that of doubling training data.

Automatic word alignment can be more challenging when translating from and to morphologically rich languages. In German and in Scandinavian languages, for instance, a compound is in fact a single token formed through concatenation of words and special infixes (*Hauptbahnhof* is the concatenation of *Haupt (main), Bahn (railway) and Hof (station)*). Stymne (2011) develops a fine-grained typology for MT error analysis which includes concatenated definite and compound nouns. For definiteness, she makes the source text look more like the target text (or vice versa) during training, thus making the learning less prone to errors by using better word alignments. In Stymne (2009), she describes her approach to noun compounds, which she splits into their single word components prior to translation. Then, after translation, she applies some post-processing rules like the reordering or merging of the components.

Pal et al. (2010) explore the extension of a Moses English–Bengali system. Significant improvements are brought by applying preprocessing steps like single-tokenisation for named entities and compound verbs. However, larger improvements (4.59 absolute BLEU points) are observed when using a statistical model for the prior alignment of named entities, allowing for their adequate transliteration.

The domain adaptation of general-purpose MT systems can also be accomplished with the integration of multiword terms. Ren et al. (2009) adapt a Chinese–English standard Moses system using three simple techniques: appending the MWE lexicon to the corpus, appending it to the phrase table, and adding a binary feature to the translation model. They found significant BLEU improvements over the baseline, especially using the extra feature.

In translation memory systems such as Similis, the translation unit can be considered as a MWE as it is an intermediary between words and sentences. The correspondences of word sequences are automatically learned from the translation memory and expressed in a multi-layer architecture including surface forms, lemmas and parts of speech (Planas and Furuse 2000).

Hierarchical and tree-based translation systems like Joshua use tree rewriting rules in order to represent the correspondences between source and target structures (Li et al. 2009). However, it is difficult to implement special rules for MWEs and to distinguish them from rules that should be applied to ordinary word combinations. Promising results in the application of MWE resources such as lexicons and thesauri show that this is a recent and apparently growing topic in the MT community.

Monti et al. (2011) compile a parallel corpus of sentences containing several types of expressions and compare the outputs of rule-based and SMT systems. While their discussion provides insightful examples, it does not help quantify the extent to which multiword expressions pose problems to MT systems. Moreover, it is not possible to know the exact details of the MT paradigms used in their experiments.

The proceedings of the 2013 MUMTTT workshop provide some pointers on different approaches for MWE translation (Mitkov et al. 2013). Our experiments on the evaluation of automatic MWE translation are presented in Chap. 7.

3.4 Summary

The underlying hypothesis in MWE acquisition is that words that form an expression will co-occur more often than if they were randomly combined. This hypothesis is applied in the design of lexical association measures (AMs) for corpus-based MWE acquisition. There are numerous AMs available for MWE acquisition (Evert 2004; Seretan 2008; Pecina 2008). For an arbitrary n-gram, we estimate its probability under MLE and scale this estimate by the total number of n-grams in the corpus, obtaining the expected count. AMs are generally based on the difference between the expected count and the observed count, like t-score, pointwise mutual information and Dice coefficient. More robust and theoretically sound AMs based on contingency tables exist for the special case of 2-grams. Examples of such measures are χ^2 and log-likelihood.

MWE acquisition comprises identification (in context) and extraction (out of context). Monolingual MWE acquisition is generally seen as a two-step process: candidate extraction and candidate filtering. In candidate extraction, POS sequences are one of the major approaches, specially for terminology (Justeson and Katz 1995; Daille 2003), but also for noun compounds (Vincze et al. 2011) and verbal expressions (Baldwin 2005). When a parser is available, syntactic patterns can be much more precise than POS sequences, specially in the extraction of non-fixed MWEs (Seretan and Wehrli 2009; Seretan 2008). Tree substitution grammars (Green et al. 2011) and structural regularities in parsing trees (Martens and Vandeghinste 2010) can also be used in order to learn syntactic MWE models from annotated corpora. During candidate filtering, some straightforward procedures are the use of stopword lists and of count thresholds. AMs are also widely employed to rank the candidates and keep only those whose association score is above a certain threshold (Evert and Krenn 2005; Pecina 2005). Supervised learning methods can be used to build a classifier modelling the optimal weights of several AMs and other features (Ramisch et al. 2008; Pecina 2008).

As for bilingual acquisition, automatic word alignments can provide lists of MWE candidates by themselves (de Medeiros Caseli et al. 2010). Bai et al. (2009) present an algorithm capable of mining translations for a given MWE in a parallel aligned corpus. The automatic discovery of non-compositional compounds from parallel data has been explored by Melamed (1997). The English-Hindi language pair presents large word order variation, and it has been shown that MWE-based features that model compositionality can help reducing alignment error rate (Venkatapathy and Joshi 2006). Zarrieß and Kuhn (2009) used syntactically analysed corpora and GIZA++ alignments to extract verb-object pairs from a German–English parallel corpus. Daille et al. (2004) performed multiword term extraction from comparable corpora in French and in English, and subsequently used the distances between the context vectors to obtain cross-lingual equivalences.

The *syntactic interpretation* of nouns compounds has been explored by Nicholson and Baldwin (2006), who distinguish three syntactic relations in noun–noun compounds: subject, direct object and prepositional object. Three-word or longer noun compounds require syntactic interpretation of the constituent hierarchy. Nakov and Hearst (2005) compare two models, based on adjacency and on dependency. Nakov and Hearst (2008) perform unsupervised *semantic interpretation* of noun compounds by generating a large number of paraphrases involving verbs related to the semantic classes and then retrieving their web counts. Kim and Nakov (2011) used a combination of data bootstrapping and web counts, using paraphrases based on parse trees. Cook and Stevenson (2006) use support vector machines to classify the meaning of the particle *up* in English phrasal verbs. Bannard (2005) investigates the extent to which the components of a phrasal verb contribute their meanings to the interpretation of the whole. A similar work is that of McCarthy et al. (2003), who propose several measures to estimate the idiomaticity of phrasal verbs.

The disambiguation of MWEs is analogous to their interpretation, except that they are considered together with the context in which they appear. Nicholson and Baldwin (2008) present a data set for noun–noun compound disambiguation where a large set of sentences has been manually annotated. Girju et al. (2005) investigate methods for their disambiguation by applying several supervised learning techniques. Fritzinger et al. (2010) manually analyse a large set of ambiguous German preposition–noun–verb constructions retrieved by a parser, classifying them as either literal, compositional or unknown. Light verbs in Japanese have also been studied by Uchiyama et al. (2005), who proposes two disambiguation methods: a statistical approach and a rule-based method. Cook et al. (2007) explore the idiomaticity of verb–noun pairs, where the noun is the direct object of the verb and may have an idiomatic (*make a face*) or literal (*make a cake*) interpretation. Fazly and Stevenson (2007) propose a more fine-grained classification for light verb–noun constructions, using a supervised learning strategy in order to perform a 4-way semantic disambiguation.

Sag et al. (2002) proposed two approaches to represent MWEs in lexicons: words-with-spaces and compositional. However, between these extremes of the compositionality spectrum, there are some other possibilities, explored in related work. Laporte and Voyatzi (2008) describe a dictionary of French adverbial expressions and their corresponding morphosyntactic patterns in the lexicon–grammar format. Graliński et al. (2010) present a qualitative and quantitative comparison between two structured representations, Multiflex and POLENG, for Polish MWEs. Grégoire (2007, 2010) uses an equivalence class method that groups similar expressions according to their syntactic characteristics. Izumi et al. (2010) suggest a rule-based method to normalise Japanese functional expressions in order to optimise their representation. Schuler and Joshi (2011) propose the use of tree-rewriting grammars to describe MWEs.

There are some target applications for which concrete results have been obtained. Constant and Sigogne (2011) present promising results for French parsing. Korkontzelos and Manandhar (2010) obtain impressing improvements by enriching a baseline shallow parser with MWEs. Zhang and Kordoni (2006) and Villavicencio et al. (2007) obtain a significant coverage increase by extending the lexicon of an English HPSG parser with MWEs. Wehrli et al. (2010) demonstrate that MWEs are not a "pain in the neck" but actually a valuable information to reduce syntactic ambiguity.

References

Acosta O, Villavicencio A, Moreira V (2011) Identification and treatment of multiword expressions applied to information retrieval. In: Kordoni V, Ramisch C, Villavicencio A (eds) Proceedings of the ALC workshop on multiword expressions: from parsing and generation to the real world (MWE 2011), Association for Computational Linguistics, Portland, pp 101–109. http://www.aclweb.org/anthology/W/W11/W11-0815

Anastasiou D, Hashimoto C, Nakov P, Kim SN (eds) (2009) Proceedings of the ACL workshop on multiword expressions: identification, interpretation, disambiguation, applications (MWE 2009), Singapore. Association for Computational Linguistics/Suntec. http://aclweb.org/anthology-new/W/W09/W09-29, 70 p.

Apresian J, Boguslavsky I, Iomdin L, Tsinman L (2003) Lexical functions as a tool of ETAP-3. In: Proceedings of the first international conference on meaning-text theory (MTT 2003), Paris

Attia M, Toral A, Tounsi L, Pecina P, van Genabith J (2010) Automatic extraction of Arabic multiword expressions. In: Laporte É, Nakov P, Ramisch C, Villavicencio A (eds) Proceedings of the COLING workshop on multiword expressions: from theory to applications (MWE 2010), Beijing. Association for Computational Linguistics, pp 18–26

Baayen RH (2001) Word frequency distributions, text, speech and language technology, vol 18. Springer, Berlin/New York

Bai MH, You JM, Chen KJ, Chang JS (2009) Acquiring translation equivalences of multiword expressions by normalized correlation frequencies. In: Proceedings of the 2009 conference on empirical methods in natural language processing (EMNLP 2009), Singapore. Association for Computational Linguistics/Suntec, pp 478–486

Baldwin T (2005) Deep lexical acquisition of verb-particle constructions. Comput Speech Lang Spec Issue MWEs 19(4):398–414

Baldwin T (2011) MWEs and topic modelling: enhancing machine learning with linguistics. In: Kordoni V, Ramisch C, Villavicencio A (eds) Proceedings of the ALC workshop on multiword expressions: from parsing and generation to the real world (MWE 2011), Portland. Association for Computational Linguistics, p 1. http://www.aclweb.org/anthology/W/W11/W11-0801

Baldwin T, Tanaka T (2004) Translation by machine of complex nominals: getting it right. In: Tanaka T, Villavicencio A, Bond F, Korhonen A (eds) Proceedings of the ACL workshop on multiword expressions: integrating processing (MWE 2004), Barcelona. Association for Computational Linguistics, pp 24–31

Baldwin T, Bannard C, Tanaka T, Widdows D (2003) An empirical model of multiword expression decomposability. In: Bond F, Korhonen A, McCarthy D, Villavicencio A (eds) Proceedings of the ACL workshop on multiword expressions: analysis, acquisition and treatment (MWE 2003), Sapporo. Association for Computational Linguistics, pp 89–96. doi:10.3115/1119282.1119294, http://www.aclweb.org/anthology/W03-1812

Banerjee S, Pedersen T (2003) The design, implementation, and use of the Ngram Statistic Package. In: Proceedings of the fourth international conference on intelligent text processing and computational linguistics, Mexico City, pp 370–381

Bannard C (2005) Learning about the meaning of verb-particle constructions from corpora. Comput Speech Lang Spec Issue MWEs 19(4):467–478

Bejček E, Stranak P, Pecina P (2013) Syntactic identification of occurrences of multiword expressions in text using a lexicon with dependency structures. In: Kordoni V, Ramisch C, Villavicencio A (eds) Proceedings of the 9th workshop on multiword expressions (MWE 2013), Atlanta. Association for Computational Linguistics, pp 106–115. http://www.aclweb. org/anthology/W13-1016

Bonin F, Dell'Orletta F, Montemagni S, Venturi G (2010a) A contrastive approach to multi-word extraction from domain-specific corpora. In: Proceedings of the seventh international conference on language resources and evaluation (LREC 2010), Valetta. European Language Resources Association

Bonin F, Dell'Orletta F, Venturi G, Montemagni S (2010b) Contrastive filtering of domain-specific multi-word terms from different types of corpora. In: Laporte É, Nakov P, Ramisch C, Villavicencio A (eds) Proceedings of the COLING workshop on multiword expressions: from theory to applications (MWE 2010), Beijing. Association for Computational Linguistics, pp 76–79

Bouamor D, Semmar N, Zweigenbaum P (2012) Identifying bilingual multi-word expressions for statistical machine translation. In: Proceedings of the eigth international conference on language resources and evaluation (LREC 2012), Istanbul. European Language Resources Association

Briscoe T, Carroll J, Watson R (2006) The second release of the RASP system. In: Curran J (ed) Proceedings of the COLING/ACL 2006 interactive presentation sessions, Sidney. Association for Computational Linguistics, pp 77–80. http://www.aclweb.org/anthology/P/P06/P06-4020

Bungum L, Gambäck B, Lynum A, Marsi E (2013) Improving word translation disambiguation by capturing multiword expressions with dictionaries. In: Kordoni V, Ramisch C, Villavicencio A (eds) Proceedings of the 9th workshop on multiword expressions (MWE 2013), Atlanta. Association for Computational Linguistics, pp 21–30. http://www.aclweb.org/anthology/W13-1003

Burnard L (2007) User reference guide for the British National Corpus. Technical report, Oxford University Computing Services

Butnariu C, Kim SN, Nakov P, Séaghdha DO, Szpakowicz S, Veale T (2010) Semeval-2 task 9: the interpretation of noun compounds using paraphrasing verbs and prepositions. In: Erk K, Strapparava C (eds) Proceedings of the 5th international workshop on semantic evaluation (SemEval 2010), Uppsala. Association for Computational Linguistics, pp 39–44. http://www. aclweb.org/anthology/S10-1007

Carpuat M, Diab M (2010) Task-based evaluation of multiword expressions: a pilot study in statistical machine translation. In: Proceedings of human language technology: the 2010 annual conference of the North American chapter of the Association for Computational Linguistics (NAACL 2003), Los Angeles. Association for Computational Linguistics, pp 242–245. http:// www.aclweb.org/anthology/N10-1029

Chen SF, Goodman J (1999) An empirical study of smoothing techniques for language modeling. Comput Speech Lang 13(4):359–394

Church K, Hanks P (1990) Word association norms mutual information, and lexicography. Comput Linguist 16(1):22–29

Constant M, Sigogne A (2011) MWU-aware part-of-speech tagging with a CRF model and lexical resources. In: Kordoni V, Ramisch C, Villavicencio A (eds) Proceedings of the ALC workshop on multiword expressions: from parsing and generation to the real World (MWE 2011), Portland. Association for Computational Linguistics, pp 49–56. http://www.aclweb.org/ anthology/W/W11/W11-0809

Constant M, Roux JL, Sigogne A (2013) Combining compound recognition and PCFG-LA parsing with word lattices and conditional random fields. ACM Trans Speech Lang Process Spec Issue Multiword Expr Theory Pract Use Part 2 (TSLP) 10(3):1–24

Cook P, Stevenson S (2006) Classifying particle semantics in English verb-particle constructions. In: Moirón BV, Villavicencio A, McCarthy D, Evert S, Stevenson S (eds) Proceedings of the COLING/ACL workshop on multiword expressions: identifying and exploiting underlying properties (MWE 2006), Sidney. Association for Computational Linguistics, pp 45–53. http://www.aclweb.org/anthology/W/W06/W06-1207

Cook P, Fazly A, Stevenson S (2007) Pulling their weight: exploiting syntactic forms for the automatic identification of idiomatic expressions in context. In: Grégoire N, Evert S, Kim SN (eds) Proceedings of the ACL workshop on a broader perspective on multiword expressions (MWE 2007), Prague. Association for Computational Linguistics, pp 41–48. http://www.aclweb.org/anthology/W/W07/W07-1106

Cook P, Fazly A, Stevenson S (2008) The VNC-tokens dataset. In: Grégoire N, Evert S, Krenn B (eds) Proceedings of the LREC workshop towards a shared task for multiword expressions (MWE 2008), Marrakech, pp 19–22

Daille B (2003) Conceptual structuring through term variations. In: Bond F, Korhonen A, McCarthy D, Villavicencio A (eds) Proceedings of the ACL workshop on multiword expressions: analysis, acquisition and treatment (MWE 2003), Sapporo. Association for Computational Linguistics, pp 9–16. doi:10.3115/1119282.1119284. http://www.aclweb.org/anthology/W03-1802

Daille B, Dufour-Kowalski S, Morin E (2004) French-English multi-word term alignment based on lexical context analysis. In: Proceedings of the fourth international conference on language resources and evaluation (LREC 2004), Lisbon. European Language Resources Association, pp 919–922

Déjean H, Gaussier É, Sadat F (2002) An approach based on multilingual thesauri and model combination for bilingual lexicon extraction. In: Proceedings of the 19th international conference on computational linguistics (COLING 2002), Taipei. http://aclweb.org/anthology-new/C/C02/C02-1166.pdf

de Medeiros Caseli H, Villavicencio A, Machado A, Finatto MJ (2009) Statistically-driven alignment-based multiword expression identification for technical domains. In: Anastasiou D, Hashimoto C, Nakov P, Kim SN (eds) Proceedings of the ACL workshop on multiword expressions: identification, interpretation, disambiguation, applications (MWE 2009), Singapore. Association for Computational Linguistics/Suntec, pp 1–8

de Medeiros Caseli H, Ramisch C, das Graças Volpe Nunes M, Villavicencio A (2010) Alignment-based extraction of multiword expressions. Lang Resour Eval Spec Issue Multiword Express Hard Going Plain Sail 44(1–2):59–77. doi:10.1007/s10579-009-9097-9, http://www.springerlink.com/content/H7313427H78865MG

Dias G (2003) Multiword unit hybrid extraction. In: Bond F, Korhonen A, McCarthy D, Villavicencio A (eds) Proceedings of the ACL workshop on multiword expressions: analysis, acquisition and treatment (MWE 2003), Sapporo. Association for Computational Linguistics, pp 41–48. doi:10.3115/1119282.1119288. http://www.aclweb.org/anthology/W03-1806

Duan J, Lu R, Wu W, Hu Y, Tian Y (2006) A bio-inspired approach for multi-word expression extraction. In: Curran J (ed) Proceedings of the COLING/ACL 2006 main conference poster sessions, Sidney. Association for Computational Linguistics, pp 176–182. http://www.aclweb.org/anthology/P/P06/P06-2023

Dunning T (1993) Accurate methods for the statistics of surprise and coincidence. Comput Linguist 19(1):61–74

Duran MS, Ramisch C, Aluísio SM, Villavicencio A (2011) Identifying and analyzing Brazilian Portuguese complex predicates. In: Kordoni V, Ramisch C, Villavicencio A (eds) Proceedings of the ALC workshop on multiword expressions: from parsing and generation to the real world (MWE 2011), Portland. Association for Computational Linguistics, pp 74–82. http://www.aclweb.org/anthology/W/W11/W11-0812

Evert S (2004) The statistics of word cooccurrences: word pairs and collocations. PhD thesis, Institut für maschinelle Sprachverarbeitung, University of Stuttgart, Stuttgart, 353p

Evert S, Krenn B (2005) Using small random samples for the manual evaluation of statistical association measures. Comput Speech Lang Spec Issue MWEs 19(4):450–466

Fazly A, Stevenson S (2007) Distinguishing subtypes of multiword expressions using linguistically-motivated statistical measures. In: Grégoire N, Evert S, Kim SN (eds) Proceedings of the ACL workshop on a broader perspective on multiword expressions (MWE 2007), Prague. Association for Computational Linguistics, pp 9–16. http://www.aclweb.org/anthology/W/W07/W07-1102

Finlayson M, Kulkarni N (2011) Detecting multi-word expressions improves word sense disambiguation. In: Kordoni V, Ramisch C, Villavicencio A (eds) Proceedings of the ALC workshop on multiword expressions: from parsing and generation to the real world (MWE 2011), Portland. Association for Computational Linguistics, pp 20–24. http://www.aclweb.org/anthology/W/W11/W11-0805

Frantzi K, Ananiadou S, Mima H (2000) Automatic recognition of multiword terms: the C-value/NC-value method. Int J Digit Libr 3(2):115–130

Fritzinger F, Weller M, Heid U (2010) A survey of idiomatic preposition-noun-verb triples on token level. In: Proceedings of the seventh international conference on language resources and evaluation (LREC 2010), Valetta. European Language Resources Association, pp 2908–2914

Gil A, Dias G (2003) Using masks, suffix array-based data structures and multidimensional arrays to compute positional n-gram statistics from corpora. In: Bond F, Korhonen A, McCarthy D, Villavicencio A (eds) Proceedings of the ACL workshop on multiword expressions: analysis, acquisition and treatment (MWE 2003), Sapporo. Association for Computational Linguistics, pp 25–32. doi:10.3115/1119282.1119286, http://www.aclweb.org/anthology/W03-1804

Girju R, Moldovan D, Tatu M, Antohe D (2005) On the semantics of noun compounds. Comput Speech Lang Spec Issue MWEs 19(4):479–496

Good IJ (1953) The population frequencies of species and the estimation of population parameters. Biometrika 40(3–4):237–264. doi:10.1093/biomet/40.3-4.237

Graliński F, Savary A, Czerepowicka M, Makowiecki F (2010) Computational lexicography of multi-word units: how efficient can it be? In: Laporte É, Nakov P, Ramisch C, Villavicencio A (eds) Proceedings of the COLING workshop on multiword expressions: from theory to applications (MWE 2010), Beijing. Association for Computational Linguistics, pp 1–9

Green S, de Marneffe MC, Bauer J, Manning CD (2011) Multiword expression identification with tree substitution grammars: a parsing tour de force with French. In: Barzilay R, Johnson M (eds) Proceedings of the 2011 conference on empirical methods in natural language processing (EMNLP 2011), Edinburgh. Association for Computational Linguistics, pp 725–735. http://www.aclweb.org/anthology/D11-1067

Grefenstette G (1999) The world wide web as a resource for example-based machine translation tasks. In: Proceedings of the twenty-first international conference on translating and the computer, ASLIB, London

Grégoire N (2007) Design and implementation of a lexicon of Dutch multiword expressions. In: Grégoire N, Evert S, Kim SN (eds) Proceedings of the ACL workshop on a broader perspective on multiword expressions (MWE 2007), Prague. Association for Computational Linguistics, pp 17–24. http://www.aclweb.org/anthology/W/W07/W07-1103

Grégoire N (2010) DuELME: a Dutch electronic lexicon of multiword expressions. Lang Resour Eval Spec Issue Multiword Expr Hard Going Plain Sail 44(1–2):23–39. doi:10.1007/s10579-009-9094-z. http://www.springerlink.com/content/7308605442W17698

Grégoire N, Evert S, Krenn B (eds) (2008) Proceedings of the LREC workshop towards a shared task for multiword expressions (MWE 2008), Marrakech, 57p. http://www.lrec-conf.org/proceedings/lrec2008/workshops/W20_Proceedings.pdf

Gurrutxaga A, Alegria I (2011) Automatic extraction of NV expressions in Basque: basic issues on cooccurrence techniques. In: Kordoni V, Ramisch C, Villavicencio A (eds) Proceedings of the ALC workshop on multiword expressions: from parsing and generation to the real world (MWE 2011), Portland. Association for Computational Linguistics, pp 2–7. http://www.aclweb.org/anthology/W/W11/W11-0802

Haugereid P, Bond F (2011) Extracting transfer rules for multiword expressions from parallel corpora. In: Kordoni V, Ramisch C, Villavicencio A (eds) Proceedings of the ALC workshop on multiword expressions: from parsing and generation to the real world (MWE 2011), Portland. Association for Computational Linguistics, pp 92–100. http://www.aclweb.org/anthology/W/W11/W11-0814

Hendrickx I, Kim SN, Kozareva Z, Nakov P, Séaghdha DO, Padó S, Pennacchiotti M, Romano L, Szpakowicz S (2010) Semeval-2010 task 8: multi-way classification of semantic relations between pairs of nominals. In: Erk K, Strapparava C (eds) Proceedings of the 5th international workshop on semantic evaluation (SemEval 2010), Uppsala. Association for Computational Linguistics, pp 33–38. http://www.aclweb.org/anthology/S10-1006

Hoang HH, Kim SN, Kan MY (2009) A re-examination of lexical association measures. In: Anastasiou D, Hashimoto C, Nakov P, Kim SN (eds) Proceedings of the ACL workshop on multiword expressions: identification, interpretation, disambiguation, applications (MWE 2009), Singapore. Association for Computational Linguistics/Suntec, pp 31–39

Hogan D, Foster J, van Genabith J (2011) Decreasing lexical data sparsity in statistical syntactic parsing – experiments with named entities. In: Kordoni V, Ramisch C, Villavicencio A (eds) Proceedings of the ALC workshop on multiword expressions: from parsing and generation to the real world (MWE 2011), Portland. Association for Computational Linguistics, pp 14–19. http://www.aclweb.org/anthology/W/W11/W11-0804

Izumi T, Imamura K, Kikui G, Sato S (2010) Standardizing complex functional expressions in Japanese predicates: applying theoretically-based paraphrasing rules. In: Laporte É, Nakov P, Ramisch C, Villavicencio A (eds) Proceedings of the COLING workshop on multiword expressions: from theory to applications (MWE 2010), Beijing. Association for Computational Linguistics, pp 63–71

Jurafsky D, Martin JH (2008) Speech and language processing, 2nd edn. Prentice Hall, Upper Saddle River, 1024p

Justeson JS, Katz SM (1995) Technical terminology: some linguistic properties and an algorithm for identification in text. Nat Lang Eng 1(1):9–27

Keller F, Lapata M (2003) Using the web to obtain frequencies for unseen bigrams. Comput Linguist Spec Issue Web Corpus 29(3):459–484

Kim SN, Baldwin T (2013) A lexical semantic approach to interpreting and bracketing English noun compounds. Nat Lang Eng Spec Issue Noun Compd 19(3):385–407. doi:10.1017/S1351324913000107, http://journals.cambridge.org/article_S1351324913000107

Kim SN, Nakov P (2011) Large-scale noun compound interpretation using bootstrapping and the web as a corpus. In: Barzilay R, Johnson M (eds) Proceedings of the 2011 conference on empirical methods in natural language processing (EMNLP 2011), Edinburgh. Association for Computational Linguistics, pp 648–658. http://www.aclweb.org/anthology/D11-1060

Kneser R, Ney H (1995) Improved backing-off for M-gram language modeling. In: Proceedings of the international conference on acoustics, speech, and signal processing (ICASSP 1995), Detroit, vol 1, pp 181–184. doi:10.1109/ICASSP.1995.479394, http://dx.doi.org/10.1109/ICASSP.1995.479394

Koehn P (2005) Europarl: a parallel corpus for statistical machine translation. In: Proceedings of the tenth machine translation summit (MT Summit 2005), Phuket. Asian-Pacific Association for Machine Translation, pp 79–86

Koehn P, Hoang H, Birch A, Callison-Burch C, Federico M, Bertoldi N, Cowan B, Shen W, Moran C, Zens R, Dyer C, Bojar O, Constantin A, Herbst E (2007) Moses: open source toolkit for statistical machine translation. In: Proceedings of the 45th annual meeting of the Association for Computational Linguistics (ACL 2007), Prague. Association for Computational Linguistics, pp 177–180

Korkontzelos I, Manandhar S (2010) Can recognising multiword expressions improve shallow parsing? In: Proceedings of human language technology: the 2010 annual conference of the North American chapter of the Association for Computational Linguistics (NAACL 2003), Los Angeles. Association for Computational Linguistics, pp 636–644. http://www.aclweb.org/anthology/N10-1089

Kulkarni N, Finlayson M (2011) jMWE: a java toolkit for detecting multi-word expressions. In: Kordoni V, Ramisch C, Villavicencio A (eds) Proceedings of the ALC workshop on multiword expressions: from parsing and generation to the real world (MWE 2011), Portland. Association for Computational Linguistics, pp 122–124. http://www.aclweb.org/anthology/W/W11/W11-0818

Lapata M (2002) The disambiguation of nominalizations. Comput Linguist 28(3):357–388

Laporte É, Voyatzi S (2008) An electronic dictionary of French multiword adverbs. In: Grégoire N, Evert S, Krenn B (eds) Proceedings of the LREC workshop towards a shared task for multiword expressions (MWE 2008), Marrakech, pp 31–34

Laporte É, Nakamura T, Voyatzi S (2008) A French corpus annotated for multiword nouns. In: Grégoire N, Evert S, Krenn B (eds) Proceedings of the LREC workshop towards a shared task for multiword expressions (MWE 2008), Marrakech, pp 27–30

Li Z, Callison-Burch C, Dyer C, Ganitkevitch J, Khudanpur S, Schwartz L, Thornton WNG, Weese J, Zaidan OF (2009) Joshua: an open source toolkit for parsing-based machine translation. In: Proceedingsof the fourth workshop on statistical machine translation (WMT 2009), Athens. Association for Computational Linguistics, pp 135–139

Manber U, Myers G (1990) Suffix arrays: a new method for on-line string searches. In: SODA '90: proceedings of the first annual ACM-SIAM symposium on discrete algorithms, San Francisco. Society for Industrial and Applied Mathematics, Philadelphia, pp 319–327

Manning CD, Schütze H (1999) Foundations of statistical natural language processing. MIT, Cambridge, 620p

Martens S (2010) Varro: an algorithm and toolkit for regular structure discovery in treebanks. In: Huang CR, Jurafsky D (eds) Proceedings of the 23rd international conference on computational linguistics (COLING 2010)—posters, Beijing. The Coling 2010 Organizing Committee, pp 810–818. http://www.aclweb.org/anthology/C10-2093

Martens S, Vandeghinste V (2010) An efficient, generic approach to extracting multi-word expressions from dependency trees. In: Laporte É, Nakov P, Ramisch C, Villavicencio A (eds) Proceedings of the COLING workshop on multiword expressions: from theory to applications (MWE 2010), Beijing. Association for Computational Linguistics, pp 84–87

McCarthy D, Keller B, Carroll J (2003) Detecting a continuum of compositionality in phrasal verbs. In: Bond F, Korhonen A, McCarthy D, Villavicencio A (eds) Proceedings of the ACL workshop on multiword expressions: analysis, acquisition and treatment (MWE 2003), Sapporo. Association for Computational Linguistics, pp 73–80. doi:10.3115/1119282.1119292, http://www.aclweb.org/anthology/W03-1810

McCarthy D, Venkatapathy S, Joshi A (2007) Detecting compositionality of verb-object combinations using selectional preferences. In: Eisner J (ed) Proceedings of the 2007 joint conference on empirical methods in natural language processing and computational natural language learning (EMNLP-CoNLL 2007), Prague. Association for Computational Linguistics, pp 369–379. http://www.aclweb.org/anthology/D/D07/D07-1039

Melamed ID (1997) Automatic discovery of non-compositional compounds in parallel data. In: Proceedings of the 2nd conference on empirical methods in natural language processing (EMNLP-2), Brown University, Providence. Association for Computational Linguistics, pp 97–108

Michou A, Seretan V (2009) A tool for multi-word expression extraction in modern Greek using syntactic parsing. In: Proceedings of the demonstrations session at EACL 2009, Athens. Association for Computational Linguistics, pp 45–48

Mikheev A (2002) Periods, capitalized words, etc. Comput Linguist 28(3):289–318

Mirroshandel SA, Nasr A, Roux JL (2012) Semi-supervised dependency parsing using lexical affinities. In: Proceedings of the 50th annual meeting of the Association for Computational Linguistics (vol 1: long papers), Jeju Island. Association for Computational Linguistics, pp 777–785. http://www.aclweb.org/anthology/P12-1082

Mitkov R, Monti J, Pastor GC, Seretan V (eds) (2013) Proceedings of the MT summit 2013 workshop on multi-word units in machine translation and translation technology (MUMTTT 2013), Nice. European Association for Machine Translation, 71p. http://www.mtsummit2013.info/workshop4.asp

Monti J, Barreiro A, Elia A, Marano F, Napoli A (2011) Taking on new challenges in multi-word unit processing for machine translation. In: Proceedings of the second international workshop on free/open-source rule-based machine translation, Barcelona

Morin E, Daille B (2010) Compositionality and lexical alignment of multi-word terms. Lang Resour Eval Spec Issue Multiword Express Hard Going Plain Sail 44(1–2):79–95. doi:10.1007/s10579-009-9098-8, http://www.springerlink.com/content/30264870R1K04744

Nakov P (2007) Using the web as an implicit training set: application to noun compound syntax and semantics. PhD thesis, EECS Department, University of California, Berkeley, 392p

Nakov P (2008a) Improved statistical machine translation using monolingual paraphrases. In: Ghallab M, Spyropoulos CD, Fakotakis N, Avouris NM (eds) Proceedings of the 18th European conference on artificial intelligence (ECAI 2008), Patras. Frontiers in Artificial Intelligence and Applications, vol 178. IOS Press, pp 338–342

Nakov P (2008b) Paraphrasing verbs for noun compound interpretation. In: Grégoire N, Evert S, Krenn B (eds) Proceedings of the LREC workshop towards a shared task for multiword expressions (MWE 2008), Marrakech, pp 46–49

Nakov P (2013) On the interpretation of noun compounds: syntax, semantics, and entailment. Nat Lang Eng Spec Issue Noun Compd 19(3):291–330. doi:10.1017/S1351324913000065, http://journals.cambridge.org/article_S1351324913000065

Nakov P, Hearst MA (2005) Search engine statistics beyond the n-gram: application to noun compound bracketing. In: Dagan I, Gildea D (eds) Proceedings of the ninth conference on natural language learning (CoNLL-2005), University of Michigan, Ann Arbor. Association for Computational Linguistics, pp 17–24. http://www.aclweb.org/anthology/W/W05/W05-0603

Nakov P, Hearst MA (2008) Solving relational similarity problems using the web as a corpus. In: Proceedings of the 46th annual meeting of the Association for Computational Linguistics: human language technology (ACL-08: HLT), Columbus. Association for Computational Linguistics, pp 452–460

Nasr A, Bechet F, Rey JF, Favre B, Roux JL (2011) MACAON an NLP tool suite for processing word lattices. In: Proceedings of the ACL 2011 system demonstrations, Portland. Association for Computational Linguistics, pp 86–91. http://www.aclweb.org/anthology/P11-4015

Newman MEJ (2005) Power laws, pareto distributions and zipf's law. Contemp Phys 46:323–351

Nicholson J, Baldwin T (2006) Interpretation of compound nominalisations using corpus and web statistics. In: Moirón BV, Villavicencio A, McCarthy D, Evert S, Stevenson S (eds) Proceedings of the COLING/ACL workshop on multiword expressions: identifying and exploiting underlying properties (MWE 2006), Sidney. Association for Computational Linguistics, pp 54–61. http://www.aclweb.org/anthology/W/W06/W06-1208

Nicholson J, Baldwin T (2008) Interpreting compound nominalisations. In: Grégoire N, Evert S, Krenn B (eds) Proceedings of the LREC workshop towards a shared task for multiword expressions (MWE 2008), Marrakech, pp 43–45

Nulty P, Costello F (2010) UCD-PN: Selecting general paraphrases using conditional probability. In: Erk K, Strapparava C (eds) Proceedings of the 5th international workshop on semantic evaluation (SemEval 2010), Uppsala. Association for Computational Linguistics, pp 234–237. http://www.aclweb.org/anthology/S10-1052

Nulty P, Costello F (2013) General and specific paraphrases of semantic relations between nouns. Nat Lang Eng Spec Issue Noun Compd 19(3):357–384. doi:10.1017/S1351324913000089, http://journals.cambridge.org/article_S1351324913000089

Pal S, Naskar SK, Pecina P, Bandyopadhyay S, Way A (2010) Handling named entities and compound verbs in phrase-based statistical machine translation. In: Laporte É, Nakov P, Ramisch C, Villavicencio A (eds) Proceedings of the COLING workshop on multiword expressions: from theory to applications (MWE 2010), Beijing. Association for Computational Linguistics, pp 45–53

Pearce D (2002) A comparative evaluation of collocation extraction techniques. In: Proceedings of the third international conference on language resources and evaluation (LREC 2002), Las Palmas. European Language Resources Association, pp 1530–1536

Pecina P (2005) An extensive empirical study of collocation extraction methods. In: Proceedings of the ACL 2005 student research workshop, Ann Arbor. Association for Computational Linguistics, pp 13–18. http://www.aclweb.org/anthology/P/P05/P05-2003

Pecina P (2008) Reference data for Czech collocation extraction. In: Grégoire N, Evert S, Krenn B (eds) Proceedings of the LREC workshop towards a shared task for multiword expressions (MWE 2008), Marrakech, pp 11–14

Pedersen T, Banerjee S, McInnes B, Kohli S, Joshi M, Liu Y (2011) The n-gram statistics package (text::NSP): a flexible tool for identifying n-grams, collocations, and word associations. In: Kordoni V, Ramisch C, Villavicencio A (eds) Proceedings of the ALC workshop on multiword expressions: from parsing and generation to the real world (MWE 2011), Portland. Association for Computational Linguistics, pp 131–133. http://www.aclweb.org/anthology/W/W11/W11-0821

Planas E, Furuse O (2000) Multi-level similar segment matching algorithm for translation memories and example-based machine translation. In: Proceedings of the 18th international conference on computational linguistics (COLING 2000), Saarbrücken. http://aclweb.org/anthology-new/C/C00/C00-2090.pdf

Ramisch C (2009) Multiword terminology extraction for domain-specific documents. Master's thesis, École Nationale Supérieure d'Informatique et de Mathématiques Appliquées, Grenoble, 79p

Ramisch C, Villavicencio A, Moura L, Idiart M (2008) Picking them up and figuring them out: verb-particle constructions, noise and idiomaticity. In: Clark A, Toutanova K (eds) Proceedings of the twelfth conference on natural language learning (CoNLL 2008), Manchester. The Coling 2008 Organizing Committee, pp 49–56. http://www.aclweb.org/anthology/W08-2107

Ramisch C, de Medeiros Caseli H, Villavicencio A, Machado A, Finatto MJ (2010) A hybrid approach for multiword expression identification. In: Proceedings of the 9th international conference on computational processing of Portuguese language (PROPOR 2010), Porto Alegre. Lecture notes in computer science (Lecture notes in artificail intelligence), vol 6001. Springer, pp 65–74. doi:10.1007/978-3-642-12320-7_9, http://www.springerlink.com/content/978-3-642-12319-1

Ren Z, Lü Y, Cao J, Liu Q, Huang Y (2009) Improving statistical machine translation using domain bilingual multiword expressions. In: Anastasiou D, Hashimoto C, Nakov P, Kim SN (eds) Proceedings of the ACL workshop on multiword expressions: identification, interpretation, disambiguation, applications (MWE 2009), Singapore. Association for Computational Linguistics/Suntec, pp 47–54

Roller S, im Walde SS, Scheible S (2013) The (un)expected effects of applying standard cleansing models to human ratings on compositionality. In: Kordoni V, Ramisch C, Villavicencio A (eds) Proceedings of the 9th workshop on multiword expressions (MWE 2013), Atlanta. Association for Computational Linguistics, pp 32–41. http://www.aclweb.org/anthology/W13-1005

Sag I, Baldwin T, Bond F, Copestake A, Flickinger D (2002) Multiword expressions: a pain in the neck for NLP. In: Proceedings of the 3rd international conference on intelligent text processing and computational linguistics (CICLing-2002), Mexico City. Lecture notes in computer science, vol 2276/2010. Springer, pp 1–15

SanJuan E, Dowdall J, Ibekwe-SanJuan F, Rinaldi F (2005) A symbolic approach to automatic multiword term structuring. Comput Speech Lang Spec Issue MWEs 19(4):524–542

Schmid H (1994) Probabilistic part-of-speech tagging using decision trees. In: Proceedings of the international conference on new methods in language processing, Manchester, pp 44–49. http://citeseerx.ist.psu.edu/viewdoc/summary?doi=10.1.1.28.1139

Schone P, Jurafsky D (2001) Is knowledge-free induction of multiword unit dictionary headwords a solved problem? In: Lee L, Harman D (eds) Proceedings of the 2001 conference on empirical methods in natural language processing (EMNLP 2001), Pittsburgh. Association for Computational Linguistics, pp 100–108

Schuler W, Joshi A (2011) Tree-rewriting models of multi-word expressions. In: Kordoni V, Ramisch C, Villavicencio A (eds) Proceedings of the ALC workshop on multiword expressions: from parsing and generation to the real world (MWE 2011), Portland. Association for Computational Linguistics, pp 25–30. http://www.aclweb.org/anthology/W/W11/W11-0806

Séaghdha DÓ, Copestake A (2013) Interpreting compound nouns with kernel methods. Nat Lang Eng Spec Issue Noun Compd 19(3):331–356. doi:10.1017/S1351324912000368, http://journals.cambridge.org/article_S1351324912000368

Seretan V (2008) Collocation extraction based on syntactic parsing. PhD thesis, University of Geneva, Geneva, 249p

Seretan V (2011) Syntax-based Collocation extraction, text, speech and language technology, vol 44, 1st edn. Springer, Dordrecht, 212p

Seretan V, Wehrli E (2006) Multilingual collocation extraction: issues and solutions. In: Witt A, Sérasset G, Armstrong S, Breen J, Heid U, Sasaki F (eds) Proceedings of the ACL workshop on multilingual language resources and interoperability, Sydney. Association for Computational Linguistics, pp 40–49. http://www.aclweb.org/anthology/W/W06/W06-1006

Seretan V, Wehrli E (2009) Multilingual collocation extraction with a syntactic parser. Lang Resour Eval Spec Issue Multiling Lang Resour Interoper 43(1):71–85. doi:10.1007/s10579-008-9075-7, http://www.springerlink.com/content/341877K50497682X

Seretan V, Wehrli E (2011) Fipscoview: on-line visualisation of collocations extracted from multilingual parallel corpora. In: Kordoni V, Ramisch C, Villavicencio A (eds) Proceedings of the ALC workshop on multiword expressions: from parsing and generation to the real world (MWE 2011), Portland. Association for Computational Linguistics, pp 125–127. http://www.aclweb.org/anthology/W/W11/W11-0819

Silva J, Lopes G (1999) A local maxima method and a fair dispersion normalization for extracting multi-word units from corpora. In: Proceedings of the sixth meeting on mathematics of language (MOL6), Orlando, pp 369–381

Silva J, Lopes G (2010) Towards automatic building of document keywords. In: Huang CR, Jurafsky D (eds) Proceedings of the 23rd international conference on computational linguistics (COLING 2010)—posters, Beijing. The Coling 2010 Organizing Committee, pp 1149–1157. http://www.aclweb.org/anthology/C10-2132

da Silva JF, Dias G, Guilloré S, Lopes JGP (1999) Using localmaxs algorithm for the extraction of contiguous and non-contiguous multiword lexical units. In: Proceedings of the 9th Portuguese conference on artificial intelligence: progress in artificial intelligence, London. EPIA 1999, pp 113–132. Springer. http://dl.acm.org/citation.cfm?id=645377.651205

Smadja FA (1993) Retrieving collocations from text: xtract. Comput Linguist 19(1):143–177

Stymne S (2009) A comparison of merging strategies for translation of German compounds. In: Proceedings of the student research workshop at EACL 2009, Athens, pp 61–69

Stymne S (2011) Pre- and postprocessing for statistical machine translation into Germanic languages. In: Proceedings of the ACL 2011 student research workshop, Portland. Association for Computational Linguistics, pp 12–17. http://www.aclweb.org/anthology/P11-3003

Szpakowicz S, Bond F, Nakov P, Kim SN (2013) On the semantics of noun compounds. In: Nat Lang Eng Spec Issue Noun Compd 19(3):289–290. Cambridge Univesity Press, Cambridge

Tanaka T, Baldwin T (2003) Noun-noun compound machine translation a feasibility study on shallow processing. In: Bond F, Korhonen A, McCarthy D, Villavicencio A (eds) Proceedings of the ACL workshop on multiword expressions: analysis, acquisition and treatment (MWE 2003), Sapporo. Association for Computational Linguistics, pp 17–24. doi:10.3115/1119282.1119285. http://www.aclweb.org/anthology/W03-1803

Tsvetkov Y, Wintner S (2010) Extraction of multi-word expressions from small parallel corpora. In: Huang CR, Jurafsky D (eds) Proceedings of the 23rd international conference on computational linguistics (COLING 2010)—posters, Beijing. The Coling 2010 Organizing Committee, pp 1256–1264. http://www.aclweb.org/anthology/C10-2144

Tsvetkov Y, Wintner S (2011) Identification of multi-word expressions by combining multiple linguistic information sources. In: Barzilay R, Johnson M (eds) Proceedings of the 2011 conference on empirical methods in natural language processing (EMNLP 2011), Edinburgh. Association for Computational Linguistics, pp 836–845. http://www.aclweb.org/anthology/D11-1077

Uchiyama K, Baldwin T, Ishizaki S (2005) Disambiguating Japanese compound verbs. Comput Speech Lang Spec Issue MWEs 19(4):497–512

Uresova Z, Hajic J, Fucikova E, Sindlerova J (2013) An analysis of annotation of verb-noun idiomatic combinations in a parallel dependency corpus. In: Kordoni V, Ramisch C, Villavicencio A (eds) Proceedings of the 9th workshop on multiword expressions (MWE 2013), Atlanta. Association for Computational Linguistics, pp 58–63. http://www.aclweb.org/anthology/W13-1009

Venkatapathy S, Joshi AK (2006) Using information about multi-word expressions for the word-alignment task. In: Moirón BV, Villavicencio A, McCarthy D, Evert S, Stevenson S (eds) Proceedings of the COLING/ACL workshop on multiword expressions: identifying and exploiting underlying properties (MWE 2006), Sidney. Association for Computational Linguistics, pp 20–27. http://www.aclweb.org/anthology/W/W06/W06-1204

Villavicencio A, Bond F, Korhonen A, McCarthy D (2005) Introduction to the special issue on multiword expressions: having a crack at a hard nut. Comput Speech Lang Spec Issue MWEs 19(4):365–377

Villavicencio A, Kordoni V, Zhang Y, Idiart M, Ramisch C (2007) Validation and evaluation of automatically acquired multiword expressions for grammar engineering. In: Eisner J (ed) Proceedings of the 2007 joint conference on empirical methods in natural language processing and computational natural language learning (EMNLP-CoNLL 2007), Prague. Association for Computational Linguistics, pp 1034–1043. http://www.aclweb.org/anthology/D/D07/D07-1110

Vincze V, Nagy TI, Berend G (2011) Detecting noun compounds and light verb constructions: a contrastive study. In: Kordoni V, Ramisch C, Villavicencio A (eds) Proceedings of the ALC workshop on multiword expressions: from parsing and generation to the real world (MWE 2011), Portland. Association for Computational Linguistics, pp 116–121. http://www.aclweb.org/anthology/W/W11/W11-0817

Wehrli E (1998) Translating idioms. In: Proceedings of the 36th annual meeting of the Association for Computational Linguistics and 17th international conference on computational linguistics, Montreal, vol 2. Association for Computational Linguistics, pp 1388–1392. doi:10.3115/980691.980795. http://www.aclweb.org/anthology/P98-2226

Wehrli E, Seretan V, Nerima L (2010) Sentence analysis and collocation identification. In: Laporte É, Nakov P, Ramisch C, Villavicencio A (eds) Proceedings of the COLING workshop on multiword expressions: from theory to applications (MWE 2010), Beijing. Association for Computational Linguistics, pp 27–35

Wermter J, Hahn U (2006) You can't beat frequency (unless you use linguistic knowledge) – a qualitative evaluation of association measures for collocation and term extraction. In: Proceedings of the 21st international conference on computational linguistics and 44th annual meeting of the association for computational linguistics (COLING/ACL 2006), Sidney. Association for Computational Linguistics, pp 785–792

Xu Y, Goebel R, Ringlstetter C, Kondrak G (2010) Application of the tightness continuum measure to Chinese information retrieval. In: Laporte É, Nakov P, Ramisch C, Villavicencio A (eds) Proceedings of the COLING workshop on multiword expressions: from theory to applications (MWE 2010), Beijing. Association for Computational Linguistics, pp 54–62

Yamamoto M, Church K (2001) Using suffix arrays to compute term frequency and document frequency for all substrings in a corpus. Comput Linguist 27(1):1–30

Zarrieß S, Kuhn J (2009) Exploiting translational correspondences for pattern-independent MWE identification. In: Anastasiou D, Hashimoto C, Nakov P, Kim SN (eds) Proceedings of the ACL workshop on multiword expressions: identification, interpretation, disambiguation, applications (MWE 2009), Singapore. Association for Computational Linguistics/Suntec, pp 23–30

Zhang Y, Kordoni V (2006) Automated deep lexical acquisition for robust open texts processing. In: Proceedings of the sixth international conference on language resources and evaluation (LREC 2006), Genoa. European Language Resources Association, pp 275–280

Part II
MWE Acquisition

Part II
MWE Acquisition

Chapter 4
Evaluation of MWE Acquisition

The result of automatic the MWE acquisition methods described in Sects. 3.2.1 and 3.2.2 can be viewed as a list of MWE candidates. We can evaluate the quality of a given approach for MWE acquisition by assessing the utility of the resulting MWE candidate list for a given application. This list has often an internal structure, and each candidate contains attached information, coming from corpora or from external resources. However, if we ignore this extra information (which is often the case), it is possible to define objective criteria for determining the quality of the list, and, indirectly, of the acquisition method.

If the list is to be evaluated on its own, we say that evaluation is intrinsic. Analogously to information retrieval systems, whose result is a list of documents, each MWE candidate can be classified as either relevant or irrelevant. Afterwards, we estimate the proportion of relevant MWEs in the list (precision), which indicates the amount of work that a human expert would need to perform, using this method, to transform a rough list of automatically acquired candidates into a lexical resource that can be used by the application. Alternatively, evaluation can be extrinsic, given a target application. In that case, we evaluate the quality of the MWE list indirectly, through the quality improvement obtained after MWE integration, as measured at the output of the application.

However, the problem of MWE acquisition is quite complex because results depend on many parameters of the acquisition context, as we will detail later in this chapter. Precision alone cannot evaluate the quality of acquisition methods. As a consequence, in this chapter our goal is two-fold: first, we would like to introduce a series of background concepts and measures commonly used in the evaluation of MWE acquisition (Sect. 4.1). Second, we would like to present the parameters of the acquisition context that may have an influence on the evaluation results (Sect. 4.2). These parameters are the reason why evaluation is a hard problem and deserves a full chapter in this book: they make results obtained in one context difficult to generalise to another context. We close this chapter with a brief discussion of the advantages and inconveniences of different evaluation types, arguing that application-oriented,

© Springer International Publishing Switzerland 2015

C. Ramisch, *Multiword Expressions Acquisition*, Theory and Applications
of Natural Language Processing, DOI 10.1007/978-3-319-09207-2_4

extrinsic evaluation is required to build solid arguments towards the utility of MWEs in NLP systems in general (Sect. 4.3).

4.1 Evaluation Context

Before starting the evaluation of a MWE candidate list, one should ask four questions:

1. What are the acquisition goals (that is, the target applications) of the resulting MWEs?
2. What is the nature of the evaluation measures that we intend to use?
3. What is the cost of the resources (dictionaries, reference lists, human experts) required for the desired evaluation?
4. How ambiguous are the target MWE types?

The answers to these questions can be modelled as a set of four independent evaluation axes that we describe in Sect. 4.1.1. These axes constitute a new typology that we propose for the evaluation of MWE acquisition. Since these axes are parameters of the *evaluation context*, they will determine the kind of annotation performed (Sect. 4.1.3) and the objective evaluation measures that are going to measure the utility of a MWE list (Sect. 4.1.2).

4.1.1 Evaluation Axes

In the literature of MWE acquisition, there are several prototypical styles of evaluation. First, some authors present the results of their methods by showing a list of the top-k MWEs returned according to some ranking criterion (da Silva et al. 1999). In terms of quantitative evaluation, it is possible to manually annotate these top-k candidates, obtaining an objective estimation of the method's precision (Seretan 2008). Traditional measures based on the information retrieval analogy report precision and recall with respect to a gold standard dictionary, trying to optimise the balance between both in order to obtain a reasonable F-measure (Ramisch 2009). In the evaluation of association measures, in order to avoid setting a hard threshold, it is possible to average precision over all recall points, thus comparing cross-measure quality through mean average precision (Evert and Krenn 2005). Given one or more objective evaluation measures, it is possible to perform a simultaneous comparative evaluation of a set of methods (Pearce 2002; Ramisch et al. 2008a). Finally, the use of the acquired MWEs in a real application can give a concrete measure of the utility of the method. In this case, evaluation of MWE acquisition is performed implicitly through the measures traditionally used to evaluate the target application (Finlayson and Kulkarni 2011; Xu et al. 2010; Carpuat and Diab 2010).

In order to provide a more structured view of the evaluation of MWE acquisition methods, we propose a new typology that classifies existing evaluation styles according to four independent axes. These axes try to bring a systematic answer to the questions asked in the introduction of Sect. 4.1.

4.1.1.1 According to the Acquisition Goals

- **Intrinsic**. Most evaluation results reported in related work are intrinsic, that is, they evaluate the MWEs by themselves, directly, as a final product in a process. This is the case, for instance, when one annotates top-k candidates or uses a gold standard to automatically calculate precision and recall (defined in Sect. 4.1.2). The problem with intrinsic evaluation is that, as the definition of MWE depends on the target application (see Sect. 2.2.2), it is often very hard to provide consistent annotation guidelines. Annotation guidelines aim at helping a human judge decide whether a word combination can be considered as a true MWE or whether it is an uninteresting word combination. The coherence and the precision of the guidelines determine the inter-annotator agreement, and a poor agreement makes evaluation of little use as it is highly unreliable. Even though it has numerous limitations, intrinsic evaluation still provides an estimation of the quality of the extracted MWEs that can be compared to related work (assuming the same available dataset).
- **Extrinsic**. Sometimes it is easier to evaluate an NLP application than a list of MWEs. For example, many linguistic tests for detecting light verb constructions use a workaround of trying to translate the expression in another language (Langer 2004). If no word for word translation can be found, this indicates that the combination needs to be treated as a unit. Therefore, manual or automatic translation can be considered as an application that is relatively easy to evaluate by a non-expert native speaker according to objective criteria such as adequacy and fluency. If confronted to the analogous problem of judging whether a word combination is a MWE, the same native speaker would probably find it more difficult. Therefore, while intrinsic evaluation often requires expert linguists to judge the data, extrinsic evaluation can be performed using the standard measures used to evaluate the target application. Furthermore, extrinsic evaluation, that is, the use of MWEs inside an external application, can be very conclusive in demonstrating whether the acquired MWEs are useful in a given task. As the evaluation axes in extrinsic evaluation depend on the target application, the remaining three evaluation axes presented below apply only for intrinsic evaluation.

4.1.1.2 According to the Nature of Measures

- **Quantitative**. A quantitative evaluation assumes the use of objective measures like precision, recall, F-measure, and mean average precision. While many papers only report precision for top-k MWEs, it is important to evaluate recall. This is rarely done but nevertheless of capital importance in assessing the utility of a method. If it extracts only a dozen expressions when there are millions to be retrieved, it will not be more effective than brute force or manual search. The amount of (new) MWEs discovered is as important as their quality, and it is hard to evaluate how many MWEs are "enough" for the automatic acquisition to be useful (Villavicencio et al. 2005; Church 2011). A summary of the measures most often used in the quantitative intrinsic evaluation of MWE acquisition is provided in Sect. 4.1.2.

- **Qualitative**. The goal of qualitative evaluation is to obtain a deep understanding of the mistakes done by the acquisition method and, as a consequence, of the target MWEs. Therefore, one tries to extract patterns of correctly/incorrectly acquired MWEs through observation of the resulting lists in terms of criteria such as POS sequences, frequency distributions and context. Qualitative evaluation is often iterative: (i) a first run of the acquisition method provides rough MWE candidates, (ii) a qualitative evaluation allows the identification of problems in the acquisition method (iii) the problems are then corrected if possible, and a new run provides a better set of MWE candidates, and so forth. Qualitative evaluation can be achieved by manual inspection of the data, statistical analysis and questionnaires. It is not impossible to perform both quantitative and qualitative analysis either simultaneously or at different steps of the acquisition.

4.1.1.3 According to the Available Resources

- **Manual annotation**. Traditionally, after acquisition is performed, one defines criteria to select a representative sample of the output (often a couple of hundred candidates). Then, a group of native speakers will go through the list, making a binary decision on whether the proposed word combination is a true MWE. This process depends on the availability of (volunteer) native speakers to perform the annotation. Ideally, a large sample should be annotated in order to obtain more consistent evaluation measures. Unfortunately, annotation can be quite time consuming and, depending on the type of expression, it may require annotation by expert native speakers like lexicographers and linguists (in opposition to laymen). Additionally, it is not possible to perform manual annotation several times, for instance if we want to optimise a certain parameter of the acquisition method automatically. Some advanced topics on data annotation for the evaluation of MWE acquisition are presented and discussed in Sect. 4.1.3.
- **Automatic annotation**. In automatic annotation, one considers that a lexical resource containing the target MWEs already exists. This lexical resource can be a regular dictionary or a simple list of MWEs, and is often referred to as *gold standard* or *reference dictionary*. For performing automatic annotation, it is necessary to assume that the existing gold standard is complete or at least that it has a broad coverage of the target MWEs. Thus, we consider that candidates contained in the gold standard are true positives (genuine/interesting MWEs)

while those not contained in the gold standard are considered as false MWEs. This is a strong assumption, as we discuss in Sect. 4.1.3.

4.1.1.4 According to the Type of MWE

• **Type-based evaluation**. Some expressions are non-ambiguous and can be annotated out of context, as entries in a lexicon. Examples include most compound nouns and technical terminology, as well as support verb constructions. The decision of whether a sequence of words is a MWE, in this kind of annotation, is independent from the context in which it occurs. On the MWE community website, several lexicons that can serve as gold standards for type-based evaluation are available. Examples include a lexicon of French adverbial expressions (Laporte and Voyatzi 2008) and a lexicon of German preposition-noun-verb constructions (Krenn 2008). A lexicon for type-based annotation can be a simple list of MWEs or it may contain additional information, useful for other MWE tasks like interpretation. Datasets including additional information contain, for example, information about the syntactic relation between the words (Nicholson and Baldwin 2008) and about semantic relations through paraphrases (Nakov 2008). In the context where no gold standard data set is available, type-based annotation must be performed manually by human judges.
• **Token-based evaluation**. Token-based evaluation must be performed whenever the target MWEs are ambiguous, such as phrasal verbs and idioms. Out of context, it is impossible to tell whether the words should be treated as a unit or separately. For example, *look up* may be an idiomatic expression meaning to consult a dictionary or a regular verb-adverb combination meaning to look to a higher position. Therefore, token-based evaluation requires manual annotation, and human judges annotate a whole sentence instead of only the MWE candidate. Data sets of sentences with token-level MWE annotations include, for example, English idiomatic verb-noun constructions (Cook et al. 2007, 2008), English verb-particle constructions (Baldwin 2008), and German verb-preposition-noun constructions (Fritzinger et al. 2010).

4.1.2 Evaluation Measures

The intrinsic quantitative evaluation of MWE acquisition uses standard measures that were originally proposed in the context of information retrieval systems. The analogy is quite straightforward: ranked candidates can be judged as interesting/uninteresting with respect to a target MWE in the same way as ranked documents are assigned relevance judgements according to a query.

First, let us model the result of MWE acquisition as a list C of MWE candidates sorted according to some numerical score (typically, AMs as those described in Sect. 3.1.4). This corresponds to the list of candidates considered as "positive" instances. There are several means to assign a binary value to each element (discussed in Sect. 4.1.3), judging its relevance as a *true positive* (TP) or as a random/uninteresting word combination. A popular evaluation metric considers the binary annotation of the first k sorted candidates (denoted $C_{[1..k]}$). When we consider the rate of true MWEs among the annotated data, the accuracy of the acquisition is denoted as *precision at k* (P@k):

$$P@k(C,k) = \frac{|\text{TPs in } C_{[1..k]}|}{k} \qquad (4.1)$$

When we set k to a reasonable value (say 100 or 200), annotation by a couple of native speakers is fast. However, it is better if we can evaluate the true precision $P(C)$ of the system by annotating the whole set of returned candidates. The precision is the proportion of candidates judged as true MWEs in the set of returned candidates:

$$P(C) = \frac{|\text{TPs in } C|}{|C|}$$

Precision measurements indicate the amount of work needed to transform the rough list of automatically acquired MWEs into a final list validated by an expert (e.g., an experienced lexicographer). However, the use of precision alone oversimplifies the evaluation. What about the elements that should have been returned and that were ignored? If a system only acquires a dozen expressions, even though its precision is close to 100 %, this is probably not enough for building a dictionary. Therefore, in addition to precision, it is crucial to calculate the recall R:

$$R(C) = \frac{|\text{TPs in } C|}{|\text{Total MWEs to acquire}|}$$

The F-measure, that is, the harmonic mean of precision and recall, is frequently used as an overall performance measure:

$$F(C) = \frac{1}{\frac{1}{2} \times \left(\frac{1}{P(C)} + \frac{1}{R(C)} \right)} = \frac{2 \times P(C) \times R(C)}{P(C) + R(C)}$$

In spite of its importance, $R(C)$ is rarely calculated because it is difficult to estimate the total number of MWEs that should be acquired by a system. If annotation is performed by humans, it means that the whole input corpus must be annotated with the target expressions, which is very onerous for small corpora and impracticable for larger corpora. If the annotation is automatic, based on the comparison with an existing dictionary, then the total number of MWEs to acquire corresponds to the size of the reference dictionary. However, this is very likely to be an underestimation, as new MWEs that were not present in the dictionary will be considered as errors.

Precision, recall and F-measure are independent of any particular ranking. When the list of candidates C is ranked according to a given AM, we can apply the mapping $rank_{AM}(c) : C \rightarrow [1..|C|]$ exactly as described in Sect. 3.1.2. Choosing a threshold below which the returned candidates are considered as negative instances is difficult, all the more because there is no systematic way to do it. Thus, it is possible to evaluate the quality of the ranked candidates through its mean averaged precision (MAP), that is, the mean of the precisions taken at each TP:

$$MAP(C) = \frac{\sum\limits_{r=1}^{|C|} P@k(C,r) \times \mathrm{isTP}(C,r)}{|\mathrm{TPs\ in}\ C|},$$

where the binary function $\mathrm{isTP}(C,r)$ is defined as follows:

$$\mathrm{isTP}(C,r) = \begin{cases} 1 \text{ if } (\exists c \in C)[rank_{AM}(c) = r \wedge c \text{ is a TP}], \\ 0 \text{ else.} \end{cases}$$

The precision $P@k(C,r)$ of a given candidate rank r is defined as in Eq. 4.1. It corresponds to the number of TPs up to rank r in C divided by the total number of candidates whose rank is less than or equal to r in C. If we plotted a graph with recall on the abscissa and precision on the ordinate, MAP would correspond to the area below the curve (Evert 2004).

Finally, it is possible to compare two rankings of the same MWE candidate list (e.g., obtained with two different AMs) by calculating the correlation between the positions of the elements in the two ranks. The use of rank correlation metrics, like Kedall's τ and Spearman, is recommended instead of Pearson's correlation index. For example, Kendall's τ correlation index estimates the probability that a MWE pair in a given rank has the same *respective* position in another rank, in spite of the distance between the MWE, which is taken into account in Speaman's correlation index.

4.1.3 Annotation

There are two types of annotation: manual and automatic. In this section, we will underline some decisions that should be taken when constituting an annotated data set for evaluation. In automatic annotation, one considers that there is a static *gold standard* (GS) or *reference*, that is, a lexicon containing the complete list of MWEs that should have been returned by the acquisition method. The candidates that are found in the GS are referred to as *true positives*. In that case, the interpretation of precision and recall, defined in Sect. 4.1.2, is as follows:

- Precision (P): proportion of MWE candidates that are present in the gold standard
- Recall (R): proportion of MWEs in the gold standard that are present in the list of candidates

Formally, the measures can be redefined in terms of set operations. For a set of candidate MWEs C and a set GS of true MWEs:

$$P(C) = \frac{|C \cap GS|}{|C|}$$

$$R(C) = \frac{|C \cap GS|}{|GS|}$$

Both measures are underestimations as they assume that candidates not in the gold standard are false MWEs, whereas they may simply be absent from dictionaries due to coverage limitations. Conversely, these measures assume that all entries in GS are true MWEs, whereas this may depend on the acquisition goal or context. The automatic evaluation of the candidates will always be limited by the coverage of the reference list. Moreover, when calculating the intersection between C and GS, one needs to be very careful to take into account the normalisation of entries. In previous experiments, for example, *Panama Canal* was considered as a true MWE whereas *US navy* was not. Both are proper names and the latter should also be included in the set of true positives. This could be the case if the lexicon uses a different capitalisation (*US Navy*) or expands acronyms (*United States navy*). Therefore, even in the case of automatic annotation, a careful data inspection must be carried out to assure that such cases are dealt with. Finally, some ambiguous cases may be difficult to judge, for example, if the set of candidates C contains the entry *human right*, should it match the *GS* entry *Human Rights*?

Automatic annotation is used to evaluate the accuracy of the acquisition method in relation to the GS, but it does not necessarily correspond to an informative evaluation of the usefulness of the acquired MWEs. In other words, it is pointless to acquire MWEs that are already known (see Sect. 4.2.3). In spite of all these disadvantages, automatic annotation is often employed. Its advantages are mainly that it represents a quite cheap and quick way to evaluate a technique. When compared to manual annotation, it provides an underestimation of recall, which is important and is hard to obtain using manual annotation. Indeed, it would be impracticable to ask annotators to go through the whole corpus and manually identify all the MWEs that should be returned by an acquisition method. The use of a GS depends on its availability or cost.

Manual annotation is rarely performed on the whole list of resulting MWEs. These lists can contain several thousand MWE candidates, and manually annotating all of them would be too onerous. Hence, a first decision that needs to be made concerns the sample of data to annotate. If the list of MWEs is ranked, the most natural choice is to annotate the top-k candidates. However, this can be biased because, if the top of the list contains mostly frequent combinations, they are likely to be known MWEs already present in a lexicon. Indeed, expert lexicographers tend to consider less frequent items as more interesting because they are more likely to be of interest for dictionary users, who are already familiar with the most frequent ones. A fairer evaluation would consider a balanced amount of candidates from high, medium and low frequency ranges. Moreover, this kind of evaluation gives an idea of a method's precision, but ignores its recall, regardless of the sampling technique employed.

The second important decision in manual annotation concerns the definition of the target public. Once the data sample is ready, designing the evaluation guidelines for the annotators requires careful planning. As MWEs are complex phenomena, a group of two or three native speakers may be enough. Depending on the availability of native speakers and on their familiarity with computers, one can develop a web interface or use crowdsourcing platforms like Amazon Mechanical Turk to gather annotations (Nakov 2008). However, if the phenomenon is hard to circumscribe, sometimes expert linguistic knowledge is required to perform the annotation. For example, it is difficult to distinguish general-purpose language like *travel photos* from more specialised cases like *lending institution* and *security institution*. For non-experts, it is not clear why the first candidate is not considered as a true MWE while the second and third ones are.

Third, it is necessary to define which candidates should be annotated as true positives, providing precise descriptions and some examples. In this case, it can be useful to define questions that help the annotators, for example: (i) *can the construction be translated word for word in another language?* or (ii) *can the meaning of this expression be derived from the meanings of its parts?*. These questions can be either based on the target application, like question (i), or on known properties of the target MWEs as described in Sect. 2.3.2, like question (ii). Even though precision and recall require yes/no judgements, when it comes to human annotators it is recommended to avoid binary answers and to allow some room for flexibility, like multiple categories (e.g., *true MWE, maybe a MWE, part of a MWE, random word combination, unknown*) or numerical scales (McCarthy et al. 2003). Posteriorly, one can homogenise the answers or keep only those candidates for which a sharp binary class has been assigned.

Fourth, once the data set has been annotated by more than one human judge (native speaker or expert), it is necessary to calculate the agreement between the annotations. It is not enough to simply calculate the proportion of identical annotations, since there is a probability that annotators agree by pure chance. Traditionally, the kappa agreement score is used to estimate how much annotators agree above of what would be expected by chance (Fleiss 1971). Fleiss' kappa is one of the most popular versions, as it allows multiple annotators per item (in opposition to Cohen's kappa, which assumes two annotators). However, its use is considered unsafe because its interpretation is controversial (is $\kappa = 0.6$ a good agreement?) and its value depends on the number of annotations per item and of available annotation categories (Eugenio and Glass 2004). Several heuristics have been used to report evaluation results based on manual annotation: a second pass of annotation can be made in order to solve the disagreements (Fazly and Stevenson 2007), or one can report both results, using the intersection and the union of MWE candidates considered as true positives, as lower and upper bounds, respectively, for the performance of the method (Linardaki et al. 2010). Regardless of its limitations, the use of agreement measures is important in any NLP annotation task, including the evaluation of MWE acquisition (Artstein and Poesio 2008).

In short, each annotation strategy has advantages and disadvantages. Automatic annotation is quick and cheap and provides an estimation of recall, but it tends to underestimate evaluation results, while manual annotation ignores recall but provides an accurate estimation of a method's precision. One advantage of automatic annotation is that it allows parameter optimisation of the acquisition method. That is, if we want to automatically tune our acquisition method so as to maximise quality on a given development set, we can only do it if automatic annotation is used. It would be impracticable to repeat manual annotation hundreds of times, for each slight modification of the parameters.

Furthermore, the choice between manual and automatic annotation is not mutually exclusive. For instance, one of the goals of manual annotation may be the creation of resources for automatic evaluation. Many such data sets exist and are freely available on the MWE community website.[1] It is also possible to use mixed automatic and manual annotation, that is, entries absent from the gold standard are manually annotated.

4.2 Acquisition Contexts

In Sect. 4.1.1, we defined four axes that describe the *evaluation context*. Here, we are interested in the *acquisition context*, that is, the set of parameters that can influence the results of evaluation. Both contexts, of acquisition and of evaluation, are closely correlated. For example, the class of acquired MWE is a characteristic of the acquisition context. Nonetheless, if the class is ambiguous (e.g., idiomatic expressions), the evaluation must be type-based. Similarly, if the acquisition context is in a language for which no gold standards are available, the evaluation must be performed manually. Therefore, the generalisation of evaluation results depends simultaneously on all the parameters of the acquisition context. This implies that a truly extensive evaluation of methods for MWE acquisition should explore all possible values for each parameter, which is impracticable. Generally, comparative evaluations of MWE acquisition tend to use a fixed test set from which conclusions are drawn (Pearce 2002; Ramisch et al. 2008a). The goal of this section is to argue that such evaluations are of limited value, as they are hard to generalise because the results depend on numerous parameters. According to our experience, the most important parameters are the characteristics of the target MWEs (Sect. 4.2.1), the size and nature of the resources from which the MWEs are acquired (Sect. 4.2.2) and the existing lexical resources present prior to acquisition (Sect. 4.2.3).

---

[1] http://multiword.sf.net

4.2.1 Characteristics of Target Constructions

The characteristics of the target MWEs influence the generalisation of evaluation results. The literature reports a plethora of methods for MWE acquisition and they are mostly motivated by different types of target MWEs. As the definition of MWE includes very heterogeneous phenomena, showing that a method performs well for a given type is not enough to conclude that its performance is superior to other methods for other types. In this section, we will provide examples of MWE evaluation results that cannot be straightforwardly generalised due to characteristics of the target constructions like their type, language and domain.

4.2.1.1 Type

In the typology proposed in Sect. 2.3.4.2, we suggest that MWEs can be classified according to the difficulty to deal with them in computational applications. Therefore, it is natural that different MWE types require different acquisition techniques and, as a consequence different evaluations. For example, a method that is usually employed for candidate extraction in the acquisition of noun compounds is the use of sequences of parts of speech. This is not adequate for extracting English verbal expressions (Villavicencio et al. 2012) or to extract flexible "true" collocations (Seretan 2008). Methods based on the flexibility of a word combination need to be adapted to each type of construction: syntactic and semantic variations are not the same for nominal expressions and verbal expressions (Pearce 2002; Ramisch et al. 2008a,b).

4.2.1.2 Language

The language is also an important characteristic of the target MWE that constitutes a parameter of the acquisition context. To start with, for a very simple reason: corpora and preprocessing tools available for different languages are not the same. For instance, one may argue that the acquisition of "true" collocations is much more efficient with the use of a deep syntactic parser, and this claim is justifiable (Seretan 2008). However, if the target language is not a major one (e.g., French, English, Russian, Chinese), for which a good deep parser is available, then it is not possible to apply such method, and shallow alternatives are required. Also, methods that depend on parallel corpora like Europarl or on large monolingual corpora like the BNC may not be easily adaptable to other languages simply because these resources do not exist in less resourced languages.

There is also another issue with cross-language adaptation, which is more related to the MWEs themselves. Even though existing typologies try to model MWEs in a generic way, so that the types are language independent, MWEs are arbitrary and depend on the language. For example, English and many Germanic languages have a large set of phrasal verbs, which are mostly absent in Romance languages. Compound nouns in German and Swedish are concatenated together as a single lexical unit, while this phenomenon is much less frequent in English (e.g., *database*, *blackboard*) and in Romance languages (e.g., chemical components in French).

4.2.1.3   Domain

Finally, the domain of the expression needs to be taken into account when evaluating MWE acquisition. Justeson and Katz (1995) suggest a list of POS patterns for the automatic acquisition of terms. However, when applied to the biomedical domain, these patterns yielded a poor performance (Ramisch 2009). The original patterns were adapted by considering characteristics of the domain such as the fact that biomedical multiword terms are longer than terms in other domains and often contain foreign words and numbers. This improved the performance of the acquisition significantly. Also, methods that are aimed at multiword terms will not necessarily perform well for acquiring general-purpose MWEs. For example, contrastive methods, such as the one used by Bonin et al. (2010) for the acquisition of legal end environmental multiword terms from Italian corpora, rely on comparing the distribution of MWEs between specialised and general-purpose corpora. In the case where these counts are similar in both corpora, as it is the case for general-purpose MWEs such as light verb constructions, contrastive methods will not work.

4.2.2   Characteristics of Corpora

The characteristics of the target construction are not the only parameter of the acquisition context that can affect evaluation results and their generalisation. For instance, a method that was optimised for a large in-domain English corpus may have a very poor performance in other languages like Portuguese, for which only general-purpose and/or small corpora are available. Among the characteristics of corpora that may heavily influence evaluation results, are its size, its nature (general-purpose, specialised, web as corpus) and the level of linguistic analysis used as preprocessing for candidate extraction.

4.2.2.1   Size

The size of the corpus from which extraction is performed can influence results at two points. First, larger corpora contain more data, so that a MWE acquisition method will be able to retrieve more candidates, increasing its coverage (recall). Second, statistical methods relying on token counts can be sensitive to data sparseness, and a larger sample allows more precise statistical measures to be deduced from it, potentially increasing the precision of the method.

An evidence for the first affirmation, that is, that larger corpora increase the recall of an acquisition method, is presented in Villavicencio et al. (2005, p. 425). In these experiments, the use of increasingly larger corpora makes an initial lexicon of around 4,000 verb-particle constructions grow to around 7,000 entries using the BNC and to around 20,000 verified entries using the web as a corpus. Analogously, in the experiments reported in Sect. 5.3, we use three fragments of increasing sizes of the Europarl corpus. The recall of n-gram approaches like NSP and the mwetoolkit increases from around 83 % in the small corpus to more than 89 % in a corpus 100 times larger (see Table 5.4).

The second advantage of using larger corpora is that they are more representative samples of language, thus yielding more reliable statistics. Sparseness is particularly dangerous when it comes to association measures. Dunning (1993), for instance, showed that normality assumptions do not hold for small samples, and that the log-likelihood ratio is much more adequate for these cases because it assumes a LNRE distribution. Pedersen (1996) suggests Fisher's exact test as a very robust measure, and Evert (2004) shows that it approximates quite well the values of Dunning's log-likelihood ratio. In all cases, when applying association measures, one should perform a frequency cut based on a minimal occurrence threshold. Thus, more data means less discarded candidates according to this criterion, in addition to more accurate AMs.

4.2.2.2 Nature

Evaluation results depend on the nature of the corpus. By *nature*, we mean its characteristics, which can be summarised as the domain and genre of the texts. Additionally, traditional text corpora differ significantly from the use of the web as a corpus. Experimental results show that, in the task of specialised noun compound extraction, the use of the web as a corpus is not recommended (Ramisch et al. 2010). The counts derived from such a generic resource are too noisy to be used as the base of association measures.

Some techniques use several corpora for acquisition, hence the nature of all of them needs to be taken into account. For example, contrastive measures for multiword term detection require the use of at least two corpora: a specialised one and a general-purpose one (Bonin et al. 2010). A bad choice in either can decrease the quality of acquired MWEs. For instance, the contrastive measure simple-csmw sharply reflects the difference between using a traditional corpus or the web as contrastive corpus, obtaining a MAP of 51.76 % for Europarl and 38.5 % for Google, even if the latter is several orders of magnitude larger than the former. This is an indication that the source of count information significantly affects the results. A traditional general-purpose corpus yielded good results even when more than 90 % of the counts were zero, since these may provide some information about the degree of specialisation of the candidate, while the web was not a good contrastive corpus because of its unboundedness.

On the other hand, the web can be quite useful in tasks that involve the extraction of more generic MWEs. As an example, Sects. 6.1 and 6.2 illustrate its usefulness in the acquisition of Greek nominal expressions and Portuguese verbal expressions, respectively. In particular, the experiments on Portuguese used traditional corpora and the web as a corpus (Duran and Ramisch 2011). The validation of sentiment expressions using the web, similarly to Villavicencio et al. (2005), was particularly useful in helping to distinguish productive patterns from more rigid expressions. In these experiments, we also noticed that the genre of the corpus has an influence on the results. Since we were interested in sentiment expressions and since our corpus contained newspaper texts of the journalistic genre, most of the acquired expressions have negative polarity. This is probably a consequence of the fact that newspapers report more often bad news like tragedies and crisis, rather than good news involving joy and happiness.

4.2.2.3 Level of Analysis

The level of linguistic abstraction used in candidate MWE extraction has an influence on the quality of the results. Existing acquisition methods vary much in the amount of linguistic preprocessing performed: from completely knowledge-free methods based on surface forms only (da Silva et al. 1999), to sophisticated methods depending on a specific type of syntactic formalism (Seretan 2008). See Sect. 3.1.1 for an overview of some linguistic analysis tools that can be used for MWE acquisition.

For the acquisition of verb-particle constructions in English, for example, Baldwin (2005) proposes four methods that use increasing levels of linguistic abstraction, according to the preprocessing tools used: a POS tagger, a chunker, a chunk grammar and a syntactic parser. The use of complete (deep) syntactic analysis has been advocated by Seretan (2008), who targets general (non-fixed) collocations such as adverb-adjective and verb-object pairs. Depending on the language, the parts of the collocation may be separated by several intervening words, thus requiring some kind of tree representation. She argues that methods based on shallow POS patterns could not appropriately capture such long-distance relations, whereas syntax-based collocation acquisition has no problem with that. In the same lines, Green et al. (2011) present and evaluate a syntax-based method for the acquisition of French MWEs, showing significant improvements over a baseline based on shallow POS patterns.

The flexibility of the target construction may justify the use of language-dependent linguistic analysis tools, which will increase the usefulness of the resulting MWE list. On the downside, linguistic analysis tools are not readily available for all languages, specially poorly resourced ones. Moreover, it remains to be proven that deeper analysis yields better results: in the experiments of Baldwin (2005), for instance, the syntactic parser does not systematically obtain the best F-measure. This may be a consequence of the heterogeneous performance of analysis tools themselves. Sometimes, it may be wiser to trust a reasonably good

POS tagger than a parser that makes too many attachment errors. In short, the level of linguistic analysis recommended for a given acquisition goal depends on the flexibility of the target construction and on the availability of tools for the target language and domain.

4.2.3 Existing Resources

The existence of lexical resources (printed and/or machine-readable dictionaries and thesauri) inventorying the target MWEs is a factor that influences the usefulness of automatic MWE acquisition methods. For example, in Sect. 6.2, we describe the acquisition of verbal MWEs in Portuguese, given the target application of (manual) semantic role labelling. In this case, the acquisition was motivated by the fact that there was no existing lexical resource containing such constructions for the Portuguese language. Therefore, the novelty of the extracted expressions was 100 % and even simple techniques that could help speed up lexicographic work compared to manual corpus inspection was considered as extremely useful by the users. In Chap. 6, we explore the use of automatically acquired MWEs to speed up lexicographic work, given that, in the absence of previously existing lexical resources, "something is better than nothing."

However, when a lexical resource covering the target constructions already exists, there are two possibilities. First, the existing lexical resource can be used as gold standard for automatic annotation, assuming that the method returns no new MWE. Second, the evaluation may report not only classical precision/recall measures but also the novelty of the acquired MWEs. The former is clearly an over-simplification, as it is unreasonable to assume that the previously existing resource has 100 % coverage (otherwise, what is the point of performing automatic MWE acquisition?).

In order to estimate the novelty of the acquisition method, it is necessary to perform manual annotation of (a sample of) the candidates that were not present in the dictionary. Then, the novelty of the method can be defined as the ratio between true positives that were not present in the initial dictionary and the total number of true positives.

In short, when MWE acquisition is performed in the context of a real NLP application (in opposition to the context of experimental research), the existence of lexical resources containing MWEs must be taken into account.

4.3 Discussion

The evaluation of MWE acquisition is an open problem. While classical measures like precision and recall based on automatic annotation assume that a complete (or at least broad-coverage) gold standard exists, manual annotation of top-k

candidates and mean average precision are labour-intensive even when applied to a small sample, emphasizing precision regardless of the number of acquired *new* expressions. Nonetheless, objective measures provide a lower bound to the ability of a tool or technique to deal with a specific type of MWE.

On the one hand, the results of intrinsic evaluation are of limited value: although they shed some light on the optimal parameters for the given scenario, they are hard to generalise and cannot be directly applied to other configurations. The quality of acquired MWEs as measured by objective criteria depends on the language, domain and type of the target construction, on corpus size and genre, on already available resources, on the preprocessing steps, among others. On the other hand, extrinsic evaluation consists of inserting acquired MWEs into a real NLP application and evaluating the impact of this new data on the overall performance of the system. For instance, it may be easier to ask a human annotator to evaluate the output of an MT system than to ask whether a sequence of words constitutes a MWE.

As pointed out by Pecina (2005), "evaluation of collocation extraction methods is a complicated task. On one hand, different applications require different [...] thresholds. On the other hand, methods give different results within different ranges of their association scores". Efforts for the evaluation of MWE acquisition approaches usually focus on a single technique or compare the quality of association measures (AMs) used to rank a fixed annotated list of MWEs. For instance, Evert and Krenn (2005) and Seretan (2008) specifically evaluate and analyse the lexical AMs used in MWE extraction on small samples of 2-gram candidates.

Some efforts have been made toward comparative evaluations of MWE acquisition techniques. Pearce (2002) systematically evaluates a set of techniques for MWE extraction on a small test set of English collocations, emphasising association measures. Similarly, Pecina (2005) and Ramisch et al. (2008a) present extensive comparisons of individual AMs and of their combination for MWE extraction in Czech, German and English. Punctual comparisons have been performed, for instance, between candidate extraction based on POS sequences and based on syntactic models (Schone and Jurafsky 2001). In Sect. 5.3, we report results of an evaluation of freely available tools compared to the framework proposed in the present work (Ramisch 2012).

One initiative aiming at more comparable evaluations of MWE acquisition approaches was in the form of a shared task (Grégoire et al. 2008). However, the experiment presented in Sect. 5.3 differs from the shared task in its aims. The latter considered only the ranking of precompiled MWE lists using AMs or linguistic filters at the end of extraction. However, for many languages and domains, no such lists are available. In addition, the evaluation results produced for the shared task may be difficult to generalise, as some of the evaluations gave priority to the precision of the techniques without considering the recall or the novelty of the extracted MWEs. To date, little has been said about the practical concerns involving MWE acquisition, like computational resources, flexibility or availability. In our experiment, we hope to help filling this gap by performing a broad evaluation of the *acquisition process as a whole*, considering many different parameters.

There have also been efforts towards the extrinsic evaluation of MWEs for NLP applications such as information retrieval (Doucet and Ahonen-Myka 2004; Xu et al. 2010; Acosta et al. 2011), word sense disambiguation (Finlayson and Kulkarni 2011), MT (Carpuat and Diab 2010; Pal et al. 2010) and ontology learning (Venkatsubramanyan and Perez-Carballo 2004).

4.4 Summary

The problem of evaluating MWE acquisition is quite complex because results depend on many parameters of the acquisition context, making results obtained in one context hard to generalise. In related work, several evaluation styles are used: showing a list of ranked top-k MWEs (da Silva et al. 1999), manually annotate the top-k candidates (Seretan 2008), measure precision and recall with respect to a dictionary (Ramisch 2009), compare the quality of association measures through mean average precision (Evert and Krenn 2005), compare different methods (Pearce 2002; Ramisch et al. 2008a), and measure the impact of acquired MWEs on NLP applications (Finlayson and Kulkarni 2011; Xu et al. 2010; Carpuat and Diab 2010). We propose the following typology for classifying the *evaluation context*:

1. **According to the acquisition goals**

    • **Intrinsic**. Results are reported by evaluating the MWEs by themselves, directly, as a final product in a process.
    • **Extrinsic**. Sometimes it is easier to evaluate an NLP application than a list of MWEs. Extrinsic evaluation can be performed by integrating MWEs into an application and then checking whether they improve its output.

2. **According to the nature of measures**

    • **Quantitative**. We evaluate the list of MWE candidates using objective measures like precision, recall, F-measure, and mean average precision.
    • **Qualitative**. The goal is to understand the mistakes done by the acquisition method. Therefore, one observes the results in terms of POS sequences, frequency distributions, context, etc.

3. **According to the available resources**

    • **Manual annotation**. A group of native speakers and/or experts will go through the list, deciding whether each proposed combination is a MWE.
    • **Automatic annotation**. Given that a broad-coverage dictionary of the target MWEs already exists, we consider that candidates contained in the dictionary are true positives (genuine/interesting MWEs) while the others are not MWEs.

4. **According to the type of MWE**

    • **Type-based evaluation**. Non-ambiguous expressions like compound nouns, terminology, and support verb constructions can be annotated out of context.

- **Token-based evaluation**. Token-based evaluation must be performed for
  ambiguous MWEs like phrasal verbs and idioms. Out of context, it is
  impossible to tell whether the words should be treated as a unit.

The *acquisition context* is the set of parameters that can influence the results of
evaluation. Results of evaluation performed on a given acquisition context are hard
to generalise because they depend on too many parameters. Some parameters of the
acquisition context are:

- **Type of MWE**. Different MWE types require different evaluations. For example,
  POS sequences are usually employed for noun compounds acquisition but this is
  not adequate for verbal expressions (Villavicencio et al. 2012).
- **Language**. Not only MWEs but also NLP resources are not equivalent in all
  languages. The use of a parser for collocation acquisition like in Seretan (2008)
  is impossible for poorly resourced languages, requiring shallow alternatives.
- **Domain**. The domain needs to be taken into account in the evaluation. For
  example, the list of POS patterns suggested by Justeson and Katz (1995) yield a
  poor performance when applied to a biomedical corpus (Ramisch 2009).
- **Corpus size**. Large corpora contain more data, so intuitively a method will be
  able to retrieve more candidates, increasing recall. Statistical methods can be
  sensitive to data sparseness, and larger samples allow more precise measures.
- **Corpus nature**. Results depend on the domain and genre of texts. Experiments
  show that, in specialised noun compound extraction, the use of the web as a
  corpus is not recommended (Ramisch et al. 2010).
- **Level of analysis**. Acquisition methods vary from knowledge-free methods
  (da Silva et al. 1999) to those depending on a syntactic formalism (Seretan 2008).
  It remains to be proven that deeper analysis yields better results (Baldwin 2005).

The evaluation of MWE acquisition remains an open problem. While precision
and recall based on automatic annotation assume the existence of a complete gold
standard, manual annotation is labour-intensive and emphasises precision regardless
of the number of acquired new MWEs. There has been some effort towards
comparative evaluation (Schone and Jurafsky 2001; Pecina 2005; Ramisch et al.
2008a) and towards extrinsic evaluation in NLP applications such as information
retrieval (Doucet and Ahonen-Myka 2004; Xu et al. 2010; Acosta et al. 2011), word
sense disambiguation (Finlayson and Kulkarni 2011), MT (Carpuat and Diab 2010;
Pal et al. 2010) and ontology learning (Venkatsubramanyan and Perez-Carballo
2004).

References

Acosta O, Villavicencio A, Moreira V (2011) Identification and treatment of multiword expressions
    applied to information retrieval. In: Kordoni V, Ramisch C, Villavicencio A (eds) Proceedings
    of the ALC workshop on multiword expressions: from parsing and generation to the real world
    (MWE 2011), Portland. Association for Computational Linguistics, pp 101–109. http://www.
    aclweb.org/anthology/W/W11/W11-0815

Artstein R, Poesio M (2008) Inter-coder agreement for computational linguistics. Comput Linguist 34(4):555–596

Baldwin T (2005) Deep lexical acquisition of verb-particle constructions. Comput Speech Lang Spec Issue MWEs 19(4):398–414

Baldwin T (2008) A resource for evaluating the deep lexical acquisition of English verb-particle constructions. In: Grégoire N, Evert S, Krenn B (eds) Proceedings of the LREC workshop towards a shared task for multiword expressions (MWE 2008), Marrakech, pp 1–2

Bonin F, Dell'Orletta F, Venturi G, Montemagni S (2010) Contrastive filtering of domain-specific multi-word terms from different types of corpora. In: Laporte É, Nakov P, Ramisch C, Villavicencio A (eds) Proceedings of the COLING workshop on multiword expressions: from theory to applications (MWE 2010), Beijing. Association for Computational Linguistics, pp 76–79

Carpuat M, Diab M (2010) Task-based evaluation of multiword expressions: a pilot study in statistical machine translation. In: Proceedings of human language technology: the 2010 annual conference of the North American chapter of the Association for Computational Linguistics (NAACL 2003), Los Angeles. Association for Computational Linguistics, pp 242–245. http://www.aclweb.org/anthology/N10-1029

Church K (2011) How many multiword expressions do people know? In: Kordoni V, Ramisch C, Villavicencio A (eds) Proceedings of the ALC workshop on multiword expressions: from parsing and generation to the real world (MWE 2011), Portland. Association for Computational Linguistics, pp 137–144. http://www.aclweb.org/anthology/W/W11/W11-0823

Cook P, Fazly A, Stevenson S (2007) Pulling their weight: exploiting syntactic forms for the automatic identification of idiomatic expressions in context. In: Grégoire N, Evert S, Kim SN (eds) Proceedings of the ACL workshop on a broader perspective on multiword expressions (MWE 2007), Prague. Association for Computational Linguistics, pp 41–48. http://www.aclweb.org/anthology/W/W07/W07-1106

Cook P, Fazly A, Stevenson S (2008) The VNC-tokens dataset. In: Grégoire N, Evert S, Krenn B (eds) Proceedings of the LREC workshop towards a shared task for multiword expressions (MWE 2008), Marrakech, pp 19–22

da Silva JF, Dias G, Guilloré S, Lopes JGP (1999) Using localmaxs algorithm for the extraction of contiguous and non-contiguous multiword lexical units. In: Proceedings of the 9th Portuguese conference on artificial intelligence: progress in artificial intelligence, (EPIA 1999), Évora. Springer, London, pp 113–132. http://dl.acm.org/citation.cfm?id=645377.651205

Doucet A, Ahonen-Myka H (2004) Non-contiguous word sequences for information retrieval. In: Tanaka T, Villavicencio A, Bond F, Korhonen A (eds) Proceedings of the ACL workshop on multiword expressions: integrating processing (MWE 2004), Barcelona. Association for Computational Linguistics, pp 88–95

Dunning T (1993) Accurate methods for the statistics of surprise and coincidence. Comput Linguist 19(1):61–74

Duran MS, Ramisch C (2011) How do you feel? investigating lexical-syntactic patterns in sentiment expression. In: Proceedings of corpus linguistics 2011: discourse and corpus linguistics conference, Birmingham

Eugenio BD, Glass M (2004) The kappa statistic: a second look. Comput Linguist 30(1):95–101

Evert S (2004) The statistics of word cooccurrences: word pairs and collocations. PhD thesis, Institut für maschinelle Sprachverarbeitung, University of Stuttgart, Stuttgart, 353p

Evert S, Krenn B (2005) Using small random samples for the manual evaluation of statistical association measures. Comput Speech Lang Spec Issue MWEs 19(4):450–466

Fazly A, Stevenson S (2007) Distinguishing subtypes of multiword expressions using linguistically-motivated statistical measures. In: Grégoire N, Evert S, Kim SN (eds) Proceedings of the ACL workshop on a broader perspective on multiword expressions (MWE 2007), Prague. Association for Computational Linguistics, pp 9–16. http://www.aclweb.org/anthology/W/W07/W07-1102

Finlayson M, Kulkarni N (2011) Detecting multi-word expressions improves word sense disambiguation. In: Kordoni V, Ramisch C, Villavicencio A (eds) Proceedings of the ALC workshop on multiword expressions: from parsing and generation to the real world (MWE 2011), Portland. Association for Computational Linguistics, pp 20–24. http://www.aclweb.org/anthology/W/W11/W11-0805

Fleiss JL (1971) Measuring nominal scale agreement among many raters. Psychol Bull 76(5):378–382

Fritzinger F, Weller M, Heid U (2010) A survey of idiomatic preposition-noun-verb triples on token level. In: Proceedings of the seventh international conference on language resources and evaluation (LREC 2010), Valetta. European Language Resources Association, pp 2908–2914

Green S, de Marneffe MC, Bauer J, Manning CD (2011) Multiword expression identification with tree substitution grammars: a parsing tour de force with French. In: Barzilay R, Johnson M (eds) Proceedings of the 2011 conference on empirical methods in natural language processing (EMNLP 2011), Edinburgh. Association for Computational Linguistics, pp 725–735. http://www.aclweb.org/anthology/D11-1067

Grégoire N, Evert S, Krenn B (eds) (2008) Proceedings of the LREC workshop towards a shared task for multiword expressions (MWE 2008), Marrakech. http://www.lrec-conf.org/proceedings/lrec2008/workshops/W20_Proceedings.pdf, 57p

Justeson JS, Katz SM (1995) Technical terminology: some linguistic properties and an algorithm for identification in text. Nat Lang Eng 1(1):9–27

Krenn B (2008) Description of evaluation resource – German PP-verb data. In: Grégoire N, Evert S, Krenn B (eds) Proceedings of the LREC workshop towards a shared task for multiword expressions (MWE 2008), Marrakech, pp 7–10

Langer S (2004) A linguistic test battery for support verb constructions. Spec Issue Linguist Investig 27(2):171–184

Laporte É, Voyatzi S (2008) An electronic dictionary of French multiword adverbs. In: Grégoire N, Evert S, Krenn B (eds) Proceedings of the LREC workshop towards a shared task for multiword expressions (MWE 2008), Marrakech, pp 31–34

Lee L, Aw A, Zhang M, Li H (2010) EM-based hybrid model for bilingual terminology extraction from comparable corpora. In: Huang CR, Jurafsky D (eds) Proceedings of the 23rd international conference on computational linguistics (COLING 2010)—Posters, The Coling 2010 Organizing Committee, Beijing, pp 639–646. http://www.aclweb.org/anthology/C10-2073

Linardaki E, Ramisch C, Villavicencio A, Fotopoulou A (2010) Towards the construction of language resources for Greek multiword expressions: extraction and evaluation. In: Piperidis S, Slavcheva M, Vertan C (eds) Proceedings of the LREC workshop on exploitation of multilingual resources and tools for central and (South) Eastern European languages, Valetta, pp 31–40

McCarthy D, Keller B, Carroll J (2003) Detecting a continuum of compositionality in phrasal verbs. In: Bond F, Korhonen A, McCarthy D, Villavicencio A (eds) Proceedings of the ACL workshop on multiword expressions: analysis, acquisition and treatment (MWE 2003), Sapporo. Association for Computational Linguistics, pp 73–80. doi:10.3115/1119282.1119292, http://www.aclweb.org/anthology/W03-1810

Nakov P (2008) Paraphrasing verbs for noun compound interpretation. In: Grégoire N, Evert S, Krenn B (eds) Proceedings of the LREC workshop towards a shared task for multiword expressions (MWE 2008), Marrakech, pp 46–49

Nicholson J, Baldwin T (2008) Interpreting compound nominalisations. In: Grégoire N, Evert S, Krenn B (eds) Proceedings of the LREC workshop towards a shared task for multiword expressions (MWE 2008), Marrakech, pp 43–45

Pal S, Naskar SK, Pecina P, Bandyopadhyay S, Way A (2010) Handling named entities and compound verbs in phrase-based statistical machine translation. In: Laporte É, Nakov P, Ramisch C, Villavicencio A (eds) Proceedings of the COLING workshop on multiword expressions: from theory to applications (MWE 2010), Beijing. Association for Computational Linguistics, pp 45–53

Pearce D (2002) A comparative evaluation of collocation extraction techniques. In: Proceedings of the third international conference on language resources and evaluation (LREC 2002), Las Palmas. European Language Resources Association, pp 1530–1536

Pecina P (2005) An extensive empirical study of collocation extraction methods. In: Proceedings of the ACL 2005 student research workshop, Ann Arbor. Association for Computational Linguistics, pp 13–18. http://www.aclweb.org/anthology/P/P05/P05-2003

Pedersen T (1996) Fishing for exactness. In: Proceedings of the south-central SAS users group conference (SCSUG-96), Austin, pp 188–200

Ramisch C (2009) Multiword terminology extraction for domain-specific documents. Master's thesis, École Nationale Supérieure d'Informatique et de Mathématiques Appliquées, Grenoble, 79p

Ramisch C (2012) A generic framework for multiword expressions treatment: from acquisition to applications. In: Proceedings of the ACL 2012 student research workshop, Jeju. Association for Computational Linguistics, pp 61–66. http://www.aclweb.org/anthology/W12-3311

Ramisch C, Schreiner P, Idiart M, Villavicencio A (2008a) An evaluation of methods for the extraction of multiword expressions. In: Grégoire N, Evert S, Krenn B (eds) Proceedings of the LREC workshop towards a shared task for multiword expressions (MWE 2008), Marrakech, pp 50–53

Ramisch C, Villavicencio A, Moura L, Idiart M (2008b) Picking them up and figuring them out: verb-particle constructions, noise and idiomaticity. In: Clark A, Toutanova K (eds) Proceedings of the twelfth conference on natural language learning (CoNLL 2008), The Coling 2008 Organizing Committee, Manchester, pp 49–56. http://www.aclweb.org/anthology/W08-2107

Ramisch C, Villavicencio A, Boitet C (2010) Web-based and combined language models: a case study on noun compound identification. In: Huang CR, Jurafsky D (eds) Proceedings of the 23rd international conference on computational linguistics (COLING 2010)—Posters, The Coling 2010 Organizing Committee, Beijing, pp 1041–1049. http://www.aclweb.org/anthology/C10-2120

Schone P, Jurafsky D (2001) Is knowledge-free induction of multiword unit dictionary headwords a solved problem? In: Lee L, Harman D (eds) Proceedings of the 2001 conference on empirical methods in natural language processing (EMNLP 2001), Pittsburgh. Association for Computational Linguistics, pp 100–108

Seretan V (2008) Collocation extraction based on syntactic parsing. PhD thesis, University of Geneva, Geneva, 249p

Venkatsubramanyan S, Perez-Carballo J (2004) Multiword expression filtering for building knowledge. In: Tanaka T, Villavicencio A, Bond F, Korhonen A (eds) Proceedings of the ACL workshop on multiword expressions: integrating processing (MWE 2004), Barcelona. Association for Computational Linguistics, pp 40–47

Villavicencio A, Bond F, Korhonen A, McCarthy D (2005) Introduction to the special issue on multiword expressions: having a crack at a hard nut. Comput Speech Lang Spec Issue MWEs 19(4):365–377

Villavicencio A, Idiart M, Ramisch C, Araujo VD, Yankama B, Berwick R (2012) Get out but don't fall down: verb-particle constructions in child language. In: Berwick R, Korhonen A, Poibeau T, Villavicencio A (eds) Proceedings of the EACL 2012 workshop on computational models of language acquisition and loss, Avignon. Association for Computational Linguistics, pp 43–50

Xu Y, Goebel R, Ringlstetter C, Kondrak G (2010) Application of the tightness continuum measure to Chinese information retrieval. In: Laporte É, Nakov P, Ramisch C, Villavicencio A (eds) Proceedings of the COLING workshop on multiword expressions: from theory to applications (MWE 2010), Beijing. Association for Computational Linguistics, pp 54–62

Chapter 5
A New Framework for MWE Acquisition

In the previous chapters, we motivated the importance of MWEs for NLP applications and provided a bibliographic review of past and present research in the area. We are now ready to present our new methodological framework for MWE acquisition. This framework was motivated by the absence of one covering all the steps of MWE acquisition in a systematic and integrated way. Thus, we have developed a methodology in which the process of MWE acquisition is divided into several independent modules that can be chained together in several ways. Each module solves a specific task using multiple and complementary techniques.

We will detail our motivations, guiding principles and methodology in Sect. 5.1. Then, we will demonstrate how the methodology can be applied to an acquisition context (a corpus in a given language and domain and a target application) through a worked out toy experiment in Sect. 5.2. In Sect. 5.3, our methodological framework is systematically compared to other similar available frameworks, underlining their differences in terms of quality but also in terms of computational resources and flexibility.

5.1 The mwetoolkit Framework

In this section, we introduce a new methodology for MWE acquisition which we baptised mwetoolkit for "multiword expressions toolkit". In the first subsection, we provide a general overview of our goals and of the main principles that guided us during the development of the methodology and of the corresponding implementation (Sect. 5.1.1). In the second subsection, we provide a detailed description of the modules composing our methodological framework and how they can be combined to achieve a given MWE acquisition goal (Sect. 5.1.2). Finally, we provide a more subjective discussion of the characteristics of the mwetoolkit. This discussion is followed by a thorough and systematic evaluation of the toolkit,

© Springer International Publishing Switzerland 2015

C. Ramisch, *Multiword Expressions Acquisition*, Theory and Applications of Natural Language Processing, DOI 10.1007/978-3-319-09207-2_5

which is described in Chaps. 6 and 7, allowing us to present our ideas for future developments, improvements and extensions.

5.1.1   General Architecture

The idea of developing a new framework for MWE acquisition originated from a real research need during previous experiments on automatic multiword terminology extraction from specialised corpora (Ramisch 2009). On that occasion, we realised that, in spite of the existence of a certain number of available tools for MWE extraction (see Sect. 3.2.3), they only dealt with part of the extraction process. For example, while UCS provides several association measures for candidate ranking, the extraction of candidates from the corpus needs to be performed externally, using regular expressions or similar tools. Moreover, it only deals with 2-grams, ignoring larger n-grams. NSP provides support for larger n-grams, but it is impossible to describe more linguistically motivated extraction patterns based on parts of speech, lemmas or syntactic relations. For a detailed comparison of the mwetoolkit with other approaches, please refer to Sect. 5.3.

In a context where existing methods only implemented part of what we needed, our primary goal was to develop a *methodology* that would cover the whole acquisition pipeline. However, given that there is no consensus about the best method for a given acquisition context,[1] the new methodology should necessarily allow *multiple solutions* for a given sub-task. Thus, decisions such as the level of linguistic analysis, length n of the n-grams, filtering thresholds and evaluation measures should not be made by the method itself. Instead, given a large range of available methods, the user should be able to chose and to tune the parameters according to his/her needs. Therefore, one of our guiding principles is *generality*. In other words, the relevant decisions in the acquisition should be taken by the users. On the one hand, this principle implies that we cannot provide a push-button simplified methodology. On the other hand, the method can be adapted and tuned to a large number of acquisition contexts, maximising its *portability* as a consequence.

The mwetoolkit was originally designed to extract multiword terminology from specialised corpora, and later extended to perform automatic acquisition of several types of MWEs in specialised and general-purpose corpora. Its implementation includes hybrid knowledge-poor techniques that can be applied virtually to any corpus, independently of the domain and of the language. The original goal of the mwetoolkit was to aid lexicographers and terminographers in the challenging task of creating language resources that include multiword entries. Therefore, we assume that, whenever a textual corpus of the target language/domain is available, it is possible to automatically acquire interesting groups of lexical units that can

---

[1] See Sect. 4.2 for a formal definition of an acquisition context.

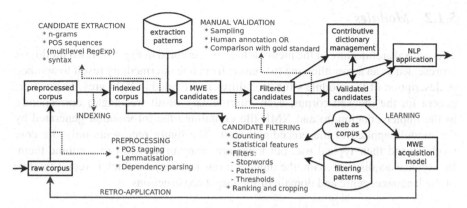

Fig. 5.1 Framework for MWE acquisition from corpora, core modules in a prototypical acquisition chain

be regarded as candidate MWEs. We assume that the existence of targeted lists containing automatically acquired MWEs can speed up the creation and improve both quality and coverage of general-purpose and specialised lexical resources (dictionaries, thesauri) and ontologies.

Basically, we employ a quite standard sub-task definition which consists of two phases: a phase of *candidate extraction* followed by a phase of *candidate filtering*, where we combine association measures (AMs), descriptive features, contrastive features and machine learning. In the first phase, one acquires candidates based either on flat *n*-grams or specific morphosyntactic patterns (of surface forms, lemmas, POS tags and dependency relations). Once the candidate lists are extracted, it is possible to filter them by defining criteria that range from simple count-based thresholds, to more complex features such as AMs. Since AMs are based on corpus word and *n*-gram counts, the toolkit provides both a corpus indexing facility and integration with web search engines (for using the web as a corpus). Additionally, for the evaluation phase, we provide validation and annotation facilities. Finally, mwetoolkit also allows easy integration with a machine learning tool for the creation of supervised MWE extraction models if annotated data is available.

The mwetoolkit methodology was implemented as a set of independent modules[2] that handle an intermediary representation of the *corpus*, the list of MWE *patterns*, the list of MWE *candidates* and the *reference* dictionaries. Each module performs a specific task in the pipeline of MWE extraction, from the raw corpus to the filtered list of MWE candidates, including their automatic evaluation if a reference (gold standard) is given. Figure 5.1 summarises the architecture of mwetoolkit, which will be described in detail in the next section.

---

[2]These modules were implemented in Python, with parts in C for efficiency reasons.

5.1.2   Modules

The general architecture of the methodology is presented in Fig. 5.1. Each module is represented as an arrow allowing to convert from one intermediary result to another. A description of the module's functionalities is provided in light grey. In practice, except for the indexed corpus, each intermediary result (rectangle) corresponds, in the implementation, to and XML file containing the information generated by the module applied to the preceding result. The figure represents only the core modules and their typical use, but there are many other ways to combine them. In a typical acquisition chain, the input is a raw text corpus which is representative of the language, genre and domain of the target constructions.

5.1.2.1   Preproccessing

- *Inputs:* raw textual monolingual corpus
- *Outputs:* preprocessed corpus

Preprocessing is actually not a module of the mwetoolkit methodology. It should be performed by external tools such as parsers and POS taggers. Preprocessing with external tools may include:

1. Consistent tokenisation
2. Lemmatisation
3. POS tagging
4. Dependency parsing

The last three steps are optional, but higher level analysis can be crucial for determining the quality of the acquired MWEs.

Additionally, case homogenisation can be performed through mwetoolkit's heuristic lowercasing rules, that tend to preserve the case of words that occur with different capitalisation throughout the corpus. However, POS taggers and parsers often already perform adequate case processing. In any case, lowercasing all words may not be a good idea because valuable information can be lost. For example, one should keep capitalisation of chemical component names (*NaCl*), person names (*Bill Gates* and *bill gates* are not the same entity) and acronyms (*SOAP* is not *soap*, *US* is a country, *us* is a pronoun).

Syntax information must be represented as dependency trees. Traditional constituent parsing trees must be somehow converted into dependency trees for use with the mwetoolkit. Our data format allows the definition of attributes on a token basis. Thus, a dependency relation can be represented as a pair ⟨parent, type⟩ where the first element is the position of the token on which the current token depends and the second element is the type of relation (e.g., object, subject, modifier, determiner).

This format is similar to the CoNLL shared task format, traditionally employed as an exchange format in many NLP tasks.[3] The preprocessed corpus should be converted from the format used by the preprocessing tool to XML or to a special text format similar to Moses factored corpora.[4] The input corpus contains a sequence of sentences, and each sentence is composed of a sequence of tokens. Each token has the following optional attributes: surface form, lemma, part of speech and dependency relation. The mwetoolkit provides useful scripts to easily convert the output formats of the TreeTagger and of the RASP parser to our input formats. For more details on preprocessing, please refer to Sect. 3.1.1, where we show the application of the TreeTagger and of the RASP parser on an example sentence.

5.1.2.2 Indexing

* *Inputs:* preprocessed corpus
* *Outputs:* indexed corpus

Processing a large corpus through its XML representation is far from being efficient. Even with the use of a minimalist library for XML parsing like SAX, the time taken to load the file and parse its elements and attributes implies in a prohibitive overhead. Therefore, the first operation performed by the mwetoolkit is the creation of index based on suffix arrays (see Sect. 3.3.3). A suffix array is a memory-efficient data structure that allows for the counts of n-grams of arbitrary length to be accessed quickly in very large corpora. For each attribute at the token level (surface form, lemma, POS and syntax), we generate a separate suffix array. Each suffix array contains three parts: a vocabulary containing the mappings between words and integer identifiers, a corpus containing the sequence of identifiers and the suffix array itself, containing the suffix indices of the corpus sorted in lexicographical order.

The n-gram counts are later retrieved during candidate extraction and filtering. During the step of candidate extraction, we use the index corpus file to match regular expressions on integers, which is faster than string operations. Later, we use the index again to count the occurrences of the whole candidate sequence as well as the individual words. We assume that the index must fit in main memory, as fast indexing depends on reasonable memory consumption, which in turn is linearly proportional to the corpus size. For instance, indexing the BNC corpus (100 million words) took about 5 min per attribute on a 3 GB RAM desktop computer.

One of the advantages of performing candidate extraction and n-gram counting as independent steps is that, in addition to the original corpus, we can obtain counts from other corpora as well. In other words, it is possible to count the n-grams not

---

[3]http://nextens.uvt.nl/depparse-wiki/DataFormat
[4]http://www.statmt.org/moses/?n=Moses.FactoredTutorial

only in the corpus from which the candidates were extracted, but also in other sources like smaller domain corpora, larger generic corpora, and the Web as a corpus. For example, the `mwetoolkit` is integrated with the search engine APIs of Google and Yahoo, which provide page hit counts.[5] Page hit counts allow us to see the web as a huge corpus, and can be used instead of or combined with standard corpus counts, offering an alternative solution to overcome data sparseness (Ramisch et al. 2010d). Since web queries can be quite time-consuming, we keep a cache file with recent queries, and this avoids sending redundant network requests.

5.1.2.3 Candidate Extraction

- *Inputs:* indexed corpus, extraction patterns
- *Outputs:* MWE candidates

This is actually the first functional module of the framework, as preprocessing and indexing are merely preparatory steps for MWE acquisition and are also required for other NLP tasks. Once the corpus has been preprocessed and indexed, this module is responsible for generating a first list of candidates based either on *raw n-grams* or on *morphosyntactic patterns*. The former, raw n-gram extraction, is a straightforward method to extract all possible word combinations using no linguistic analysis at all. The only parameters that should be defined are the minimal and maximal n-gram length to be extracted, n_{min} and n_{max}. The module returns all word sequences from n_{min} to n_{max} words contained the corpus, respecting sentence boundaries. This extraction method will return a very large number of candidates, but most of them will probably not be interesting MWEs. Nonetheless, such strategy can be used as backoff when no linguistic information is available. If tools like a POS tagger and/or parser are not available for a given language and/or domain, it is possible to generate simple n-gram lists, even though the quality will most probably be poor. In this case, a relatively cheap workaround would be to filter out candidates on a keyword basis, for example, from a list of stopwords, during candidate filtering. This extraction method is identical to the n-gram extraction functionality provided by Text::NSP.

Morphosyntactic patterns allow the definition of fine-grained morphosyntactic constraints on the extracted sequences. For example, suppose we want to extract *noun–noun* and *adjective-noun* pairs, or collocations involving the adjective *strong*, or direct objects of the verb *remove*. In this module, it is possible to define patterns containing wildcards and to extract semi-fixed expressions with intervening words, using a formalism similar to regular expressions. Such patterns are multilevel, that is, it is possible to match simultaneously one or more token attributes among surface

---

[5]As search engines may update or shut down their APIs, the `mwetoolkit` cannot always be updated accordingly. For example, in 2012, Yahoo announced that their service would no longer be supported. See (Kilgarriff 2007) for an interesting discussion on this kind of limitation.

Fig. 5.2 Pattern 1 matches
noun phrases of the form DT?
J* N+, pattern 2 matches
sequences N₁ P N₁

```
<pat id="1">
    <pat repeat="?"><w pos="DT"/></pat>
    <pat repeat="*"><w pos="J"/></pat>
    <pat repeat="+"><w pos="N"/></pat>
</pat>
<pat id="2">
    <w pos="N" id="@noun1"/>
    <w pos="P"/>
    <backw lemma="@noun1" pos="@noun1"/>
</pat>
```

forms, lemmas, parts of speech and syntax. Multilevel patterns are correctly handled during pattern matching, in spite of individual per-attribute indices. Actually, our implementation merges the individual corpus indices on the fly, according to the extraction patterns, producing a combined index (e.g., for n-gram counting).

This module supports all the operators shown in Fig. 5.2 and some additional ones. In the examples below, we use the same notation as the one used in our implementation, which in turn is borrowed from standard regular expressions.

- Repetition of items: an arbitrary number of times (*), once or more (+), between a and b times ({a,b}), at least a times ({a,}), at most b times ({,b})
- Optional items: may or may not appear (?), multiple choice among the defined patterns (either element)
- Backreference: the current word is identical to a previously matched word (backw element)
- Negation: any word whose attributes are different from the defined ones (neg attribute)
- Wildcard: underspecified words and in-word attributes (<w/> matches any word and *writ** matches *written, writing, . . .*)
- Syntactic dependencies: a special operator to match a word that depends syntactically on another word defined in the pattern (syndep attribute)
- Ignored parts: a part of the pattern that must be matched but will not be present in the resulting MWE candidate (ignore attribute)

In Fig. 5.2, the use of the two first items is illustrated in pattern 1 while the third item is illustrated in pattern 2. Pattern 1 returns noun phrases, such as *the duck*, *children* and *the big green apple tree*, pattern 2 returns a pair of equal nouns linked by a preposition, such as *hand in hand, word for word* and *little by little*.

The optimal set of patterns for a given domain, language and MWE type can be defined based on several factors. First, it is possible to define patterns based on linguistic intuition and/or expert knowledge about the target MWE type. Second, it is possible to perform empirical observation of some positive and negative examples in order to match only the positive ones. Finally, a combination of these two steps is often required. Initial intuition can be validated by performing a first extraction step and an evaluation of a sample of extracted candidates. Then, the patterns can

be improved and a second round of candidate extraction is performed. The process
is repeated until a good trade-off is obtained.

Up-to-date documentation and a manual showing how to define morphosyntactic
patterns in our tool can be found on the website http://mwetoolkit.sf.net.

5.1.2.4   Candidate Filtering

* *Inputs:* MWE candidates
* *Outputs:* filtered MWE candidates

Candidate filtering takes as input the list of MWE candidates extracted from
the corpus and tries to remove as many as possible noisy candidates, keeping only
genuine MWEs. In a first moment, the initial candidate list can be filtered in order
to exclude candidates that contain spurious punctuation, n-grams occurring less
frequently than a given threshold or specific words and POS. This first filtering
step can be carried out mostly using heuristics that will help cleaning the data.
For example, statistics calculated on events occurring only once are unreliable, thus
hapax candidates can be excluded from the list.

In a second step, each candidate is enriched with a set of *features*. These features
can represent any information that helps distinguish true MWEs from random
word combinations that were accidentally captured by the morphosyntactic patterns.
Features can be used either directly for setting threshold values (unsupervised
model) or indirectly through the application of machine learning (supervised
model). In the current implementation, we provide tools for generating four kinds
of features: descriptive features, association measures, contrastive measures and
variations. However, the features are independent from the implementation and any
kind of feature could be appended to the candidates.

Descriptive features are simply a structured representation of the properties of
the MWE candidate itself. Examples of descriptive features are: length of n-gram,
sequence of POS tags, presence of dashes/slashes and capitalisation. Many other
descriptive features can be added according to the type of target expression. Even
if these features are not directly interpretable, their presence may correlate with the
class of the candidate (true MWE or random word combination). Thus, a machine
learning algorithm could use them to build an automatic MWE classifier.

The *association measures* estimate the degree of independence between the
counts of the MWE candidate and the counts of the individual words that compose
it. The following AMs are available, even though it would be straightforward to add
other measures according to the acquisition context:

* `mle`: relative frequency, that is, the n-gram count divided by the number of
  tokens in the corpus, as defined in Sect. 3.1.2;
* `t-score`: Student's t test statistic, as defined in Eq. 3.7;
* `pmi`: pointwise mutual information, as defined in Eq. 3.8;
* `dice`: Dice's coefficient, as defined in Eq. 3.9;

- **ll**: log-likelihood, based on contingency tables, as defined in Eq. 3.12 (applicable only to 2-grams).

Association measures involve operations on the number of occurrences of the MWE candidate and of the words composing it. These counts are not included in the result of candidate extraction, but are obtained a posteriori from the index. This allows the use of other information sources to count the candidates, like a different corpus or web hits. Frequency information sources can be either compared or combined, and this can help overcoming data sparseness problems (Ramisch et al. 2010d). However, when dealing with non-contiguous candidates, it is possible to count the candidates during extraction, otherwise the counts returned by looking up the n-gram index will be incorrect.

Contrastive measures estimate how specialised a multiword term candidate is with respect to its occurrences in general-purpose texts (the *contrast* corpus). The main difference between AMs and contrastive measures is that the former are designed for general MWE identification whereas the latter aim at automatic term recognition. The measure implemented in the mwetoolkit is inspired by the CSmw measure proposed by (Bonin et al. 2010a,b), only we simplify the original function into a rank-equivalent variant:

$$\text{simple-csmw} = \log_2 c(w_1^n) \times \frac{c(w_1^n)}{c_{contrast}(w_1^n)} \qquad (5.1)$$

We denote as $c_{contrast}(w_1^n)$ the number of occurrences of the multiword term candidate in a contrastive frequency source. In a typical configuration, $c(\cdot)$ is the count in the original specialised corpus while $c_{contrast}(\cdot)$ corresponds to the count in a larger general-purpose corpus.

Finally, *variation entropy* estimates the degree of syntactic and/or semantic variability of the candidate. In order to calculate variation entropy, it is necessary to first artificially generate variations of the original n-gram. In order to create syntactic variations, it is possible to generate simple permutations by randomly changing word order (Zhang et al. 2006; Villavicencio et al. 2007), or alternatively to use knowledge about the syntactic behaviour of the target constructions in order to generate syntactically valid permutations (Ramisch et al. 2008a). In order to create semantic variations, it is possible to replace parts of the candidate by a semantically equivalent word, for instance a Wordnet synonym (Pearce 2001; Ramisch et al. 2008b) or a word in the same lexical field (Duran et al. 2011).

Once we have gathered a set of variations $\{v_1, \ldots, v_m\}$ for a given candidate w_1^n, we obtain their counts in a corpus. The sum of all the counts over the variations is denoted as $M = \sum_{i=1}^{m} c(v_i)$ and then the entropy is computed as follows:

$$H(w_1^n) = -\sum_{i=1}^{m} \frac{c(v_i)}{M} \log \frac{c(v_i)}{M} \qquad (5.2)$$

The interpretation of variation entropy is as follows: high values close to the maximum $\log m$ indicate a homogeneous distribution, that is, variations are roughly equally likely. Lower values closer to zero show that one of the variations is much more likely than the others, showing a pronounced preference for that variation. In other words, low values indicate less variability (syntactic or semantic, depending on the type of variation employed), and flexibility is related to low productivity, which is one of the characteristics of MWEs (see Sect. 2.3).

5.1.2.5 Manual Validation

• *Inputs:* filtered MWE candidates
• *Outputs:* validated MWE candidates

The output of candidate filtering is still a rough stone: a set of MWE candidates that require further validation. However, it can provide a straightforward starting point for lexicographic work, speeding up the construction of language resources, especially for poorly resourced languages and domains.

Numerical features can be used as sorting keys, in order to rank a list of candidates. Thus, given a single feature calculated during candidate filtering, it is possible to remove all candidates whose feature value is below a given threshold. As there is no systematic way of deciding which features should be used to rank candidates, this is often performed on a trial-and-error basis. Therefore, our tool provides a simple export functionality to comma-separated format, so that the candidate lists and their features can be visualised using a spreadsheet viewer.

Depending on the acquisition context, a list of filtered MWE candidates can have different uses. One alternative is the manual validation of candidates by an expert human lexicographer, thus generating a list of validated MWEs directly. This manual annotation task can be defined, in a first moment, as a binary classification task whose goal is to separate interesting and genuine target MWEs from random word combinations. The interesting MWEs will further be included in a lexical resource, which can be a printed and/or machine-readable dictionary, thesaurus or ontology. In addition to validation, the expert lexicographer may want to use the features to annotate the characteristics of the MWE. The evaluation of MWEs acquired automatically by expert lexicographers is described in Chap. 6.

An alternative to direct annotation by a single lexicographer is the use of a software platform for the collaborative creation and management of lexical resources. An example of such platform is the Jibiki system (Mangeot and Chalvin 2006). Collaborative annotation allows for multiple users to create the dictionary as a joint collective effort, thus speeding up and optimising the process. The system can incrementally and interactively generate a list of validated MWEs, possibly enriched with further lexical information. This corresponds to the bidirectional arrow on Fig. 5.1.

Finally, the resulting list of validated MWEs can be used directly in a NLP application. Examples of such applications are described in Sect. 3.3.4. In Chap. 7, we describe possible ways to integrate MWEs into a statistical machine translation system. Depending on the target application, the phase of manual validation can be skipped. This means that, despite potential noise in the candidate list, the target application can appropriately use the automatically acquired MWEs, particularly when quantity is more important than quality.

5.1.2.6 Learning

- *Inputs:* validated MWE candidates
- *Outputs:* MWE acquisition model

If a gold standard reference list of MWEs is available, we can automatically annotate each candidate to indicate whether it is contained in the gold standard. Therefore, an evaluation facility is provided so that, if a (potentially limited) reference gold standard is present, the class of the candidate is automatically inferred. That is, if the candidate is contained in the reference list, it is a true MWE, otherwise we assume that it is a random word combination. This assumption is strong, as a candidate absent from the gold standard can simply be a newly acquired MWE. The pros and cons of automatic evaluation are discussed in Sect. 4.1.3.

The class annotation is not used to filter the lists, but by a machine learning algorithm that builds a classifier based on the relation between the features and the MWE class of the candidate in the training set. This is particularly useful because, to date, it remains unclear which features perform best for a particular MWE type or language, and the classifier applies measures according to their efficiency in filtering the candidates.

The mwetoolkit package provides a conversion facility that allows the importing of a candidate list into the machine learning package WEKA.[6] Once the data set is imported into WEKA, a plethora of machine learning algorithms and models can be applied, our problem being handled as a traditional classification problem in artificial intelligence. Some preliminary experiments have shown that polynomial support vector machines perform quite well in the task of automatic MWE candidate filtering (Ramisch 2009). Equally good candidates for efficient machine learning technique are logistic linear regression and artificial neural networks (Pecina 2008).

If we have an existing machine learning model for MWE acquisition, we can apply it on a new data set. Thus, once each new candidate has a set of associated features generated by the filtering module, we can apply an existing machine learning model to distinguish true and false positives based on the characteristics of another MWE data set. However, this should be performed carefully, as we cannot assume that a model that works well on a given language and domain will work well on other languages and domains. The generalisation of a model for MWE

---

[6]http://www.cs.waikato.ac.nz/ml/weka/

acquisition is a hypothesis that remains to be validated, and experiments in other fields of NLP show that overfitting is a challenging problem.

5.1.2.7 Auxiliary Modules

In addition to the core modules, some auxiliary tools are available in the `mwetoolkit` software package. These include scripts for performing simple operations on XML files, like counting the number of words, lines and characters (like Unix's `wc`), keeping only the first or last n lines of a file (like Unix's `head` and `tail`), or sorting a list of candidates according to the numeric or lexicographic order of a given feature domain (like Unix's `sort`). Finally, some useful scripts perform the conversion of XML files into several formats including TXT, CSV,[7] ARFF,[8] UCS[9] and OWL.[10]

5.1.3 Discussion

To date, there is little agreement on whether there is a single best method for MWE acquisition, or whether a different subset of methods is better for a given MWE type. Most of recent work on MWE treatment focuses on candidate extraction from preprocessed text (Seretan 2008) and on the automatic filtering and ranking through association measures (Evert 2004; Pecina 2010), but few authors provide a whole picture of the MWE treatment pipeline. The main contribution of our methodology, rather than a revolutionary approach to MWE acquisition, is the systematic integration of the processes and tasks required for acquisition, from sophisticated corpus queries, like in CQP (Christ 1994) and Manatee (Rychlý and Smrz 2004), to candidate extraction, like in Text::NSP (Banerjee and Pedersen 2003), filtering, like in UCS (Evert 2004), and machine learning.

One of the advantages of the framework proposed here is that it models the whole acquisition process in a modular approach that can be configured in several ways, each task having multiple available alternatives. Therefore, it is highly customisable and allows for a large number of parameters to be tuned according to the target MWE types. For instance, one of the advantages of our candidate extraction step is that we separate pattern matching from n-gram counting. Therefore, it is possible to match the patterns in a corpus A and then use count information from sources B and C.

---

[7]Comma-separated values, readable by most spreadsheet software like Microsoft Excel and OpenOffice Calc.

[8]Format supported by WEKA.

[9]Special CSV format supported by the UCS toolkit.

[10]Web ontology language, standard format in the web semantic community.

The mwetoolkit can be used not only to speed up the work of lexicographers and terminographers in the creation of lexical resources for new domains and languages, but also to contribute to the porting of NLP systems such as machine translation and information extraction across languages and domains. The methodology employed in the toolkit is not based on symbolic knowledge or pre-existing dictionaries, and the techniques that are incorporated in it are language independent. Moreover, the techniques that we have developed do not depend on a fixed length of candidate expression nor on adjacency assumptions, as the words in an expression might occur several words away. Thanks to this generality, this methodology can be applied to virtually any language, MWE type and domain, not strictly depending on a given formalism or tool.[11] Intuitively, for a given language, if some preprocessing tools like POS taggers and/or parsers are available, the results will be much better than running the methods on raw text. But since such tools are not available for all languages, the methodology was designed to be applicable even in the absence of preprocessing.

In sum, the mwetoolkit methodology allows users to perform systematic MWE acquisition with consistent intermediary files and well defined modules and arguments (avoiding the need for a series of ad hoc separate processes). Even if some basic knowledge about how to run Python scripts and how to pass arguments to the command line is necessary, the user is not required to be a computer programmer.

We believe that there is room for improvement at several points of the mwetoolkit acquisition methodology. Nested MWEs are a problem in the current approach. For example, if the two 2-grams *International Cooperation* and *Cooperation Agreement* were acquired, both would be evaluated separately. However, they could be considered as parts of a larger MWE *International Cooperation Agreement*. If the reference dictionary only contains the larger expression, the shorter sub-expressions will count as negative results even though they are part of a MWE. With the current methodology, it is not possible to detect this kind of situation. Another problematic case would be the inverse case, that is, the candidate contains a MWE, like in the example *pro-human right*. In this case, it would be necessary to separate the prefix from the MWE, that is, to re-tokenise the words around the MWE candidate. In the case of multiple overlapping candidates matching a pattern, the current strategy returns all possibilities.

We expect, in the future, to integrate a higher number of features of the MWE candidates into the classifiers. Other features that could potentially improve classification results are new descriptive features, deep syntax, semantic classes, semantic relations, domain-specific keywords, context-based measures and context words. In addition, we would like to integrate information coming from peripheral sources such as parallel corpora (word alignments) and general-purpose or domain-specific simple word dictionaries. While for poorly resourced languages we can

---

[11]However, it is designed to deal with languages that use spaces to separate words. Thus, when working with Chinese, Japanese, or even with German compounds, some additional preprocessing is required.

only count on shallow linguistic information, it is unreasonable to ignore available information for other languages like English, Spanish, French and German.

Related work showed that association measures based on contingency tables are more robust to data sparseness (Evert and Krenn 2005). However, they are based on pairwise comparisons and their application on arbitrarily long n-grams is not straightforward. A heuristic to adapt these measures consists in applying them recursively over increasing n-gram lengths. In the future, we would like to test several heuristics to handle nested candidates and longer n-grams.

Moreover, we would like to provide better integration between the candidate extraction step and the classifier construction step. Currently, the latter is performed externally using WEKA, but we believe that if this step were integrated into the toolkit's pipeline, we would increase its ease of use. Still under the perspective of usability, we would like to develop or adapt an interface for manual evaluation of the candidates and for testing the results in the context of lexical resources construction.

One of our goals for future versions is to be able to automatically extract bilingual MWEs from parallel or comparable corpora. This could be done through the inclusion of automatic word alignment information. Some previous experiments show, however, that this may not be enough, as automatic word alignment uses almost no linguistic information and its output is often quite noisy (Ramisch et al. 2010a). Combining alignment and linguistic information seems a promising solution for the automatic extraction of bilingual MWEs. Another method that we would like to explore is the generation of compositional translations to be validated against corpora evidence. The potential uses of bilingual MWE lexicons are multiple, but the most obvious applications are machine translation and multilingual technical writing. On the one hand, MWEs could be used to guide the word alignment process. For instance, this could solve the problem of aligning a language having a writing system where compounds are made of separate words, like French, with a language that joins compound words together, like German. In statistical machine translation systems, MWEs could help to filter phrase tables or to boost the scores of phrases whose words are likely to be multiword expressions.

We would like to evaluate our method on several data sets, varying the languages, domains and target MWE types. This extensive evaluation could allow the development of standard machine learning models for MWE acquisition in different domains. Thus, we would be able to compare the similarities and differences between domains based on the models that are created for them. Additionally, we could evaluate how well the classifiers perform across languages and domains.

The mwetoolkit is an important first step toward robust and reliable MWE treatment by NLP applications. It is a freely available core application providing powerful tools and coherent up-to-date documentation, and these are essential characteristics for the extension and support of any computer tool. Thus, we would like to keep making periodical releases of a stable software version. Therefore, we would need extensive testing and constant documentation update.

5.2   A Toy Experiment

In the present section, we describe a step-by-step example of MWE acquisition from a corpus. In the following toy experiment, we used the `mwetoolkit` to extract *multiword terms* (MWTs) from the Genia corpus, composed of a set of 2,000 English abstracts of scientific articles from the biomedical domain (Ohta et al. 2002). It contains around 18K sentences and around 490K tokens. In order to train machine learning models and test them, the original corpus was divided into a training set and a test set, with the latter containing 895 sentences ($\approx$4.9 % of the corpus), and the former containing all other sentences (17,543).

5.2.1   Candidate Extraction

In order to unify the spelling of the words throughout the corpus, we preprocessed it uniformly according to the following criteria:

- Capitalised words were lowercased using the heuristics described in Sect. 5.1.2.1.
- POS tags were simplified to match a set of patterns (e.g., NN, NNS, NP... → N)
- Words containing dashes and slashes were retokenised, as these symbols are not used consistently in the Genia corpus (e.g., *T cell* and *T-cell*). Therefore, any word that contained these symbols was split into independent parts as the symbols were removed (e.g., *T-cell* becomes *T cell*).
- Acronyms were recognised and removed when they occurred between parentheses (e.g., *human immunodeficiency virus (HIV) type 1* was changed to *human immunodeficiency virus type 1*).
- Nouns were lemmatised to their singular form.

These preprocessing steps aim to reduce the problem of data sparseness, which is particularly acute for MWEs and specific domains, and has a significant impact on the quality of the results. We estimate, for instance, that precision and recall are reduced by more than 50 % if the lemmatisation and retokenisation steps are not performed. This happens because the reference dictionary only contains canonical forms and because the counts of lemmatised words are less sparse than those of inflected ones.

In this experiment, we used a set of 57 morphosyntactic patterns based on the POS sequences defined by (Justeson and Katz 1995). Their original set of patterns was augmented through the use of a heuristic that enables the extraction of longer sequences of contiguous nouns and adjectives than originally defined. For instance, using these patterns, it is possible to extract candidates that match POS patterns containing sequences of two to seven adjacent nouns and adjectives (e.g., *T cell*, *thromboxane receptor gene*), foreign words (e.g., in vitro) and numbers (e.g., *nucleotide 46*).

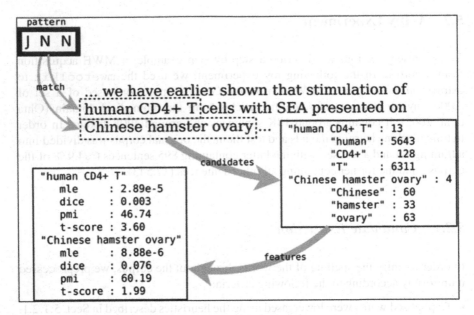

Fig. 5.3 Example of MWT candidates extracted from the Genia corpus

From the Genia corpus sentence shown in Fig. 5.3, we selected two candidates that match the sequence adjective-noun-noun (J N N): *human CD4+ T* and *Chinese hamster ovary*. The former, although part of a longer MWT in this sentence (*human CD4+ T cell*) is a false positive if seen as a 3-gram.[12]

5.2.2 Candidate Filtering

This initial list of candidates can be further validated using some criteria, in order to, insofar as possible, remove false positives from the list, and only keep genuine MWTs. This validation is done using a set of AMs as basis for building a classifier. In order to calculate the AMs for each candidate, the mwetoolkit determines the corpus counts for the candidate as well as for the individual words that compose it. In Fig. 5.3, the *n*-gram and word counts of the Genia corpus are represented.

After obtaining the corpus counts, the toolkit uses this information as input to the formulae that calculate four association scores for each candidate in each corpus (the 11 measure was not used because it can only be applied to 2-grams). All

---

[12]This sentence exemplifies the problem that arises from ignoring nested MWTs. Here, each part of a MWT is treated independently from any other part. As the original MWT (*human CD4+ T cell*) matches different POS patterns, it forms three different candidates which are treated independently: *human CD4+ T* (J N N), *CD4+ T cell* (N N N) and *human CD4+ T cell* (J N N N).

```
<cand candid="4582">
    <ngram>
        <w lemma="Chinese" pos="A" >
            <freq name="genia" value="60" />
            <freq name="yahoo" value="1460000000" />
        </w>
        <w lemma="hamster" pos="N" >
            <freq name="genia" value="33" />
            <freq name="yahoo" value="42600000" />
        </w>
        <w lemma="ovary" pos="N" >
            <freq name="genia" value="63" />
            <freq name="yahoo" value="12300000" />
        </w>
        <freq name="genia" value="4" />
        <freq name="yahoo" value="723000" />
    </ngram>
    <occurs>
        <ngram>
            <w surface="Chinese" pos="A" />
            <w surface="hamster" pos="N" />
            <w surface="ovary" pos="N" />
            <freq name="corpus" value="4" />
        </ngram>
    </occurs>
    <features>
        <feat name="pos_pattern" value="A#S#N#S#N" />
        <feat name="n" value="3" />
        <feat name="mle_genia" value="8.8833220071e-06" />
        <feat name="pmi_genia" value="60.193312488" />
        <feat name="t_genia" value="1.99999969239" />
        <feat name="dice_genia" value="0.0769230769231" />
        <feat name="mle_yahoo" value="1.31454545455e-05" />
        <feat name="pmi_yahoo" value="82.8386600941" />
        <feat name="t_yahoo" value="849.996644814" />
        <feat name="dice_yahoo" value="0.00143177767509" />
    </features>
    <tpclass name="genia-reference" value="True" />
</cand>
```

Fig. 5.4 XML fragment describing a MWT candidate extracted from the Genia corpus with
`mwetoolkit`

AMs are used as features for the classifier and it then decides on the best feature
combination to use in order to choose whether a candidate should be kept in the list
or be discarded as noise.

Figure 5.4 shows an example of XML representation obtained for one of our
example candidates extracted from the Genia corpus: *Chinese hamster ovary*.
For each individual word and for the whole candidate, the `freq` elements show their

corpus counts in two different corpora: Genia (as `genia`) and Yahoo (as `yahoo`). The idea is to use two heterogeneous data sources so that we do not loose in accuracy because of the sparseness of the former or because of the rough approximations done by the latter. The first two features are descriptive properties of the candidate such as the number of words and the POS sequence and the remainder of the features correspond to the AMs in the Genia corpus and in Yahoo. After the list of features, the special element `tpclass` indicates the class of the candidate with respect to the reference list. This information, when available, can be used to build a new classifier for a given language or domain. In our toy experiment, its utility is two-fold: (1) on the training corpus, it is used as class information for a supervised learning algorithm that will build our MWT classifier; (2) in the test corpus, it determines whether a candidate is correctly classified as a true positive (or as a true negative), helping us evaluate the performance of the `mwetoolkit`.

5.2.3 Results

We evaluate the performance of the MWT identification in terms of precision (P), recall (R) and F-measure, using the Genia ontology as MWT gold standard (see Sect. 4.1). The Genia ontology is a manually-built resource that contains, among other information, the set of terms found in the Genia corpus (Kim et al. 2006). For a given portion of the Genia corpus, the MWT *reference list* is composed of the multiword entries of the Genia ontology that occur in that portion of the corpus.

The candidates were fed into a learning algorithm that produced a *support vector machine* (SVM) classifier. In previous experiments performed, among all tested machine learning models, SVM with polynomial kernel presented the best balance between precision and recall (Ramisch 2009). We applied this model to the test corpus (the remaining unannotated 895 sentences of the Genia corpus) and evaluated the output in terms of precision and recall.

Table 5.1 shows three different filtering configurations applied (both during training and testing) to the candidates extracted by the `mwetoolkit` from the test portion of the Genia corpus. In the first condition, we considered all candidates without any frequency threshold. In the second, we considered all the candidates which occurred more than once in the test corpus, while in the third, we kept all the

Table 5.1 Performance of the `mwetoolkit` considering (a) no filtering threshold, (b) a threshold of $t = 1$ occurrence and (c) a threshold of $t = 5$ occurrences

	$t = 0$	$t = 1$	$t = 5$
# cand	763	739	174
# ref	2,009	2,009	2,009
# TP	401	420	129
P	52.56 %	56.83 %	74.14 %
R	19.96 %	20.91 %	6.42 %
F	28.93 %	30.57 %	11.82 %

candidates that occurred at least five times. The results show us that, as expected, statistical AMs calculated including candidates that occur only once are not reliable ($t = 0$), and discarding them helps to improve precision and recall ($t = 1$). A higher threshold like $t = 5$ provides even better precision at the price of drastically reducing recall, but even so recall and F-measure in this configuration are still higher than those of the baseline systems with which we compared the mwetoolkit (Ramisch 2009).

For a given application, the exact value of the threshold can be customised according to whether the preference is for a higher recall or for a higher precision. For instance, if the goal is to create a terminological dictionary, a higher recall may be desirable with manual validation of the results. The mwetoolkit allows parametrisation and customisation of its various modules according to a particular application without being language- or domain-dependent. Therefore, its performance could be improved even further with better tuning to the domain or postprocessing of the results.

A detailed tutorial explaining the application of the scripts, the parameters and intermediary files can be found on the website http://mwetoolkit.sf.net.

5.3 Comparison with Related Approaches

In this section, we compare the mwetoolkit methodology, presented in the previous sections, with three other similar approaches. We consider only freely available, downloadable and openly documented tools. Therefore, outside the scope of this comparison are proprietary tools, terminology and lexicography tools, translation aid tools and published techniques for which no available implementation is provided. The experimental setup used in our comparison is presented in Sect. 5.3.2. In Sect. 5.3.3, we evaluate the following acquisition dimensions: quality of extracted candidates and of association measures, use of computational resources and flexibility. Thus, this comparative investigation indicates the best cost-benefit ratio in a given context (language, type, corpus size).

5.3.1 Related Approaches

We examine as parameters of the experimental context: the language (English and French), the type of target MWE (verbal and nominal) and the size of corpus (small, medium, large).

We focus our comparative evaluation on MWE acquisition methods that follow the general trend in the area of using shallow linguistic (lemmas, POS, stopwords) and/or statistical (counts, AMs) information to distinguishing ordinary sequences (e.g., *yellow dress*, *go to a concert*) from MWEs (e.g., *black box*, *go by a name*).

Our evaluation compares the mwetoolkit with the three first approaches described in Sect. 3.2.3.1, namely:

- The LocalMaxs reference implementation (LocMax);
- The N-gram statistics package (NSP); and
- The UCS toolkit.

In addition to the brief description provided in Sect. 3.2.3.1, Sect. 5.3.3.4 underlines the main differences between the mwetoolkit and these approaches.

As the focus of our comparison is on MWE acquisition, other tasks related to MWE treatment are not considered. This is the case, for instance, of approaches for dictionary-based in-context MWE token identification requiring an initial dictionary of valid MWEs, like jMWE.

5.3.2 Comparison Setup

We investigate the acquisition of MWEs in two languages, English (en) and French (fr), analysing nominal and verbal expressions in English and nominal expressions in French. As French does not present many verb-particle constructions and due to the lack of availability of resource for other types of French verbal expressions (e.g., light verb constructions), only nominal expressions are considered. The candidate MWEs were obtained through the following patterns:

- **Nominal expressions en**: a noun preceded by a sequence of one or more nouns or adjectives (e.g., *European Union, clock radio, clown anemone fish*).
- **Nominal expressions fr**: a noun followed by either an adjective or a preposi-tional complement (with the prepositions *de, à* and *en*) followed by an optionally determined noun (e.g., *algue verte, aliénation de biens, allergie à la poussière*).
- **Verbal expressions en**: verb-particle constructions formed by a verb (except *be* and *have*) followed by a prepositional particle[13] not further than five words after it,[14] (e.g., *give up, switch the old computer off*).

To test the influence of corpus size on performance, three fragments of the English and French parts of the Europarl corpus v3, were used as test corpora: (S)mall, (M)edium and (L)arge, summarised in Table 5.2.

The extracted MWEs were automatically evaluated against the following gold standards: WordNet 3, the Cambridge Dictionary of Phrasal Verbs, and the VPC

---

[13]*up, off, down, back, away, in, on.*

[14]In theory, a particle could occur further than five positions away, like in the example **take** *patient risk factors and convenience* **into account** (googled on May 6, 2012). However, such cases are rare and, for verb-particle constructions, empirical studies showed that the longest noun phrase separating a verb from a particle contains three words (Baldwin 2005).

Table 5.2 Number of
sentences and of words of
each fragment of the Europarl
corpus in fr and in en

	Small	Medium	Large
# sentences	5,000	50,000	500,000
# en words	133,859	1,355,482	13,164,654
# fr words	145,888	1,483,428	14,584,617

Table 5.3 Dimensions of the
reference gold standards used
and of the respective number
of entries that occur at least
twice in the S, M and L
corpora

type	lang.	# entries			
		total	S	M	L
Nominal	en	59,683	122	764	2,710
Nominal	fr	69,118	220	1,406	4,747
Verbal	en	1,846	699	1,846	1,846

(Baldwin 2008) and CN (Kim and Baldwin 2008) datasets [15] for en; the Lexique-
Grammaire[16] for fr. The total number of entries is listed in Table 5.3, along
with the number of entries occurring at least twice in each corpus, which was the
denominator used to calculate recall in Sect. 5.3.3.1.

5.3.3   Results

We performed MWE acquisition using four tools: mwetoolkit, LocMax, NSP
and UCS. We includes both versions of LocMax: *LocalMaxs Strict*, which gives
priority to high precision (henceforth LocMax-S), and *LocalMaxs Relaxed* which
focuses on high recall (henceforth LocMax-R). As approaches differ in the way
they allow the description of extraction criteria, we present the results of candidate extraction (Sect. 5.3.3.1) separately from the results of AMs (Sect. 5.3.3.2).
Additionally, we go beyond traditional evaluation by presenting the trade-off
between the usefulness of the acquired MWEs and the computational resources
used (Sect. 5.3.3.3). We close this section with a discussion about the suitability
of the techniques in each extraction context (Sect. 5.3.3.4).

5.3.3.1   Extracted Candidates

We consider as *MWE candidates* the initial set of sequences before any AM is
applied. Candidate extraction is performed through the application of patterns
describing the target MWEs in terms of POS sequences, as described in Sect. 5.3.2.

The quality of candidates extracted from the medium-size corpus (M) varies
across MWE types/languages, as shown in Fig. 5.5. UCS is unable to process

---

[15]The latter are available from http://multiword.sf.net/

[16]http://infolingu.univ-mlv.fr/

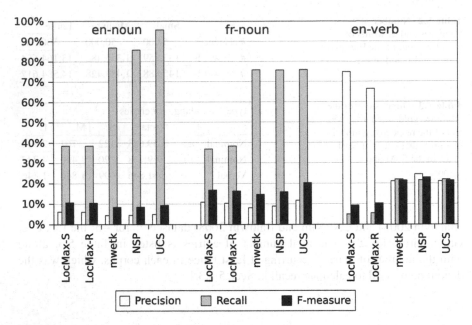

Fig. 5.5 Quality of candidates extracted from medium corpus, comparison across languages/MWE types

candidates longer than two words. Therefore, the candidates for UCS are obtained by keeping only the 2-grams in the candidate list returned by the mwetoolkit. For nominal MWEs, the approaches have similar patterns of performance in the two languages, with high recall and low precision yielding an F-measure of around 10–15 %. The variation between en and fr can be partly explained by the differences in size of the gold standards for each of these languages. Further experiments would be needed to determine to what degree the characteristics of these languages and the set of extraction patterns influence these results. For verbal expressions, LocMax has high precision (around 70 %) but low recall while the other approaches have more balanced P and R values around 20 %. This is partly due to the need for simulating POS filters for extraction of verbal MWE candidates with LocMax. The filter consists of keeping only contiguous n-grams in which the first and the last words matched verb+particle pattern and removing intervening words.

The techniques differ in terms of extraction strategy: (i) mwetoolkit and NSP allow the definition of linguistic filters while LocMax only allows the application of grep-like filters after extraction; (ii) there is no preliminary filtering in mwetoolkit and NSP, they simply return all candidates matching a pattern, while LocMax filters the candidates based on the local maxima criterion; (iii) LocMax only extracts contiguous candidates while the others allow discontiguous candidates. The way mwetoolkit and NSP extract discontiguous candidates differs: the former extracts all verbs with particles no further than five positions to the right. NSP extracts 2-grams in a window of five words, and then filters the list, keeping

Table 5.4 (P)recision and (R)ecall of en nominal candidates, comparison across corpus sizes: (S)mall, (M)edium and (L)arge

	LocMax-S		LocMax-R		mwetoolkit		NSP		UCS	
	P	R	P	R	P	R	P	R	P	R
S	7.53	42.62	7.46	42.62	6.50	83.61	6.61	83.61	6.96	96.19
M	6.18	38.48	6.02	38.48	4.40	86.78	4.46	85.73	4.91	95.65
L	4.50	37.42	–	–	2.35	89.23	2.48	89.41	2.77	96.88

Table 5.5 Intersection of the candidate lists extracted from medium corpus. Nominal candidates en in bottom left, verbal candidates en in top right

	LocMax-S	LocMax-R	mwetk	NSP	UCS	Total verbs
LocMax-S	–	124	124	122	124	124
LocMax-R	4,747	–	156	153	156	156
mwetoolkit	4,738	4,862	–	1,565	1,926	1,926
NSP	4,756	4,879	14,611	–	1,565	1,629
UCS	4,377	4,364	13,407	13,045	–	1,926
Total nouns	4,760	4,884	15,064	14,682	13,418	

only those in which the first word is a verb and that contain a particle. However, the results are similar, with slightly better values for NSP.

The evaluation of en nominal candidates according to corpus size is shown in Table 5.4.[17] For all approaches, precision decreases when the corpus size increases as more false MWEs are returned, while recall increases for all except LocMax. This may be due to the latter ignoring shorter n-grams when longer candidates containing them become sufficiently frequent, as is the case when the corpus increases. Table 5.5 shows that the candidates extracted by LocMax are almost completely covered by the candidates extracted by the other approaches. The relaxed version extracts slightly more candidates, but still much less than mwetoolkit, NSP and UCS, which all extract a similar set of candidates. In order to distinguish the performance of the approaches, we need to analyse the AMs they use to rank the candidates.

5.3.3.2   Association Measures

Traditionally, to evaluate an AM, the candidates are ranked according to it and a threshold value is applied, below which the candidates are discarded. However, if we take the average of precision considering all true MWEs as threshold points,

---

[17]It was not possible to evaluate LocMax-R on the large corpus as the provided implementation did not support corpora of this size.

Table 5.6 Mean average precision of AMs in the large corpus

| | en | fr | en | | en | fr | en |
	noun	noun	verb		noun	noun	verb
Baseline				NSP			
rand	2.75	6.11	17.21	pmi	2.99	7.68	62.17
freq	4.75	8.79	22.72	ps	5.40	12.38	57.62
				tmi	2.108	4.89	19.80
LocMax-S							
glue	6.99	12.94	87.06	UCS			
				z.score	6.12	11.77	46.87
mwetoolkit				Poisson	6.59	12.82	32.77
dice	5.78	9.54	46.36	MI	5.15	9.34	53.56
t	5.09	8.68	26.42	rel.risk	5.10	9.29	46.67
pmi	2.76	2.92	53.56	odds	5.04	9.21	50.22
ll	3.17	5.52	45.88	gmean	6.01	11.52	45.61
				local.MI	6.43	12.78	29.99

we obtain the mean average precision (MAP) of the measure without setting a hard threshold (see Sect. 4.1.2).

Table 5.6 presents the MAP values for the tested AMs applied to the candidates extracted from the large corpus (L), where the larger the value, the better the performance. We used as baseline the assignment of a random score and the use of the raw relative frequency for the candidates. Except for mwetoolkit's t-score and pmi, all MAP values are significantly different from the two baselines, with a two-tailed t test for difference of means assuming unequal sample sizes and variances (p-value < 0.005).

LocMax's glue performs best for all types of MWEs, suggesting local maxima as a good generic MWE indicator and glue as an efficient AM to generate highly precise results (considering the difficulty of this task). On the other hand, this approach returns a small set of candidates and this may be problematic for some tasks (e.g., for building a wide-coverage lexicon). For mwetoolkit, the best overall AM is dice; the other measures are not consistently better than the baseline, or perform better for one MWE type than for the other. The Poisson-Stirling (Poisson) measure performed quite well, while the other two measures tested for NSP performed below baseline for some cases. Finally, the AMs applied by UCS perform all above baseline and, for nominal MWEs, are comparable to the best AM (e.g., Poisson and local.MI). The MAP for verbal expressions varies much for UCS (from 30 to 53 %), but none of the measures comes close to the MAP of glue (87.06 %).

5.3.3.3   Computational Resources

In the decision of which AM to adopt, factors like the degree of MWE variability and computational performance may be taken into account. For instance, `dice` can be applied to *n*-grams of any length quite fast while more sophisticated measures like `Poisson` can be applied only to 2-grams and sometimes use considerable computational resources. Even if one could argue that we can be lenient towards a slow offline extraction process, the extra waiting may not be worth a slight quality improvement. Moreover, memory limitations are an issue if no large computer clusters are available.

In Fig. 5.6, we plotted in log-scale the time in seconds used by each approach to extract nominal and verbal expressions in en, using a dedicated 2.4 GHz quad-core Linux machine with 4 GB RAM. For nominal expressions, time increases linearly with the size of the corpus, whereas for verbal expressions it seems to increase faster than the size of the corpus. UCS is the slowest approach for both MWE types while NSP and LocMax-S are the fastest. However, it is important to emphasize that NSP consumed more than 3 GB memory to extract 4- and 5-grams from the large corpus and LocMax-R could not handle the large corpus at all. In theory, all techniques can be applied to arbitrarily large corpora if we used a map-reduce approach (e.g., NSP provides tools to split and join the corpus). However, the goal of this evaluation is to discover the performance of the techniques with no manual optimisation. In this sense, mwetoolkit provides a good trade-off between quality and resources used.

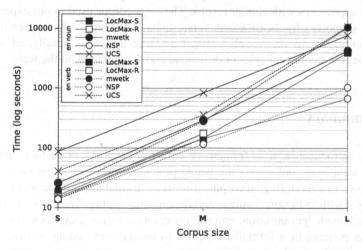

Fig. 5.6 Time (seconds, log scale) to extract en nouns (*bold line*) and verbs (*dashed line*) from corpora

Table 5.7 Summary of tools for MWE acquisition

	LocMax	mwetoolkit	NSP	UCS
Candidate extraction	Yes	Yes	Yes	No
N-grams with $n > 2$	Yes	Yes	Yes	No
Discontiguous MWE	No	Yes	Yes	–
Linguistic filter	No	Yes	No	No
Robust AMs	No	No	Yes	Yes
Large corpora	Partly	Yes	Yes	No
Availability	Free	Free	Free	Free

5.3.3.4 Generality

Table 5.7 summarises the characteristics of the approaches. Among them, UCS does not extract candidates from corpora but takes as input a list of 2-grams and their counts. While it only supports n-grams of size 2, NSP implements some of the AMs for 3 and 4-grams and mwetoolkit and LocMax have no constraint on the number of words. The AMs implemented by LocMax and mwetoolkit are thus less statistically sound than the clearly designed measures used by UCS and, to some extent, by NSP (Fisher test). LocMax extracts only contiguous MWEs while mwetoolkit allows the extraction of unrestrictedly distant words and NSP allows the specification of a window of maximum w ignored words between each two words of the candidate. Only mwetoolkit integrates linguistic filters on the lemma, POS and syntax, but this was performed using external tools (sed/grep) for the other approaches with similar results. The large corpus used in our experiments was not supported by LocMax-R version, but LocMax-S has a version that deals with large corpora, as well as mwetoolkit and NSP. Finally, all of these approaches are freely available for download and documented on the web.

5.4 Summary

We have introduced a new framework called mwetoolkit, which integrates multiple techniques and covers the whole pipeline of MWE acquisition. One can preprocess a raw monolingual corpus, if tools are available for the target language, enriching it with POS tags, lemmas and dependency syntax. Then, based on expert linguistic knowledge, intuition, empiric observation and/or examples, one defines multilevel patterns in a formalism similar to regular expressions to describe the target MWEs. The application of these patterns on an indexed corpus generates a list of candidate MWEs. For filtering, a plethora of methods is available, ranging from simple frequency thresholds to stopword lists and association measures. Finally, the resulting filtered candidates are either directly injected into a NLP application or further manually validated. An alternative use for the validated candidates is to train a machine learning model which can be applied on new corpora in order to automatically identify and extract MWEs based on the characteristics of the previously acquired ones. This is summarised in the schema of Fig. 5.1. Further details are provided on the tool website and in previous publications (Ramisch et al. 2010b,c).

The main contribution of our methodology is the systematic integration of the processes and tasks required for acquisition. One of its main advantages is that it models the whole acquisition process in a modular approach, thus being customisable and allowing for a large number of parameters to be tuned. The mwetoolkit can be used to speed up lexicographic and terminographic work and contribute to the porting of NLP systems across languages and domains. The methodology employed in the toolkit is not based on symbolic knowledge or pre-existing dictionaries, and the techniques are language independent. Moreover, they do not depend on fixed candidate length nor adjacency. Thanks to this generality, this methodology can be applied to virtually any language, MWE type and domain, not strictly depending on a given formalism or tool. In sum, the mwetoolkit methodology allows users to perform systematic MWE acquisition with consistent intermediary files and well defined modules and arguments.

We compared the mwetoolkit methodology with three other freely available, downloadable and openly documented tools: the LocalMaxs reference implementation (LocMax), the N-gram statistics package (NSP), and the UCS toolkit. We investigated the acquisition of MWEs in two languages, English (en) and French (fr), analysing nominal and verbal expressions in English and nominal expressions in French. The extracted MWEs were automatically evaluated against existing gold standards.

For nominal MWEs, the approaches have similar patterns of performance, with high recall and low precision. For verbal expressions, LocMax has high precision (around 70%) but low recall while the other approaches have more balanced P and R values around 20%. The techniques differ in terms of extraction strategy: (i) mwetoolkit and NSP allow the definition of linguistic filters while LocMax only allows the application of grep-like filters after extraction; (ii) there is no preliminary filtering in mwetoolkit and NSP, they simply return all candidates matching a pattern, while LocMax filters the candidates based on the local maxima criterion; (iii) LocMax only extracts contiguous candidates while the others allow discontiguous candidates.

Aspects like the degree of MWE variability and computational performance influence the decision of which AM to adopt. For instance, dice can be easily applied to any n-gram, while more sophisticated measures like Poisson are defined only for 2-grams and are sometimes computationally heavy. UCS does not extract candidates from corpora but takes as input a list of 2-grams. NSP implements some of the AMs for 3 and 4-grams and mwetoolkit and LocMax have no constraint on the number of words. LocMax extracts only contiguous MWEs while mwetoolkit and NSP allow the extraction of non-adjacent words. Only mwetoolkit integrates linguistic filters on the lemma, POS and syntax. This can be performed using external tools (sed/grep) for the other approaches.

The mwetoolkit is an important first step toward robust and reliable MWE treatment by NLP applications. It is a freely available core application providing powerful tools and coherent up-to-date documentation. These are essential characteristics for the extension and support of any computational tool.

References

Baldwin T (2005) Deep lexical acquisition of verb-particle constructions. Comput Speech Lang Spec Issue MWEs 19(4):398–414

Baldwin T (2008) A resource for evaluating the deep lexical acquisition of English verb-particle constructions. In: Grégoire N, Evert S, Krenn B (eds) Proceedings of the LREC workshop towards a shared task for multiword expressions (MWE 2008), Marrakech, pp 1–2

Banerjee S, Pedersen T (2003) The design, implementation, and use of the Ngram statistic package. In: Proceedings of the fourth international conference on intelligent text processing and computational linguistics, Mexico City, pp 370–381

Bonin F, Dell'Orletta F, Montemagni S, Venturi G (2010a) A contrastive approach to multi-word extraction from domain-specific corpora. In:Proceedings of the seventh international conference on language resources and evaluation (LREC 2010), Valetta. European Language Resources Association

Bonin F, Dell'Orletta F, Venturi G, Montemagni S (2010b) Contrastive filtering of domain-specific multi-word terms from different types of corpora. In: Laporte É, Nakov P, Ramisch C, Villavicencio A (eds) Proceedings of the COLING workshop on multiword expressions: from theory to applications (MWE 2010), Beijing. Association for Computational Linguistics, pp 76–79

Christ O (1994) A modular and flexible architecture for an integrated corpus query system. In: COMPLEX 1994, Budapest, pp 23–32

Duran MS, Ramisch C, Aluísio SM, Villavicencio A (2011) Identifying and analyzing Brazilian Portuguese complex predicates. In: Kordoni V, Ramisch C, Villavicencio A (eds) Proceedings of the ALC workshop on multiword expressions: from parsing and generation to the real world (MWE 2011), Portland. Association for Computational Linguistics, pp 74–82. http://www.aclweb.org/anthology/W/W11/W11-0812

Evert S (2004) The statistics of word cooccurrences: word pairs and collocations. PhD thesis, Institut für maschinelle Sprachverarbeitung, University of Stuttgart, Stuttgart, 353p

Evert S, Krenn B (2005) Using small random samples for the manual evaluation of statistical association measures. Comput Speech Lang Spec Issue MWEs 19(4):450–466

Justeson JS, Katz SM (1995) Technical terminology: some linguistic properties and an algorithm for identification in text. Nat Lang Eng 1(1):9–27

Kilgarriff A (2007) Googleology is bad science. Comput Linguist 33(1):147–151

Kim JD, Ohta T, Teteisi Y, Tsujii J (2006) GENIA ontology. Technical report, Tsujii Laboratory, University of Tokyo

Kim SN, Baldwin T (2008) Standardised evaluation of English noun compound interpretation. In: Grégoire N, Evert S, Krenn B (eds) Proceedings of the LREC workshop towards a shared task for multiword expressions (MWE 2008), Marrakech, pp 39–42

Mangeot M, Chalvin A (2006) Dictionary building with the jibiki platform: the GDEF case. In: Proceedings of the sixth international conference on language resources and evaluation (LREC 2006),Genoa. European Language Resources Association, pp 1666–1669

Ohta T, Tateishi Y, Kim JD (2002) The GENIA corpus: an annotated research abstract corpus in molecular biology domain. In: Proceedings of the second human language technology conference (HLT 2002), San Diego. Morgan Kaufmann, pp 82–86

Pearce D (2001) Synonymy in collocation extraction. In: WordNet and other lexical resources: applications, extensions and customizations (NAACL 2001 Workshop), Pittsburgh, pp 41–46

Pecina P (2008) Reference data for Czech collocation extraction. In: Grégoire N, Evert S, Krenn B (eds) Proceedings of the LREC workshop towards a shared task for multiword expressions (MWE 2008), Marrakech, pp 11–14

Pecina P (2010) Lexical association measures and collocation extraction. Lang Resour Eval (Spec issue Multiword Expr: Hard Going Plain Sail) 44(1–2):137–158. doi:10.1007/s10579-009-9101-4. http://www.springerlink.com/content/DRH83N312U658331

Ramisch C (2009) Multiword terminology extraction for domain-specific documents. Master's thesis, École Nationale Supérieure d'Informatique et de Mathématiques Appliquées, Grenoble, 79p

Ramisch C, Schreiner P, Idiart M, Villavicencio A (2008a) An evaluation of methods for the extraction of multiword expressions. In: Grégoire N, Evert S, Krenn B (eds) Proceedings of the LREC workshop towards a shared task for multiword expressions (MWE 2008), Marrakech, pp 50–53

Ramisch C, Villavicencio A, Moura L, Idiart M (2008b) Picking them up and figuring them out: verb-particle constructions, noise and idiomaticity. In: Clark A, Toutanova K (eds) Proceedings of the twelfth conference on natural language learning (CoNLL 2008), Manchester. The Coling 2008 Organizing Committee, pp 49–56. http://www.aclweb.org/anthology/W08-2107

Ramisch C, de Medeiros Caseli H, Villavicencio A, Machado A, Finatto MJ (2010a) A hybrid approach for multiword expression identification. In: Proceedings of the 9th international conference on computational processing of Portuguese language (PROPOR 2010), Porto Alegre. Lecture notes in computer science (Lecture notes in artificail intelligence), vol 6001. Springer, pp 65–74. doi:10.1007/978-3-642-12320-7_9. http://www.springerlink.com/content/978-3-642-12319-1

Ramisch C, Villavicencio A, Boitet C (2010b) Multiword expressions in the wild? The mwetoolkit comes in handy. In: Liu Y, Liu T (eds) Proceedings of the 23rd international conference on computational linguistics (COLING 2010)—Demonstrations, Beijing. The Coling 2010 Organizing Committee, pp 57–60. http://www.aclweb.org/anthology/C10-3015

Ramisch C, Villavicencio A, Boitet C (2010c) mwetoolkit: a framework for multiword expression identification. In: Proceedings of the seventh international conference on language resources and evaluation (LREC 2010), Valetta. European Language Resources Association, pp 662–669

Ramisch C, Villavicencio A, Boitet C (2010d) Web-based and combined language models: a case study on noun compound identification. In: Huang CR, Jurafsky D (eds) Proceedings of the 23rd international conference on computational linguistics (COLING 2010)—Posters, Beijing. The Coling 2010 Organizing Committee, pp 1041–1049. http://www.aclweb.org/anthology/C10-2120

Rychlý P, Smrz P (2004) Manatee, bonito and word sketches for Czech. In: Proceedings of the second international conference on corpus linguisitcs, Saint-Petersburg, pp 124–131. http://www.fit.vutbr.cz/research/view_pub.php?id=7700

Seretan V (2008) Collocation extraction based on syntactic parsing. PhD thesis, University of Geneva, Geneva, 249p

Villavicencio A, Kordoni V, Zhang Y, Idiart M, Ramisch C (2007) Validation and evaluation of automatically acquired multiword expressions for grammar engineering. In: Eisner J (ed) Proceedings of the 2007 joint conference on empirical methods in natural language processing and computational natural language learning (EMNLP-CoNLL 2007), Prague. Association for Computational Linguistics, pp 1034–1043. http://www.aclweb.org/anthology/D/D07/D07-1110

Zhang Y, Kordoni V, Villavicencio A, Idiart M (2006) Automated multiword expression prediction for grammar engineering. In: Moirón BV, Villavicencio A, McCarthy D, Evert S, Stevenson S (eds) Proceedings of the COLING/ACL workshop on multiword expressions: identifying and exploiting underlying properties (MWE 2006), Sidney. Association for Computational Linguistics, pp 36–44. http://www.aclweb.org/anthology/W/W06/W06-1206

Part III
Applications

Chapter 6
Application 1: Lexicography

This chapter shows the results of the evaluation of the mwetoolkit methodology for the creation of MWE dictionaries. First, we explore the creation of a dictionary containing Greek nominal expressions (Sect. 6.1). Second, we present the creation of two lexical resources for Brazilian Portuguese. They contain complex predicates (verbal expressions) and are aimed at two real applications: semantic role labelling and sentiment analysis (Sect. 6.2). These two languages were chosen because: (a) they are poorly resourced in terms of MWE lexicons, and (b) there was a real need to build MWE lexicons for a given application.

6.1 A Dictionary of Nominal Compounds in Greek

The main goal of this section is to evaluate the effectiveness of the MWE acquisition approach proposed in Chap. 5 for the automatic construction of a MWE dictionary for Greek.[1] We present the results of experiments carried out in order to create a dictionary of MWEs for Greek using automatic extraction followed by human validation. In Sect. 6.1.1 we discuss some related work on the construction of language resources for the Greek language. We performed extraction using the mwetoolkit, based on POS patterns applied to the Greek portion of the Europarl corpus (Sect. 6.1.2). The results obtained by AMs on the Greek Europarl corpus are compared and contrasted with those obtained by the same measures using the web as a corpus (Sect. 6.1.3). The manual evaluation of the results by Greek native speakers led to the creation of an available lexical resource.

---

[1]Work reported in this section was previously published in the paper *Towards the Construction of Language Resources for Greek Multiword Expressions: Extraction and Evaluation* (Linardaki et al. 2010). It was carried out with the collaboration of Evita Linardaki, Aline Villavicencio and Aggeliki Fotopoulou.

© Springer International Publishing Switzerland 2015
C. Ramisch, *Multiword Expressions Acquisition*, Theory and Applications
of Natural Language Processing, DOI 10.1007/978-3-319-09207-2_6

Table 6.1 Example sentences in Greek where MWEs can be at the root of translation problems. The source and reference texts were taken from the Europarl corpus. The last column shows the number of occurrences of the highlighted Greek MWE in the corpus

Greek source	Result of MT	English reference	Count
όπως αυτό ορίζεται από την ανθρώπινη **οπτική γωνία**	*as this is fixed by the* human **optical corner**	*as seen from the* human **point of view**	131
Το **ξέπλυμα βρώμικου χρήματος** αντιπροσωπεύει το 2 έως 5 %	*The* **rinsing of dirty money** *represents the 2 until 5 %*	**Money laundering** *represents between 2 and 5 %*	21
Για τα **εργοστάσια ατομικής ενέργειας** η Ευρωπαϊκή Ένωση έχει αναλάβει δράσεις για την υψηλότερη ασφάλεια	*For the* **factories of individual energy** *the European Union has undertaken action for the higher safety*	**Nuclear power stations** *in the European Union have the highest safety standards*	8

6.1.1 Greek Nominal Compounds

In the state of the art presented in Chap. 3, we show that the performance of techniques for the automatic acquisition of MWEs has been assessed on languages like English, Spanish, French and German. As a consequence, the construction of MWE resources for these languages is picking up pace, whereas for languages like Greek, computational approaches for the automatic or semi-automatic construction of language resources are still underexploited. However, the Greek language is as rich in MWEs as main European languages. Some examples of MWEs in Greek are: κάλιο αργά παρά πατέ (*better late than ever*—idiom), πλυντήριο πιάτων (*washing machine*—noun compound), οπτική ίνα (*optical fiber*—terminology). These examples indicate the wide range of linguistic structures that can be classified as MWEs in Greek.

Table 6.1 illustrates the importance of MWE treatment in the context of MT. It shows a set of sentence fragments taken from the Greek portion of the Europarl corpus along with an English translation generated by a commercial MT system.[2] The corresponding reference translations from the English portion of the Europarl corpus show that the expected translations of the highlighted MWEs in the source text are clearly not equivalent to the actual output of the system.

The linguistic properties of MWEs in Greek have been the focus of considerable work (Fotopoulou 1993; Moustaki 1995; Fotopoulou 1997). However, published results about a purely computational treatment are still very limited. One of the few works concerning the acquisition of MWEs for Greek is the one of Fotopoulou et al. (2008). Their approach combines grammar rules and statistical measures in an attempt to extract from a 142,000,000-word collection of Greek texts as many nominal MWEs as possible while at the same time ensuring consistency of results.

---

[2]The result of MT was obtained through Systran's online translation service, available at http://www.systranet.com/

Another approach is that of Michou and Seretan (2009). They describe a Greek version of the *FipsCo* system that is able to extract collocations from corpora. Their method uses a hand-crafted generative parser for Greek built upon the *Fips* framework to analyse the sentences of the Europarl corpus and then extract MWE candidates based on syntactic patterns. The candidates are further filtered according to their association strength through the log-likelihood measure. Their system also allows the potential extraction of bilingual Greek–French MWEs when parallel corpora is available.

Despite the methodological similarities, our acquisition experiments differ from related work not only in the techniques used in each extraction step, but also in its goal: instead of building a hand-crafted specialised deep analysis tool aimed at the identification of Greek MWEs, we use the language-independent mwetoolkit methodology to extract shallow MWE candidates. Then, we evaluate the effectiveness of several AMs implemented by the toolkit using both textual corpora and the World Wide Web as a corpus.

The general characteristics of Greek nominal MWEs are the same as those described in Sect. 2.3.2. They also vary to a great extent in terms of the fixedness of their morphosyntactic structure and of their semantic interpretation, that can be more or less transparent depending on the type of MWE (idioms tend to be less transparent than specialised terms, for example). The decision to investigate nominal MWEs (as opposed to verbal ones) was largely based on the fact that they are less heterogeneous in nature and can, therefore, be more easily encoded (Mini and Fotopoulou 2009).

The most common types of Greek nominal MWEs identified in the literature are (Anastasiadi-Symeonidi 1986; Fotopoulou et al. 2008)[3]:

- J + N: In this case we have an adjective followed by a noun which constitutes the head of the phrase, for example, φορητός υπολογιστής (*laptop*), ομφάλιος λώρος (*umbilical cord*).
- N + N: MWEs of this type consist of two nouns that:

  - Carry the same weight and have the same case, for example, κράτος μέλος (*member state*), παιδί θαύμα (*child prodigy*).
  - The second is in genitive and modifies the first, for example, σύνοδος κορυφής (*summit*), Υπουργείο Εξωτερικών (*ministry of foreign affairs*).

- N + DT + N: These MWEs have a noun phrase modifying a preceding noun, for example, κοινωνία της πληροφορίας (*information society*), μήλο της Έριδος (*apple of discord*).
- N + P + N: In this case we have a prepositional phrase modifying a preceding noun, for example, σκλήρυνση κατά πλάκας (*multiple sclerosis*), φόνος εκ προμελέτης (*premeditated murder*).

---

[3] See Appendix D.1 for a description of the generic POS tags used in this chapter.

- P + N + N: MWEs in this category are very similar to those in the previous
  one in terms of their grammatical composition, the only difference being that the
  modifier precedes the noun it modifies, for example, διά βίου μάθηση (*lifelong
  learning*), κατά κεφαλήν εισόδημα (*per capita income*).

In addition to these, we are going to examine two more categories:

- N + J + N: MWEs in this category consist of an adjectival phrase in the genitive
  case modifying a preceding noun, for example, ξέπλυμα βρώμικου Χρήματος
  (*money laundering*), εμπόριο λευκής σαρκός (*white slavery*).
- N + CC + N: In this last category we come across phrases that consist of two
  conjoined nouns, for example, σάρκα και οστά (*[take] shape*), τελεία και παύλα
  (*full stop*).

6.1.2   Automatic Acquisition Setup

The candidate extraction process was carried out on the Greek portion of the
Europarl (EP) v3 corpus (Koehn 2005). It consists of 962,820 sentences and
26,306,875 words was five at the time this was written. Even though EP does not
contain a great variation of text types, it can be assumed to constitute a relatively
representative sample of general-purpose Greek language, mainly due to its size.

Before feeding the corpus into the mwetoolkit, we preprocessed it using
external tools, as described in Sect. 5.1.2.1. We used the Greek POS tagger
developed at ILSP by Papageorgiou et al. (2000). Since Greek is a morphologically
rich language, the tagset used for the description of the various morphosyntactic
phenomena is very large compared to tagsets used by annotation schemata in other
languages (584 vs 36 tags in the Penn Treebank). These labels were reduced to simplified POS tags. The word lemmas were determined using the ILSP morphological
dictionary which contains around 80,000 lemmas corresponding to approximately
2,500,000 fully inflected entries.

Once the corpus was cleaned, tagged and lemmatised, it was fed as input to the
mwetoolkit. The seven POS patterns in Fig. 6.1 are defined on the basis of the
types discussed in Sect. 6.1.1. Their application on the Greek EP corpus produced
526,012 word sequences. In order to reduce the effects of data sparseness and avoid
computational overhead, we disregarded candidates that occurred less than 10 times.
The size of the list of candidates reduced to 25,257 word sequences.

For each candidate entry, we obtained individual word counts both in EP and
in the web through Yahoo! search API. These, combined with the candidate's joint
count, are used to calculate four statistical AMs for each MWE candidate: pointwise
mutual information (pmi), maximum likelihood estimator (mle), Student's *t* score
(t-score) and Dice's coefficient (dice), as described in Sect. 3.1.4.

The mwetoolkit outputs a list containing the following information on each
MWE candidate: the lemma forms and POS tags of its individual words, the counts

```
<?xml version="1.0" encoding="UTF-8"?>
<!DOCTYPE patterns SYSTEM "mwttoolkit-patterns.dtd">
<patterns>
<pattern><w pos="J"/> <w pos="N"/></pattern><!--φορητός υπολογιστής -->
<pattern><w pos="N"/><w pos="N"/></pattern><!--κράτος μέλος, Υπουργείο Εσωτερικών-->
<pattern><w pos="N"/><w pos="DT"/><w pos="N"/></pattern><!--φαινόμενο του θερμοκηπίου-->
<pattern><w pos="N"/><w pos="J"/> <w pos="N"/></pattern><!--εμπόριο λευκής σαρκός-->
<pattern><w pos="N"/><w pos="P"/><w pos="N"/></pattern><!--σκλήρυνση κατά πλάκας-->
<pattern><w pos="P"/><w pos="N"/><w pos="N"/></pattern><!--κατά κεφαλήν εισόδημα-->
<pattern><w pos="N"/><w pos="CC"/><w pos="N"/></pattern><!--τελεία και παύλα-->
</patterns>
```

Fig. 6.1 XML file containing the description of the relevant POS patterns for extraction

```
<cand candid="13421">
  <ngram>
    <w lemma="αχίλλειος" pos= "J" >
      <freq name="EP" value="14" /><freq name="WWW" value="16700" /></w>
    <w lemma="πτέρνα" pos="N" >
      <freq name="EP" value="14" /><freq name="WWW" value="49900" /></w>
    <freq name="EP" value="14" /><freq name="WWW" value="15400" />
  </ngram>
  <occurs>
    <ngram><w surface="αχίλλειος" lemma="αχίλλειος" pos="J" />
           <w surface="πτέρνα" lemma="πτέρνα" pos="N" />
           <freq name="EP" value="8" /></ngram>
    <ngram><w surface="Αχίλλειος" lemma="aq'illeios" pos="J" />
           <w surface="πτέρνα" lemma="pt'erna" pos="N" />
           <freq name="EP" value="1" /></ngram>
    <ngram><w surface="αχίλλειος" lemma="aq'illeios" pos="J" />
           <w surface="πτέρνα" lemma="pt'erna" pos="N" />
           <freq name="EP" value="5" /></ngram>
  </occurs>
  <features>
    <feat name="pos-pattern" value= "J#S#N#S" /><feat name="n" value="2" />
    <feat name="mle-EP" value="7.4773e-07" /><feat name="pmi-EP" value="44.5092" />
    <feat name="t-EP" value="3.7416" /><feat name="dice-EP" value="1.0" />
    <feat name="mle-WWW" value="3.08e-07" /><feat name="pmi-WWW" value="55.3587" />
    <feat name="t-WWW" value="124.0966" /><feat name="dice-WWW" value="0.4624" />
  </features>
</cand>
```

Fig. 6.2 Extract of the XML output file with MWE candidates and their AM scores

of these words as well as of the entire *n*-gram sequence both in EP and in the web, all the surface forms of each candidate together with their counts in the original corpus (EP) and a set of features that correspond to the candidate's score for each AM. Figure 6.2 shows an example of an extracted candidate.

6.1.3   Results

Evaluation was performed manually by three native speakers. In terms of the typology proposed in Chap. 4, our evaluation is intrinsic and quantitative, involves manual annotation, and is type-based. Our evaluation is based on precision as

Fig. 6.3 Precision based on
the EP counts

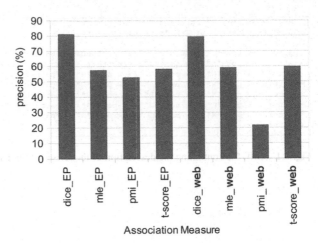

performance measure, in spite of its limitations and oversimplification, as discussed in Sect. 4.3. In order to calculate recall, however, we would need to know how many MWEs exist in EP, in the web, or more generally in the Greek language. It is almost impossible to know and very difficult to estimate these values.

Due to the size of the candidate list (25,257 candidates), it was not possible to perform exhaustive manual judgement of all the candidates. Instead, the human judges annotated a sample containing the first 150 candidates proposed by each measure. From these, we manually removed the most striking cases of noise (introduced by the tagger) such as single words or candidates that appeared more than once based on a different grammatical classification. In short, each annotator classified around 1,200 entries in one of the following categories:

1. mwe: the candidate is a nominal compound, that is, a true positive;
2. maybe: the candidate is ambiguous, but it may be considered as a compound depending on the context of use;
3. part: the candidate includes a or is part of a compound or;
4. not: the candidate is not a MWE, but a regular sequence of words with no particularity.

In the following evaluation steps, we considered MWEs to be those that were classified as such (mwe) by at least two out of three of our judges. This is a conservative evaluation scheme that does not take into account other categories such as maybe and part.

Our initial anticipation, given evaluation results reported in the literature (Evert and Krenn 2005), was that the dice coefficient or pmi would be the best AMs, followed by t-score and then mle. As Fig. 6.3 shows, this was not exactly the case. Considering only EP counts, the dice$_{EP}$ coefficient did indeed have the highest precision, 81.08 %. This result surpassed all our expectations since it is one of the highest reported in the Greek literature. The second highest precision

(58.21 %) is achieved by t-score$_{EP}$, followed by the mle$_{EP}$ at approximately the same levels (57.43 %), leaving pmi$_{EP}$ behind with a precision of 52.66 %.

The web-based precision for each AM other than the pmi$_{web}$ reached the same levels as the EP-based one. More precisely, the dice$_{web}$ coefficient yielded a precision of 79.43 %, corresponding to a marginal decrease of approximately 2 % with respect to EP. mle$_{web}$ and t-score$_{web}$, on the other hand, did show an increase of 2.6–2.7 %, with their exact precision values being 58.99 and 59.71 % respectively. These values seem to confirm our earlier assumption that EP, despite its lack of textual genre variation, can reasonably be assumed to contain a representative sample of the Greek language, mainly due to its size. The most striking result about the web-based results, however, is the dramatic decrease (almost 60 % lower) in the precision of pmi$_{web}$ (a very unimpressive 21.62 %).

The pmi score seems to overestimate the importance of rare word sequences, since the candidate lists consisted entirely of less frequent three-word candidates both in the case of EP and web as opposed to, say, the dice coefficient whose candidate lists consisted of entirely of 2-grams (something that can be attributed to their higher number of occurrences in general language use). A large proportion of the candidates proposed by pmi included partial MWEs, which were not proposed as a unit by themselves, but in combination with some other word. To be more precise, out of the 148 candidates evaluated, 32 were classified as MWEs while 50 included some MWE, which in the majority of cases was εν λόγω (*in question*). Indeed, some of the candidates classified as part or maybe should be manually analysed for deciding whether to include them as entries in the dictionary, as they could constitute interesting MWEs.

As an additional evaluation, we quantified the difficulty of the classification task for the human judges. Therefore, we calculated the inter-judge agreement rate using Fleiss's kappa coefficient. The results for each analysed AM are summarised in Table 6.2: the first four columns correspond to the individual agreement proportions for each of the categories while the last column contains the kappa value.

The agreement coefficients are very heterogeneous, ranging from $\kappa = 40$ to $\kappa = 74$ %. If we look in detail at the proportion of agreement for each category,

Table 6.2 Inter-annotator agreement for each of the four categories and each evaluated AM in both corpora, as well as Fleiss' kappa coefficient (κ)

	mwe (%)	maybe (%)	part (%)	not (%)	κ (%)
dice$_{EP}$	78	10	3	9	40
mle$_{EP}$	55	9	3	33	65
pmi$_{EP}$	50	9	16	26	52
t-score$_{EP}$	56	9	3	32	61
dice$_{web}$	78	8	2	12	56
mle$_{web}$	58	6	1	36	74
pmi$_{web}$	21	7	36	36	63
t-score$_{web}$	58	6	1	35	70

we can see that annotators are quite at ease to identify true MWEs, whereas, for the other classes, the agreement is much lower (e.g., annotators cannot truly distinguish maybe from part). While, on the one hand, this might be caused by ambiguous annotating guidelines, on the other hand, it is also an indicator of how difficult it is for a human annotator to identify and classify MWEs.

The results of manual evaluation by the three native speakers were joined and resulted in a lexicon of 815 nominal MWEs in Greek. The dictionary was made freely available on the MWE community website.[4] Moreover, our methodology allowed a fine-grained evaluation of some parameters of the evaluation, such as the association measures and the frequency source. Thus, this evaluation experiment of the mwetoolkit methodology resulted in (a) a list of nominal compounds in Greek that may help building other NLP applications, and (b) a set of experimental results that may help designing new MWE acquisition methods in similar contexts.

6.2   A Dictionary of Complex Predicates in Portuguese

In this section, we describe the creation of two related lexical resources for NLP applications processing texts in Brazilian Portuguese.[5] Both resources are dictionaries including complex predicates, that is, verbal MWEs which act as a predicate in a sentence and which are composed of a verb and a complement.

The first dictionary was constructed based on a concrete need of a semantic role labelling task. Semantic role labelling annotation depends on the correct identification of predicates, before identifying arguments and assigning them role labels. However, many predicates are not constituted only by a verb: they constitute *complex predicates* (CPs) not readily available in most computational lexicons. In order to create a dictionary of CPs aimed at semantic role labelling (henceforth, CP-SRL), we employed the mwetoolkit using POS tag sequences instead of a limited list of verbs or nouns, in contrast to similar studies. The resulting CPs include (but are not limited to) light and support verb constructions.

The second lexicon constructed using a the mwetoolkit also contains CPs, but is aimed at a different application: sentiment analysis. Sentiment verbs like *temer (fear)*, *odiar (hate)* and *invejar (envy)* are examples of lexical units specifically used to express feelings. The same meaning may be conveyed through other verbs associated to sentiment nouns. We firstly identify 7 recurrent patterns of sentiment expression through CPs and then employ these patterns to identify sentiment nouns associated to them. We will refer to the lexical resource resulting from these experiences as CP-SENT.

---

[4]http://multiword.sourceforge.net/PHITE.php?sitesig=FILES&page=FILES_20_Data_Sets

[5]Work reported in this section was previously published in the papers *Identifying and Analysing Brazilian Portuguese Complex Predicates* (Duran et al. 2011) and *How do you feel? Investigating lexical-syntactic patterns in sentiment expression* (Duran and Ramisch 2011). It was carried out with the collaboration of Magali Sanchez Duran, Sandra Maria Aluisio and Aline Villavicencio.

The remainder of this section is structured as follows: we start by introducing and exemplifying the characteristics of CPs in Brazilian Portuguese in Sect. 6.2.1. Then, in Sect. 6.2.2 we present the corpus, the POS patterns employed and the acquisition methodology using the mwetoolkit. Then, we present the analysis of the results and the creation of the CP-SRL lexicon in Sect. 6.2.3.1, and analogously, for CP-SENT in Sect. 6.2.3.2. We conclude with a discussion on the role of the mwetoolkit in the creation of both resources (Sect. 6.2.3.3).

6.2.1 Portuguese Complex Predicates

Complex predicates can be defined as "predicates which are multi-headed: they are composed of more than one grammatical element" (Alsina et al. 1997, p. 1), like *give a try, take care–take a shower*. The correct identification of CPs is a crucial step in *semantic role labelling* (SRL) and for sentiment analysis. We examine the behaviour and importance of CPs for these two applications separately in Sects. 6.2.1.1 and 6.2.1.2.

6.2.1.1 Complex Predicates and Semantic Roles

Independently of the approach adopted, SRL comprehends two steps before the assignment of role labels: (a) the delimitation of argument takers and (b) the delimitation of arguments. If the argument taker is not correctly identified, the argument identification will propagate the error. Argument takers are predicates, represented by a verb or by a CP.

The verbal phrases identified by a parser are usually used to automatically identify argument takers, but do no suffice. A lexicon of CPs is also required for the fully automatic identification of argument takers. The first part of our experiments reports the creation of the CP-SRL lexicon, in order to meet the needs arisen from a SRL annotation task in a corpus of Brazilian Portuguese.[6]

Consider the sentence *John takes care of his business* in three alternatives of annotation:

1. [John]$_{ARG}$ [takes]$_{PRED}$ [care of his business]$_{ARG}$
2. [John]$_{ARG}$ [takes]$_{PRED}$ [care] $_{ARG}$ [of his business]$_{ARG}$
3. [John]$_{ARG}$ [takes care]$_{PRED}$ [of his business]$_{ARG}$

The first annotation shows *care of his business* as a unique argument, masking the fact that this segment is constituted of a predicative noun, *care*, and its internal argument, *of his business*. The second annotation shows *care* and *of his business* as arguments of *take*, which is incorrect because *of his business* is clearly an argument

---

[6]CPs constituted by verbal chains (e.g., *have been working*) are not considered here.

of *care*. The third annotation is the best for SRL purposes: as a unique predicate—*take care*—*take* shares its external argument with *care* and *care* shares its internal argument with *take*. Such complex predicates as *take care* are a type of verbal MWE which must be taken into account for manual and automatic SRL. Our goal is to apply the `mwetoolkit` methodology to build a comprehensive machine-readable dictionary of CPs for SRL.

Complex predicates are also called in the literature *light verb constructions* (LVCs) or *support verb constructions* (SVCs), with slightly different definitions. They have been studied in several languages from different points of view (Salkoff 1990; Stevenson et al. 2004; Barreiro and Cabral 2009; Hwang et al. 2010). Work focusing on the automatic extraction of LVCs or SVCs often take as starting point a list of recurrent light verbs (Hendrickx et al. 2010) or a list of nominalisations (Teufel and Grefenstette 1995; Dras 1995; Hwang et al. 2010). These approach is not adopted in out experiment because our goal is precisely to identify which verbs, nouns and other lexical elements take part in CPs.

Similar motivation to study LVCs/SVCs (that is, for SRL) is found within the scope of Framenet (Atkins et al. 2003) and Propbank (Hwang et al. 2010). These projects have taken different decisions on how to annotate such constructions. Framenet annotates the head of the construction (noun or adjective) as argument taker (or frame evoker) and the light verb separately; Propbank, on its turn, first annotates separately light verbs and the predicative nouns (as ARG-PRX) and then merges them, annotating the whole construction as an argument taker.

6.2.1.2 Complex Predicates and Sentiment Analysis

Sentiment analysis and opinion mining are a growing topic of interest in the last few years due to the large amount of texts produced through web facilities, like social networking, blogs, e-mail and chats. These texts contain information about what people think and feel, which constitute valuable information (Pang and Lee 2008).

Although sentiment verbs are lexical items specifically used to express feelings, they are not the only option. In Portuguese, it is possible and frequent to express feelings using other verbs associated to sentiment nouns. For example, in the sentence *João tem inveja de você. (lit. João has envy of you = João envies you)*, the sentiment expressed is *inveja (envy)*, *João* is the one who feels envy and *você (you)* is the cause (or stimulus) for *João* feeling envy.

It would be interesting, indeed, that a Portuguese sentiment lexicon includes collocations like *ter inveja*, which corresponds to the verb *invejar (to envy)*. Analogously to the problem of SRL described above, it is relevant for sentiment data mining to know how to determine who is feeling the expressed sentiment and what is causing the expressed sentiment. Hence, our experiments aim to explore recurrent MWEs used to express feelings in Portuguese.

Besides the identification of sentiment words, there are studies dedicated to enriching the description of these words, aggregating features that enable clustering the gathered information. Up to this date, features regarding sentiment words are almost always related to their polarity, as may be seen in Kim and Hovy (2004), in SentiWordNet (Esuli and Sebastiani 2006) and in SentiLexPT,[7] this latter being a lexical resource for Portuguese. In Portuguese, there are few reported studies related to sentiment analysis (Silva et al. 2009; Carvalho et al. 2011). The growing need for lexical resources aimed at sentiment analysis and the role played by CPs in sentiment expression motivate our efforts toward the creation of the CP-SENT lexicon, using the `mwetoolkit` methodology.

6.2.2 Automatic Acquisition Setup

We use the `mwetoolkit` to automatically acquire candidate CPs from the corpus, and then we manually analyse the candidate lists to distinguish CPs from fully compositional word sequences. For the automatic acquisition step, we used the PLN-BR-FULL corpus. This corpus was built in the context of the PLNBR project.[8] It contains 29,014,089 tokens of news text from *Folha de São Paulo*, a Brazilian newspaper, from 1994 to 2005. The corpus was first preprocessed for sentence splitting, case homogenisation, lemmatisation and POS tagging using PALAVRAS, a deep syntactic parser for Portuguese (Bick 2000).

Differently from the studies referred to in Sect. 6.2.1, we did not presume any closed list of light verbs or nouns as starting point to our searches. The search criteria we used in order to acquire CPs for SRL are composed of seven POS patterns observed in examples collected during previous corpus annotation tasks[9]:

1. V + N + P: *abrir mão de* (*give up*, lit. *open hand of*);
2. V + P + N: *deixar de lado* (*ignore*, lit. *leave at side*);
3. V + DT + N + P: *virar as costas para* (*ignore*, lit. *turn the back to*);
4. V + DT + R: *dar o fora* (*get out*, lit. *give the out*);
5. V + R: *ir atrás* (*follow*, lit. *go behind*);
6. V + P + R: *dar para trás* (*give up*, lit. *give to back*);
7. V + J: *dar duro* (*work hard*, lit. *give hard*).

We will refer to this set of POS patterns as PAT-SRL. This strategy is suitable to extract occurrences from active sentences, both affirmative and negative. We ignore cases which present intervening material between the verb and the other elements of the CP. After generating separate lists of candidates for each pattern with the `mwetoolkit`, we filtered out all those occurring less than 10 times. This threshold was set based on the analysis presented in Fig. 6.4. The graphic shows that precision increases slowly while the drop in recall is roughly linear. A good compromise (F-measure) can be obtained by setting the threshold at 10 occurrences.

---

[7]http://dmir.inesc-id.pt/reaction/SentiLex-PT_01

[8]http://www.nilc.icmc.usp.br/plnbr

[9]See Appendix D.1 for a description of the POS tags.

Fig. 6.4 Quality comparison
of threshold values

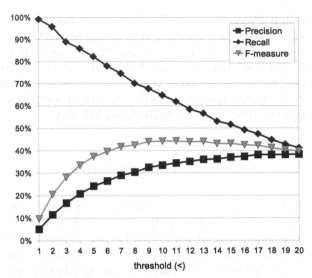

In order to create the CP-SRL lexicon, we manually analysed the candidates
generated by the `mwetoolkit`. During this analysis, we accidentally identified
constructions containing sentiment nouns. These findings motivated the creation of
the second lexicon, CP-SENT, using the following patterns[10]:

1. *sentir* N *de* (*to feel* N *of*)
2. *sentir* N *por* (*to feel* N *for*)
3. *ter* N *de* (*to have* N *of*)
4. *ter* N *por* (*to have* N *for*)
5. *ficar com* N *de* (*to become with* N *of*)
6. *estar com* N *de* (*to be with* N *of*)
7. *dar* N *em* (*to give* N *in*)

We identified these syntactic patterns empirically based on observation of the
data in the CP-SRL lexicon and on trial and error. We will refer to this set of
patterns as PAT-SENT. Notice that, instead of using abstract POS like for CP-SRL,
we used the identified lemmas of the support verbs of sentiment nouns. This was
necessary because these patterns correspond to syntactic configurations in which,
in most cases, the sentiment noun is part of a CP instead of being the topic of
conversation. If we had used POS instead of lemmas, the resulting list would be
too noisy to be useful for lexicographic purposes.

The patterns in PAT-SENT allowed us to manually identify 98 sentiment nouns.
We combine all the nouns with all the patterns in PAT-SENT, thus artificially
generating 686 variations that were automatically looked up in the web using
the `mwetoolkit`. Web hit counts were used because the original corpus is not

---

[10]The placeholder N stands for a sentiment noun.

Table 6.3 Variations artificially generated for the noun *consciência* (*conscience*)

dar | *dá* | *deu* | *dava consciência em*	0
*ficar | *fica* | *ficou* | *ficava com consciência de*	3
estar | *está* | *esteve* | *estava com consciência de*	2
*sentir | *sente* | *sentiu* | *sentia consciência de*	6
sentir | *sente* | *sentiu* | *sentia consciência por*	0
*ter | tem | teve | tinha consciência de	47, 600
*ter | *tem* | *teve* | *tinha consciência por*	179

large enough to allow the distinction between unacceptable constructions and constructions that were not found in the corpus due to its limited size. Web search engines do not allow search by lemmas. To overcome this limitation, we generated inflected forms for each variation. For instance, the candidate *ter medo de (to have fear of)* became *ter* \| *tem* \| *teve* \| *tinha medo de (to have* \| *has* \| *had* \| *was having fear of)*.

Table 6.3 shows the queries and the resulting number of hits generated for the target sentiment word *consciência (conscience)*. The query in bold corresponds to the preferred pattern, that is, the pattern that maximises the hit counter for the target noun. The queries preceded by a star (*) are acceptable patterns, that is, patterns that return three hits or more. This is an example of variation features that can be generated using the `mwetoolkit` for estimating variation entropy, as described in Sect. 5.1.2.4.

6.2.3 Results

In spite of sharing the construction methodology that uses morphosyntactic patterns, both lexicons, CP-SRL and CP-SENT have different purposes. Therefore, we present the analysis of the results of automatic acquisition in two parts. First, we analyse each of the patterns used for CP acquisition in the context of SRL, focusing on idiomaticity and single-verb paraphrases (Sect. 6.2.1.1). Second, we analyse the patterns used for sentiment analysis, in terms of their precision and of the polarity and source of the acquired sentiment nouns (Sect. 6.2.1.2).

6.2.3.1 Analysis of the CP-SRL Lexicon

Each of the POS patterns contained in the PAT-SRL set returned a large number of candidates. Our expectation was to identify CPs among the most frequent candidates. First we annotated "interesting" candidates, and then we judged their idiomaticity. In Table 6.4, we show the total number of candidates extracted before applying any threshold (extracted), the number of analysed candidates using a threshold of 10 (analysed) and the number of CPs correctly identified divided into

Table 6.4 Number of candidates extracted from the corpus and analysed

pattern	extracted	analysed	less idiomatic	idiomatic
V + N + P	69,264	2,140	327	8
V + P + N	74,086	1,238	77	8
V + DT + N + P	178,956	3,187	131	4
V + DT + R	1,537	32	0	0
V + R	51,552	3,626	19	41
V + P + R	5,916	182	0	2
V + R	25,703	2,140	145	11
Total	407,014	12,545	699	74

two columns: idiomatic and less idiomatic CPs. In addition to the idiomaticity judgement, each CP was annotated with one or more single-verb paraphrases. Sometimes, it is not a simple task to decide whether a candidate constitutes a CP, specially when the verb is a very polysemous one and is often used as support verb. For example, *fazer exame em/de alguém/alguma coisa* (lit. *make exam in/of something/somebody*) is a CP corresponding to *examinar* (*exam*). But *fazer exame* in another use is not a CP and means to submit oneself to someone else's exam or to perform a test to pass examinations (*take an exam*).

In total, we identified 699 less idiomatic CPs and observed the following recurrent pairs of paraphrases:

• V = V + deverbal N, for example, *tratar = dar tratamento* (*treat = give treatment*);
• Denominal V = V + N, for example, *amedrontar = dar medo* (*frighten = give fear*);
• Deadjectival V = V + J, for example, *responsabilizar = tornar responsável* (lit. *responsibilise = hold responsible*).

Further extensions of the CP-SRL lexicon can consider this fact, as we may search for denominal and deadjectival verbs (which may be automatically recognised through infix and suffix rules) to manually identify corresponding CPs. Moreover, the large set of verbs involved in the analysed CPs, summarised in Fig. 6.5, shows that any study based on a closed set of light verbs will be limited, as it cannot capture common exceptions and non-prototypical constructions. The use of the mwetoolkit methodology allowed us to test several variants of the patterns and frequency thresholds, which would otherwise not be possible.

The CP-SRL lexicon containing idiomaticity and paraphrase information is available at the MWE community website.[11] A detailed description of the linguistic properties of the CPs extracted using each pattern is provided in the original article from which the current section was adapted (Duran et al. 2011).

---

[11]http://multiword.sourceforge.net/PHITE.php?sitesig=FILES&page=FILES_20_Data_Sets

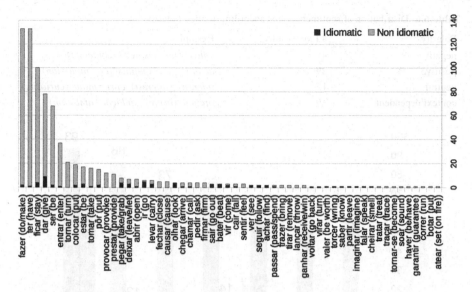

Fig. 6.5 Distribution of verbs involved in CPs, total number of CPs (all patterns)

Table 6.5 Number of candidates extracted and validated per pattern

	Pattern	Candidates	TPs	Precision (%)	Coverage (%)
1	*sentir* N *de*	49	22	44.9	12.7
2	*sentir* N *por*	18	13	**72.2**	7.5
3	*ter* N *de*	1,218	69	5.7	**39.9**
4	*ter* N *por*	131	29	22.1	16.8
5	*ficar com* N *de*	51	14	27.4	8.1
6	*estar com* N *de*	92	16	17.4	9.2
7	*dar* N *em*	215	10	4.7	5.8

6.2.3.2   Analysis of the CP-SENT Lexicon

The application of the patterns PAT-SENT on the PLN-BR-FULL corpus resulted in seven candidate lists, one for each pattern, with the collocated nouns and their respective count in the corpus. The 1,774 candidates are distributed as described in Table 6.5. Human annotators manually analysed the extracted MWE candidates lists, distinguish nouns denoting sentiments from other nouns, for example *ter ódio de* vs *ter camisa de* (lit. *to have hate of* vs *to have shirt of*). The analysis of these lists identified 173 combinations of sentiment nouns used with the patterns. The proportion of candidates analysed (column 1) which was validated as being a CP (column 2) corresponds to the precision of each pattern (column 3). This measure indicates how much a pattern is associated with sentiment nouns.

The pattern *ter* N *de* returned the largest number of validated candidates, but, at the same time, it is the one that presented one of the largest amounts of noise. This is

Table 6.6 Distribution of sentiment nouns according to their polarity

Polarity	# Expressions	Examples
negative	45	*ódio (hate), desprezo (contempt)*
positive	29	*amor (love), compaixão (compassion)*
neutral	15	*interesse (interest), curiosidade (curiosity)*
context dependent	9	*orgulho (pride), ambição (ambition)*

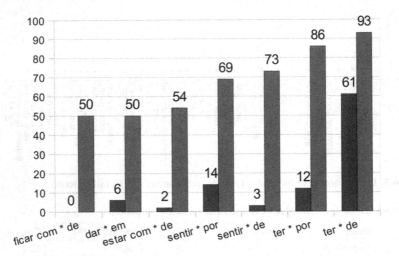

Fig. 6.6 Number of sentiment nouns (*y* axis) that prefer (*dark bars*) and accept (*light bars*) each pattern

most probably due to the high polysemy of the verb *ter (to have)*. The patterns *sentir* N *de* and *sentir* N *por* are much less ambiguous and their precision ranges from 44.9 to 72.2 %, respectively. Patterns 5 and 6 have a similar profile; both are responsible for 8 and 9 % of the final list, with a precision between 17.4 % for *estar* and 27.4 % for *ficar*. Pattern 7 presents the lowest precision, 4.7 %, which is expected as the verb *dar* is highly polysemous in Portuguese.

The 173 validated candidates present some repetitions of nouns which occur in more than one pattern. Eliminating the redundancies, we obtained a list of 98 sentiment nouns. Two human judges annotated the polarity associated to these sentiment nouns, shown in Table 6.6. We notice that most of the expressions express negative emotions. We propose two hypotheses to explain this fact: either this is a bias from our newspaper corpus (there are often more bad news than good news in general newspapers) or Brazilian Portuguese native speakers prefer to use the identified patterns instead of sentiment verbs because they somehow diminish/blur the impact of the negative emotion expressed.

After the corpus-based extraction, we generated web-based variations for each identified sentiment noun, as described in Sect. 6.2.2. The graphic shown in Fig. 6.6 shows how many sentiment nouns take each pattern as preferred pattern. The pattern

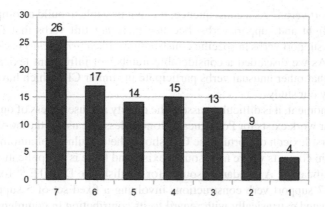

Fig. 6.7 Number of nouns (*y* axis) vs number of patterns accepted (*x* axis)

ter N *de* is the preferred one for expressing 61 of a total of 98 sentiment nouns. All patterns but one (*ficar com* N *de*) are preferred by at least one sentiment noun.

In Fig. 6.7, we present the number of sentiment nouns that accept[12] one or more patterns. With these data, we are able to distinguish more variable constructions from more fixed ones. Lexicalised constructions present zero count for all alternative patterns except for the preferred one. This is the case of four sentiment nouns. Most of the nouns, however, are quite variable and accept several patterns, although it is not clear whether alternative patterns express the same sentiment with the same connotation.

6.2.3.3 Discussion

We strongly believe that our patterns are sensitive to corpus genre, because the CPs identified are typical of colloquial register. The same patterns could be applied on a corpus of spoken Brazilian Portuguese, as well as other written genres like blog posts. A corpus of speech transcriptions, blogs (Gill et al. 2008) or social networking posts would more likely present CPs and sentiment expression. Due to its size and availability, web-based corpora would also allow us to obtain better frequency estimators.

We underline, however, that we should not underestimate the value of our original corpus, as it contains a large amount of unexplored material. We observed that only the context can tell us whether a given verb is being used as a full verb or as a light

---

[12]We say that a noun "accepts" a pattern if the count returned by the web search engine is greater than 3 pages, thus avoiding noise probably due to typos and artificial results.

and/or support verb.[13] As a consequence, it is not possible to build a comprehensive lexicon of light and support verbs, because there are full verbs that function as light and/or support verbs in specific constructions, like *correr* (*run*) in *correr risco* (*run risk*). As we discarded a considerable number of infrequent lexical items, it is possible that other unusual verbs participate in similar CPs which have not been identified by our study.

For the moment, it is difficult to assess the quality and usefulness of our resource, as no similar work exists for Portuguese. Nonetheless, the use of the mwetoolkit to build a first lexicon of Portuguese CPs shows the usefulness of automatic MWE acquisition in contexts where no resource exists and there is an application need for MWE identification. A standard resource for English like DANTE,[14] for example, contains 497 support verb constructions involving a fixed set of 5 support verbs. It was evaluated extrinsically with regard to its contribution in complementing the FrameNet data (Atkins 2010). Likewise, we would like to evaluate our resource in the context of SRL annotation, to measure its contribution in automatic argument taker identification. It would also be interesting, for instance, to compare, across genres, utterances using sentiment verbs with utterances using the patterns we have identified.

There are many possible extensions to the present experiments, which could help build a broad-coverage lexicon of CPs in Brazilian Portuguese. This lexicon may contribute to different NLP applications, in addition to SRL and sentiment analysis. Computer-assisted language learning systems and other material for learning Portuguese as a second language may include CPs. Systems for automatic textual entailment may use the relationship between CPs and paraphrases to infer equivalences between propositions. Computational language generation systems may also want to choose the most natural verbal construction to use when generating texts in Portuguese. Furthermore, these MWEs may be used to improve bilingual dictionaries with information on how to express sentiments from the point-of-view of a Brazilian speaker.

6.3 Summary

This chapter presented a first evaluation of the mwetoolkit framework in the context of computer-aided lexicography. We have collaborated with colleagues who are experienced linguists and lexicographers in order to create new lexical resources containing MWEs in Greek and in Portuguese. The created data sets are freely available.[15]

---

[13]A verb is not light or support in the lexicon, it is light and/or support depending on the combinations in which it participates.

[14]http://www.webdante.com

[15]http://multiword.sourceforge.net/PHITE.php?sitesig=FILES&page=FILES_20_Data_Sets

For Greek, considerable work has been done to study the linguistic properties of MWEs, but computational approaches are still limited (Fotopoulou et al. 2008). In our experiments, we used the mwetoolkit to extract an initial list of MWE candidates from the Greek Europarl corpus. We extracted words matching the following patterns: adjective-noun, noun-noun, noun-determiner-noun, noun-preposition-noun, preposition-noun-noun, noun-adjective-noun and noun-conjunction-noun. For filtering these candidates, we applied a set of statistical association measures using counts collected both from the corpus and from the web. The top-150 ranked candidates produced by four AMs applied on two different corpora were manually evaluated by three native speakers. Each annotator judged around 1,200 candidates and in the end the annotations were joined, creating a lexicon with 815 Greek nominal MWEs.

Based on these judgements, the AM that produced better results was dice, which significantly outperformed the other measures, followed by the t-score. The performance of the latter, however, is surprisingly similar to the performance of raw counts, suggesting that sophisticated measures are not needed when enough data is available. In relation to the use of the web as a corpus, it has a number of advantages over standard corpora, the most salient being its availability and accessibility. However, in our experiments, the results obtained with web counts did not bring considerable improvements. In sum, our results indicate that automatic methods can indeed be used for extending NLP resources with MWE information, and improving the quality of NLP systems that support Greek.

The goal of the work with Portuguese complex predicates (CPs) was to perform a qualitative analysis of these constructions. We generated two lexical resources based on two target applications: CP-SRL is aimed at semantic role label annotation while CP-SENT is aimed at sentiment analysis. For both resources, we POS-tagged the PLN-BR-FULL corpus and extracted sequences of words matching specific POS patterns using the mwetoolkit.

Semantic role label annotation depends on the correct identification of predicates, before identifying arguments and assigning them role labels. However, many predicates are not constituted only by a verb: they constitute CPs not available in a computational lexicon. In order to create the dictionary CP-SRL, we used POS sequences instead of a limited list of verbs or nouns: verb-[determiner]-noun-preposition, verb-preposition-noun, verb-[preposition/determiner]-adverb and verb-adjective. The extraction process resulted in a list of 407,014 candidates which were further filtered using statistical AMs. An expert human annotator manually validated 12,545 candidates, from which 699 were annotated as compositional verbal expressions and 74 as idiomatic verbal expressions. Results include (but are not limited to) light and support verb constructions.

For the creation of CP-SENT, our goal was to investigates how sentiments are expressed in Brazilian Portuguese. Sentiment verbs like *temer (fear), odiar (hate)* and *invejar (envy)* are examples of lexical units specifically used to express feelings, but the same meaning may be conveyed through other verbs associated to sentiment nouns. We first identify seven recurrent patterns of sentiment expression without sentiment verbs and then employ these patterns to identify sentiment nouns associated to them. We also combined the patterns with the sentiment nouns identified in the candidates, and searched the combinations in the web. Analysis of the patterns showed that combining sentiment nouns with the seven patterns may be useful to automatically identify sentiment expression and additionally know who is feeling and who or what is causing the feeling.

References

Alsina A, Bresnan J, Sells P (eds) (1997) Complex predicates. CSLI Publications, Stanford, 514p

Anastasiadi-Symeonidi A (1986) Neology in modern Greek (in Greek). PhD thesis, Aristotle University of Thessaloniki

Atkins S (2010) The DANTE database: its contribution to English lexical research, and in particular to complementing the FrameNet data. In: de Schryver GM (ed) A way with words: recent advances in lexical theory and analysis. A Festschrift for Patrick Hanks. Menha Publishers, Kampala

Atkins S, Fillmore C, Johnson CR (2003) Lexicographic relevance: selecting information from corpus evidence. Int J Lexicogr 16(3):251–280

Barreiro A, Cabral LM (2009) ReEscreve: a translator-friendly multi-purpose paraphrasing software tool. In: Proceedings of the workshop beyond translation memories: new tools for translators, the twelfth machine translation summit, Ottawa, pp 1–8

Bick E (2000) The parsing system Palavras. Aarhus University Press, Aarhus, 411p

Carvalho P, Sarmento L, Teixeira J, Silva MJ (2011) Liars and saviors in a sentiment annotated corpus of comments to political debates. In: Proceedings of the 49th annual meeting of the Association for Computational Linguistics: human language technology (ACL HLT 2011), Portland. Association for Computational Linguistics, pp 564–568. http://www.aclweb.org/anthology/P11-2099

Dras M (1995) Automatic identification of support verbs: a step towards a definition of semantic weight. In: Proceedings of the eighth Australian joint conference on artificial intelligence. World Scientific Press, Canberra, pp 451–458

Duran MS, Ramisch C (2011) How do you feel? Investigating lexical-syntactic patterns in sentiment expression. In: Proceedings of corpus linguistics 2011: discourse and corpus linguistics conference, Birmingham

Duran MS, Ramisch C, Aluísio SM, Villavicencio A (2011) Identifying and analyzing Brazilian Portuguese complex predicates. In: Kordoni V, Ramisch C, Villavicencio A (eds) Proceedings of the ALC workshop on multiword expressions: from parsing and generation to the real world (MWE 2011), Portland. Association for Computational Linguistics, pp 74–82. http://www.aclweb.org/anthology/W/W11/W11-0812

Esuli A, Sebastiani F (2006) SENTIWORDNET: a publicly available lexical resource for opinion mining. In: Proceedings of the sixth international conference on language resources and evaluation (LREC 2006), Genoa. European Language Resources Association, pp 417–422

Evert S, Krenn B (2005) Using small random samples for the manual evaluation of statistical association measures. Comput. Speech Lang Spec Issue MWEs 19(4):450–466

Fotopoulou A (1993) Une classification des phrases à compléments figés en grec moderne: étude morphosyntaxique des phrases figées. PhD thesis, Université Paris VIII, 248p

Fotopoulou A (1997) L'ordre des mots dans les phrases figées à un complément libre en grec moderne. In: Fiala P, Lafon P, Piguet MF (eds) La locution: entre lexique, syntaxe et pragmatique. INALF, Saint-Cloud, pp 37–48

Fotopoulou A, Giannopoulos G, Zourari M, Mini M (2008) Automatic recognition and extraction of multiword nominal expressions from corpora (in Greek). In: Proceedings of the 29th annual meeting, Department of Linguistics, Aristotle University of Thessaloniki, Greece

Gill AJ, French RM, Gergle D, Oberlander J (2008) The language of emotion in short blog texts. In: Proceedings of the 2008 ACM conference on computer supported cooperative work (CSCW '08)San Diego. Association for Computing Machinery

Hendrickx I, Mendes A, Pereira S, Gonçalves A, Duarte I (2010) Complex predicates annotation in a corpus of Portuguese. In: Proceedings of the ACL 2010 fourth linguistic annotation workshop, Uppsala, pp 100–108

Hwang JD, Bhatia A, Bonial C, Mansouri A, Vaidya A, Zhou Y, Xue N, Palmer M (2010) Propbank annotation of multilingual light verb constructions. In: Proceedings of the ACL 2010 fourth linguistic annotation workshop, Uppsala, pp 82–90

Kim SM, Hovy E (2004) Determining the sentiment of opinions. In: Proceedings of the 20th international conference on computational linguistics (COLING 2004), Geneva. International Committee on Computational Linguistics, pp 1367–1373. http://aclweb.org/anthology-new/C/C04/C04-1200.pdf

Koehn P (2005) Europarl: a parallel corpus for statistical machine translation. In: Proceedings of the tenth machine translation summit(MT Summit 2005), Phuket. Asian-Pacific Association for Machine Translation, pp 79–86

Linardaki E, Ramisch C, Villavicencio A, Fotopoulou A (2010) Towards the construction of language resources for Greek multiword expressions: extraction and evaluation. In: Piperidis S, Slavcheva M, Vertan C (eds) Proceedings of the LREC workshop on exploitation of multilingual resources and tools for central and (South) Eastern European languages, Valetta, May 2010, pp 31–40

Michou A, Seretan V (2009) A tool for multi-word expression extraction in modern Greek using syntactic parsing. In: Proceedings of the demonstrations session at EACL 2009, Athens. Association for Computational Linguistics, pp 45–48

Mini M, Fotopoulou A (2009) Typology of multiword verbal expressions in modern Greek dictionaries: limits and differences (in Greek). In: Proceedings of the 18th international symposium of theoretical & applied linguistics, School of English, Aristotle University of Thessaloniki, Thessaloniki, pp 491–503

Moustaki A (1995) Les expressions figées $\epsilon'\iota\mu\alpha\iota$/être prép C W en grec moderne. PhD thesis, Université Paris VIII, 476p

Pang B, Lee L (2008) Opinion mining and sentiment analysis. Found Trends Inf Retr 2(1–2):135p. Now Publishers Inc. doi:http://dx.doi.org/10.1561/1500000011

Papageorgiou H, Prokopidis P, Giouli V, Piperidis S (2000) A unified POS tagging architecture and its application to Greek. In: Proceedings of the second international conference on language resources and evaluation (LREC 2000), Athens. European Language Resources Association, pp 1455–1462

Salkoff M (1990) Automatic translation of support verb constructions. In: Proceedings of the 13th international conference on computational linguistics (COLING 1990), Helsinki, pp 243–246

Silva MJ, Carvalho P, Sarmento L, Oliveira E, Magalhães P (2009) The design of OPTIMISM, an opinion mining system for Portuguese politics. In: Proceedingsof the fourteenth Portuguese conference on artificial intelligence (EPIA 2006), Aveiro, pp 565–576

Stevenson S, Fazly A, North R (2004) Statistical measures of the semi-productivity of light verb constructions. In: Tanaka T, Villavicencio A, Bond F, Korhonen A (eds) Proceedings of the ACL workshop on multiword expressions: integrating processing (MWE 2004), Barcelona. Association for Computational Linguistics, pp 1–8

Teufel S, Grefenstette G (1995) Corpus-based method for automatic identification of support verbs for nominalizations. In: Proceedings of the 7th conference of the European chapter of the association for computational linguistics (EACL 1995), Dublin Association for Computational Linguistics, pp 98–103

Chapter 7
Application 2: Machine Translation

Throughout the previous chapters, we have demonstrated that MWEs are a source of errors for machine translation (MT) systems and for human non-native speakers of a language. As Manning and Schütze (1999, p. 184) point out, "a nice way to test whether a combination is a collocation [MWE] is to translate it into another language. If we cannot translate the combination word by word, then there is evidence that we are dealing with a collocation". In Sect. 2.3.2, we argue that the fact that MWEs cannot be translated word-for-word is a consequence of their limited syntactic and semantic compositionality. Adequate solutions for the variable syntactic/semantic fixedness of MWEs are not easy to find, especially in the context of statistical MT models. However, for high quality MT, it is important to detect MWEs, to disambiguate them semantically and to treat them appropriately in order to avoid generating unnatural translations or losing information.

The automatic translation of MWEs can generate unnatural and sometimes funny translations, as exemplified in Tables 6.1 and 1.1 and in Appendix A. While sometimes a MWE in the source language is translated as another MWE in the target language, MWEs may imply lexical and grammatical asymmetries between languages. In other words, an expression in the source language can be translated as a single word in the target language, and vice versa. This particular case is the focus of our experiments in this chapter. Concretely, we will deal with *phrasal verbs* (PVs), so abundant in English, but absent in other languages like Portuguese and French, where the particle may be omitted (e.g., *clean up* as *limpar/nettoyer*, literally *clean*). However, as PVs are often semantically non-compositional, their contribution may involve a more complex translation to another language with the target verb being unrelated to the source verb and possibly the inclusion of additional material (e.g., *they made out* as *eles se beijaram/ils se sont embrassés*, literally *they kissed themselves*).

Our experiments investigate how PVs affect the output of English–French SMT systems. Our long-term goal is to explore possible ways for integrating them into the systems in order to improve translation quality for these constructions. In the

© Springer International Publishing Switzerland 2015
C. Ramisch, *Multiword Expressions Acquisition*, Theory and Applications
of Natural Language Processing, DOI 10.1007/978-3-319-09207-2_7

ideal scenario, the results of automatic MWE acquisition are plugged directly into the translation model, generating improved translations for the correctly identified MWEs. Since this is an ambitious goal, we were required to simplify many aspects of the experiments. The experiments in this chapter are restricted to in-depth automatic and manual *evaluation* of automatic PV translation. Our analysis shows how the linguistic, semantic and distributional characteristics of PVs affect the results obtained. We show that current statistical MT technology cannot deal with PVs and that further efforts need to be made in MT evaluation for taking them into account.[1]

The MWEs under consideration, that is, English phrasal verbs, are identified only on the source side using monolingual identification. The use of bilingual identification would probably be more helpful and would generate significant improvements in translation quality if integrated into the MT models. While the acquisition of bilingual MWEs has been the focus of some related work (see Sect. 3.2.2), this is far from being a solved problem and the quality of results is still below our expectations, specially when it comes to the asymmetric constructions. Thus, we apply monolingual identification with the mwetoolkit hoping that, in the future, this can be replaced by automatically acquired bilingual MWEs (assuming that the techniques for bilingual MWE acquisition evolve).

When it comes to complex linguistic phenomena like MWEs, traditional expert systems have more sophisticated mechanisms to deal with them and would be the natural choice for our experiments. However, statistical systems are a very popular MT paradigm that has received much emphasis in the last years. Moreover, there are many open source and freely available tools to create a competitive system from scratch quite quickly. In short, as discussed by Stymne (2011b) SMT is "a very successful approach, and has received much research focus. Other approaches [...] have the drawback of being more complex [and] can still gain from preprocessing."

One advantage of SMT systems is that their models are relatively language independent, and a new language pair may be added to the MT system with little effort.[2] However, in order to allow this straightforward adaptation, one needs a very large volume of parallel data to train the model on, and this is not readily available for every language pair. Even though SMT seems to be the current trend in MT, the approach seems to reach its limitations when it comes to domain adaptation, traceability of errors, integration of external lexical, syntactic and semantic knowledge. The experiments reported in Sect. 7.2 represent a step toward the integration of external lexical resources containing MWEs into SMT systems. Nonetheless, we believe that it is necessary to investigate and propose new

---

[1]Experiments on the integration of PVs into English-Portuguese MT are described in the original version of the thesis. However, since these experiments do not show conclusive results yet, we prefer to report in this book the use of the mwetoolkit as a tool for studying and evaluating MT quality rather than integrating MWEs into MT systems.

[2]Some languages, however, require some linguistic preprocessing. This is the case of Chinese word segmentation, for instance.

translation models, capable of modelling MWE information more adequately than current SMT models.

This chapter starts with a brief introduction of empirical methods used to train statistical MT systems in Sect. 7.1. A discussion of some existing techniques used in expert and statistical MT systems for dealing with MWEs was presented in Sect. 3.3.4.4 and complements the current chapter. Finally, Sect. 7.2 presents the results of experiments on the evaluation of phrasal verb translation by two MT systems, where the phrasal verbs were identified using the mwetoolkit methodology.

7.1 A Brief Introduction to SMT

In the following experiments, we use a *statistical machine translation* (SMT) framework to learn translation models automatically from parallel corpora (Lopez 2008; Koehn 2010). We refer to SMT as opposed to *expert MT* systems, which are also sometimes called *rule-based* or *transfer-based* MT systems. In practice, however, this distinction is not always possible, since any system, expert or statistical, will probably contain both transfer rules *and* statistics at some point of processing. What distinguishes these two paradigms is not the translation model itself, but the way the model is built. In SMT, we learn the translation rules empirically from data, while in expert MT the rules are provided by human translation experts.

In order to build an SMT system, we need to obtain a parallel corpus of the source-target language pair. A *parallel corpus* is a set of texts in two or more languages, in which the documents are the translations of each others. Examples of parallel corpora found in everyday life include film subtitles translated into several languages, the multilingual instructions manual of your new hair drier, phrase books and restaurant menus for tourists. In SMT, most large parallel corpora come from international political institutions such as the United Nations, the World International Patent Organisation or from the transcriptions of multilingual parliaments such as those of Canada (Hansard corpus) or the European Union (Europarl corpus).

Once we have gathered a set of parallel documents, it is necessary to align them, both at the sentence level and at the word level. There are many algorithms and tools for performing sentence alignment of a parallel corpus. Anchors like numbers, question marks, dates and proper names can be used to find equivalent fragments in both languages. One of the most popular algorithms for sentence alignment is based on a statistical model of sentence length, assuming that equivalent sentences have roughly the same length (Gale and Church 1993).

After sentence alignment, it is necessary to tokenise the text so that words are represented coherently throughout the text (see Sect. 3.1.1). Then, it is usual to lowercase the corpus in order to avoid double representation of the same word depending on its position (at the beginning or in the middle of the sentence).

However, as discussed in Sect. 3.1.1, one should apply lowercasing with parsimony, especially on domain-specific corpora.

After these preparatory steps (sentence alignment, cleaning, tokenisation and lowercasing), the corpus can be word-aligned. A parallel corpus aligned on the sentence level does not contain links between the individual source and target words. Most current SMT systems rely on some word alignment software such as GIZA++ to align the words in the parallel corpus (Och and Ney 2000, 2004, 2003). In the latter, word alignment is modelled using probabilities. Given one source word s_i in a sentence, there is a probability $p(t_j|s_i)$ that it is translated as any of the words t_j on the target side, and each of these probabilities is a parameter of the model. More sophisticated word alignment models include parameters for words to be inserted (fertility), removed (null word) and reordered. This progression of translation models of increasing complexity, trained using the expectation-maximisation algorithm, is referred to as the IBM models.

One of the problems of the IBM models is that, while one-to-many alignments are possible, many-to-one alignments cannot be represented. Phrase-based SMT (PB-SMT) models emerged as an attempt to overcome this limitation. While they still strongly rely on the IBM models for word alignment, they try to combine them in order to generate larger translation chunks, better taking into account the local context of words.

The main component of the SMT translation model is the phrase table, that is, a table containing sentence fragments (the "phrases") in the source language and the corresponding sentence fragment or phrase in the target language, as the example shown in Table 7.1.[3] Each bilingual phrase (also called bi-phrase) has several associated probabilities that are integrated into a log-linear model as features. In order to create the phrase table, a PB-SMT model usually combines word alignments generated in both directions (source → target and target → source),

Table 7.1 Example of phrase table containing bi-phrases with English source (s), Portuguese target (t), phrase translation probabilities ($p(t|s)$ and $p(s|t)$) and lexical translation probabilities ($lex(t|s)$ and $lex(s|t)$)

Source s	Target t	$p(t|s)$	$lex(t|s)$	$p(s|t)$	$lex(s|t)$
a baby being born blind	uma criança cega	1	0.0106327	1	0.026239
a backward step .	de uma regressão .	1	0.0280532	0.5	0.002579
a backward step .	uma regressão .	1	0.0280532	0.5	0.027814
a backward step	de uma regressão	1	0.0287083	0.5	0.002676
a backward step	uma regressão	1	0.0287083	0.5	0.028855
a bad foundation for	uma má base para	1	0.0009332	1	0.004316
a bad foundation	uma má base	1	0.0036263	1	0.018618
a bad	uma má	1	0.1378	1	0.049648

[3]The term *phrase* is used here to denote any sequence of words, in opposition to its standard use in linguistic to denote a well formed linguistic constituent.

calculating their intersection. Afterwards, some heuristics are used to group word pairs that maximize the total translation probability. When the phrases in the table are n-grams, we say that the model is phrase-based. If the phrase contain non-terminal variable elements, we say that the translation model is hierarchical.

Besides the features represented in the phrase table, it is possible to learn generation and reordering models from the parallel data. Additionally, a target n-gram language model is usually required, and can be built using larger monolingual texts and software like the SRILM toolkit (Stolcke 2002). The features coming from these different models (translation, generation, reordering and target language) are joined using a log-linear combination in which each feature f_k has a weight λ_k. These weights can be optimised using a statistical parameter optimisation technique. The optimisation of the λ_k weights is a classical machine learning search problem called *tuning*. It requires a held-out *tuning set* of a few thousand parallel sentences. One of the most popular strategies for tuning in SMT is minimum error rate training (Shinozaki and Ostendorf 2008).

The translation of a new sentence is a search problem in a huge search space. In a phrase-based model, this space consists of all possible replacements of source phrases by target phrases until the source sentence is completely covered. That is, translating a sentence corresponds to choosing the bi-phrases that cover the source sentence and maximise the joint translation probabilities considering all features f_k weighted by the λ_k coefficients. While finding an exact solution for this problem is NP-hard (Knight 1999), reasonable heuristics like A* and beam search can be used with satisfactory results (Tillmann and Ney 2003).

The evaluation of machine translation has been a very active research topic for many years, and still seems to be an open problem. Subjective evaluation relies on human judgements. There are many subjective measures, such as readability, fidelity, grammaticality and usability. Since the advent of large MT evaluation campaigns, two objective measures have been particularly popular: adequacy and fluency. *Adequacy* is the amount of meaning transferred from the source sentence to the target sentence, and *fluency* is the naturalness and grammaticality of the target sentence. Other objective evaluation metrics can involve human-related factors such as average reading or post-editing times.

When it comes to SMT systems, evaluation is often performed automatically by comparing the automatic translation with a (set of) reference translation(s) proposed by human translators. Several metrics exist for calculating the similarity between automatic and reference translations. Some of the most popular evaluation scores used in current SMT technology are BLEU, TER and METEOR. BLEU is a precision score that takes into account the proportion of shared n-grams between the automatic translation and the references (Papineni et al. 2002). METEOR is a score based on BLEU that, instead of calculating n-gram precision, focuses on direct word matches. In order to calculate the METEOR metric, the automatic and reference translations are aligned taking into account not only word forms, but also stems, Wordnet synonyms and paraphrases, thus including more linguistic information than BLEU (Banerjee and Lavie 2005). BLEU and METEOR values closer to 100 indicate good translation quality while values closer to 0 indicate low agreement with the reference translations and, as a consequence, low translation quality. Finally, the TER score and its variants (WER, pWER) are error metrics that take into account the number of edit operations needed to convert the automatic translation into one of the references (Snover et al. 2006). Contrary to BLEU and METEOR, low TER values indicate good translation quality as they require little changes in order to look like the reference translations.

Even though automatic evaluation measures are very popular in SMT, in our experiments we will not rely on them. MWEs are a complex phenomenon and their translation cannot be evaluated automatically.

In the following experiments, we use the Moses toolkit,[4] a popular software for training SMT systems (Koehn et al. 2007). Moses uses word-aligned corpora as input, from which it learns a statistical translation model composed of several different components that are combined using a log-linear feature model (Knight and Koehn 2003; Koehn et al. 2003).

7.2 Evaluation of Phrasal Verb Translation

Most of the published results to date on MWE translation focus on automatic evaluation measures and only deal with fixed constructions like noun compounds (see Sect. 3.3.4.4).[5] This section presents an evaluation focusing on a more flexible type of MWE, phrasal verbs, which are not correctly dealt with by simple integration strategies (Carpuat and Diab 2010; Stymne 2009). We base our findings on qualitative and quantitative results obtained from a large-scale human evaluation experiment. Moreover, we do not intend to improve an SMT system with multiword unit processing: our goal is rather to evaluate and quantify how hard it is to translate these constructions. The mwetoolkit methodology is useful in this context since it allows the fast identification of phrasal verbs for creating training and test material for MT. We believe that these results can help conceiving more linguistically informed models for treating multiword units in MT systems in the future, as opposed to heuristic trial-and-error strategies that can be found in the literature.

English *phrasal verbs* (PVs) like *take off, give up* and *pull out* represent a particularly challenging class of multiword expressions for MT. We carry out an evaluation in order to quantify how hard it is for current MT technology to translate these constructions. We focus on split PV occurrences because, as explained in

---

[4]http://www.statmt.org/moses/

[5]Work reported in this section was previously published in the paper *How hard is it to automatically translate phrasal verbs from English to French?* (Ramisch et al. 2013). It was carried out with the collaboration of Laurent Besacier and Alexander Kobzar.

Sect. 7.2.1, these constructions present a specific syntactic and semantic behaviour that makes them hard to model in current MT paradigms.

We want to evaluate the quality of PV translation in phrase-based and hierarchical English-French SMT systems. Therefore, we design and apply a generic evaluation protocol suitable to circumscribe a particular linguistic phenomenon (in our case, PVs) and manually annotate translation quality. Automatic evaluation measures such as BLEU and METEOR estimate the similarity between candidate and reference translations by comparing their n-grams. In our case, manual annotation is crucial, because these automatic metrics do not provide insights into the nature of errors. Our analysis aims to answer the questions:

- What proportion of PVs is translated correctly/acceptably by each SMT paradigm?
- Which MT paradigm, phrase-based or hierarchical, can better handle these constructions?
- What are the main factors that influence translation quality of PVs?

7.2.1 English Phrasal Verbs

Phrasal verbs are recurrent MWEs in English. They are composed by a main verb (*take*) combined with a preposition (*take on* in *take on a challenge*) or adverb (*take away* in *I take away your books*). Even if "it is often said that phrasal verbs tend to be rather colloquial or informal and more appropriate to spoken English than written" (Sinclair 1989, p. iv), PVs are pervasive and appear often in all language registers. PVs present a wide range of variability both in terms of syntax and semantics. Thus, they are challenging not only for NLP, but also for students learning English as a second language (Sinclair 1989).

7.2.1.1 Syntactic Characterisation

Phrasal verbs can be intransitive, that is, taking no object (*the aircraft takes off*, *she will show up later*) or transitive (*he took off his shoes, we made up this story*). Many PVs can appear in both intransitive and transitive configurations, having either related senses (*the band broke up, the government broke up monopolies*) or unrelated senses (*the aircraft takes off, he took off his shoes*). In this work, we will focus only on transitive PV occurrences.

In terms of syntactic behaviour of transitive PVs, one must distinguish two types of constructions: verb-particle constructions like *put off*, *give up* and *move on*, and prepositional verbs like *talk about*, *rely on* and *wait for*. In verb-particle constructions, the particle depends syntactically (and semantically) on the verb, while in prepositional verbs it depends on the object, constituting a PP-complement of a regular verb. Prepositional verbs are syntactically rigid, selecting for particular prepositions and requiring a complement after the preposition (Lohse et al. 2004). Verb-particle constructions, however, can occur in different subcategorisation frames and in different word orders, in a joint (*make up something*) or split configuration (*make something up*).

Moreover, as particles in English tend to be homographs with prepositions and adverbs (*up, out, in, off*), a verb followed by a particle may be syntactically ambiguous (*eat up [ten apples], eat [up in her room], eat [up to ten apples]*). This affects how they are to be identified, interpreted, and translated automatically, as explained in Sect. 7.2.2. A simple way to test whether an occurrence is a true verb-particle construction or a prepositional verb is to replace its object by the pronoun *it*. For example, *make up* is a verb-particle construction (*make it up* vs **make up it*) while *rely on* is a prepositional verb (**rely it on* vs *rely on it*). In this chapter, the term *phrasal verb* (PV) denotes transitive verb-particle constructions. Furthermore, we focus on split occurrences of PVs, that is, with at least one intervening word between the verb and its particle.

7.2.1.2   Semantic Characterisation

PVs can be described according to a three-way classification as (a) literal or compositional like *take away*, (b) aspectual or semi-idiomatic like *fix up*, and (c) idiomatic combinations like *pull off* (Bolinger 1971). The first two classes capture the core meaning of particles as adding a sense of motion-through-location (*carry NP up*) and of completion or result (*fix NP up*) to the verb. Semi-productive patterns can be found in these combinations (e.g. verbs of cleaning + *up*). For idiomatic cases, however, it is not possible to straightforwardly determine their meanings by interpreting their components literally (e.g. *make out* → *kiss*). However, the borders between these classes are fuzzy, as "there is a general shading of meaning from one extreme to the other" (Sinclair 1989).

Like simple verbs, PVs are often polysemous and their interpretation is not straightforward. Metaphor can change the sense and the interpretation (literal or idiomatic) of the PV, like in *wrap up the present* vs *wrap up the presentation*. While some PVs have limited polysemy (e.g. *figure out* and *look up* have only 1 sense in Wordnet), others can have multiple uses and senses (e.g. *pick up* has 16 senses and *break up* has 19 senses in Wordnet).

Many PVs seem to follow a productive pattern of combination of semantically related verbs and a given particle (Fraser 1976), like verbs used to join material (*bolt, cement, nail* + *down*). While some verbs form combinations with almost every particle (*get, fall, go*), others are selectively combined with only a few particles (*book, sober* + *up*), or do not combine well with them at all (*know, want, resemble*). This productivity is specially high in spoken registers, as we verified in the test data (see Sect. 7.2.2).

7.2.2 Translation Setup

The goal of our evaluation is to quantify the translation quality of PVs by current SMT paradigms. Therefore, we build phrase-based and hierarchical SMT systems from the same parallel English-French corpus. We also identify the sentences containing PVs on the English side, and then use them as test set for manual error analysis.

7.2.2.1 Parallel Corpus and Preprocessing

For all the experiments described in this Section—extraction and translation of PVs—the English-French portion of the *TED Talks* corpus was used (Cettolo et al. 2012).[6] It contains transcriptions of the TED conferences, covering a great variety of topics. The colloquial and informal nature of the talks favours the productive use of PVs. Talks are given in English, and are translated by volunteers worldwide. The corpus contains 141,390 English-French aligned sentences with around 2.5 million tokens in each language.

Before feeding the corpus into the MT training pipeline, we performed tokenisation. Tokenisation was performed differently on both languages. Since we wanted to identify PVs in English automatically, we had to parse the English corpus. Therefore, we used the RASP system v2 (Briscoe et al. 2006) to generate the full syntactic analysis of the English sentences. Since the parser contains an embedded tokeniser, we ensured consistency by using this tokenisation as preprocessing for MT as well. On the French side, we applied the simplified tokeniser provided as part of the Moses suite.

After preprocessing, we performed automatic PV detection on the corpus using the mwetoolkit, as described in Sect. 7.2.2.3. This resulted in a set of 2,071 sentences in the corpus which contain split PVs (henceforth *PV set*). We used around half of the PV set as test data, while the other half was kept as training data, included in the larger set of training sentences with no split PVs. However, since we wanted to maximise the amount of translated data to analyse, we built two similar MT systems (1 and 2) for each paradigm.[7] System 1 uses the first half of the PV set as training data and the second half as test, while for system 2 the sets are swapped. Table 7.2 summarises the data sets. Since the systems are comparable, we can concatenate the two test sets after translation to obtain 2,071 French sentences.[8] This ensures that training and test sets are disjoint and that the systems have seen enough occurrences to be able to learn the constructions.

---

[6] Available at the Web Inventory of Transcribed and Translated Talks: https://wit3.fbk.eu/

[7] In total, 4 MT systems were built.

[8] These were further cleaned, as described in Sect. 7.2.2.3.

Table 7.2 Training,
development and test set
dimensions for MT systems
1 and 2

	# sentences	
	Sys. 1	Sys. 2
Shared training set	137,319	137,319
PVs training set	1,034	1,037
Shared dev. set	2,000	2,000
PVs test set	1,037	1,034
Total	141,390	141,390

7.2.2.2   MT Systems

We compare SMT systems of two paradigms: a *phrase-based system* (PBS) and
a *hierarchical system* (HS). The main difference between these two paradigms is
the representation of correspondences in the translation model. While the PBS uses
word sequences, the HS uses synchronous context-free grammars, allowing the use
of non-terminal symbols in the phrase table. Intuitively, the HS should be more
suitable to translate PVs because it can generalize the intervening words between
the verb and the particle. In other words, while the PBS enumerates all possible
intervening sequences explicitly (*make up*, *make it up*, *make the story up*, ...), the
HS can replace them by a single variable (*make X up*).

   Both PBS and HS were built using the Moses toolkit (Koehn et al. 2007) and
standard training parameters, described in more detail on the Moses online documentation, at http://www.statmt.org/moses/?n=Moses.Baseline. The preprocessed
training sets described in Table 7.2 were used as input for both systems. The corpus
was word-aligned using GIZA++ and the phrase tables were extracted using the
grow-diag-final heuristic. Language models were estimated from the French part of
the parallel training corpus using 5-grams with IRSTLM. For the HS, the maximum
phrase length was set to 5. The model weights were tuned with minimum error rate
training, which converged in at most 16 iterations. The training scripts and decoder
were configured to print out word alignment information, required to identify which
part of a French translated sentence corresponds to a PV in English.

7.2.2.3   Phrasal Verb Detection

PVs were detected in three steps: automatic extraction, filtering heuristics and
manual validation.

Automatic Extraction

As described in Sect. 7.2.2.1, we parsed the English corpus using RASP. It
performs full syntactic analysis and generates a set of grammatical relations,
similar to dependency syntax. The parser includes a lexicon of phrasal verbs and

represents them using a special grammatical relation (see the RASP tagset in Appendices D.2 and D.3). Since we are only interested in split PVs, we used the `mwetoolkit` to extract only sentences that match the morphosyntactic pattern `Verb + Object + Particle`, where:

- `Verb` is a content verb (POS starts with `VV`);
- `Object` is a sequence of at least 1 and at most 5 words, excluding verbs;
- `Particle` is a preposition or adverb tagged as `II`, `RR` or `RP` which depends syntactically on the verb with a `ncmod_part` relation.

Filtering Heuristics

The application of this pattern on the parsed corpus generates the PV set (2,071 sentences). Manual inspection allowed us to formulate further heuristics to filter the set. We used the `mwetoolkit` simple filter module to automatically remove 243 sentences that match one of the following rules around the identified PV.

- Verbs *go, walk, do, see* + locative words: Locative words are prepositions or adverbs that indicate locations and/or directions, like *up, down, in, out*. Even though this filtering rule removes some authentic PVs (*walk somebody out*), most of the time it matches regular verb+prepositional phrase constructions wrongly parsed as PVs (*walk up the steps*).
- Constructions involving the particles *about, well, at*: These words are more often used to introduce propositional complements and adjuncts than as particles.
- Constructions with locative words followed by the words *here* and *there*, or preceded by the word *way*: Most of the time the identified particle is actually an adverbial complement indicating a location or direction.
- Constructions involving the expressions *upside down, inside out, all over*: The parser sometimes identifies the words *upside, inside* and *all* as direct objects of a PV, when they are actually fixed adverbial locutions that modify the verb.
- Verbs with double particles, that is, with a particle as intervening word: Even though these constructions are authentic PVs, the parser attaches the second particle to the verb instead of the first one (*walk out on somebody* as *walk on* instead of *walk out + PP*).

Manual Validation

The extraction pattern and the filtering heuristics generate a precise set of sentences in a fully automatic manner using the methodology proposed in Chap. 5. However, we require that the test set to be presented to our annotators contains 100 % correctly identified PVs. Therefore, we manually inspected the resulting set of sentences and manually removed 266 of them. These were mainly due to parsing errors. The resulting set of sentences containing PVs has 1,562 sentences (705 different PVs), meaning that the fully automatic identification had a precision of around 85.5 % on this data set. PV frequencies vary from 1 to 44, and 637 PVs occur only once. Almost a half of all identified PVs, 452, were present in both training and test sets.

7.2.3 Results

The MT systems described in Sect. 7.2.2.2 were used to translate the test set of English sentences containing PVs. For each English sentence, two corresponding translations in French were generated by the PBS and HS. We developed an evaluation protocol that allows human annotators to assess the quality of PV translation in the sentences in terms of adequacy and fluency.

7.2.3.1 Evaluation Protocol

An annotator was presented with a pair of sentences, the English source and the French target translated by one of the MT systems. In order to avoid duplicated annotation effort, we only present once those sentences for which the PBS and the HS generate similar PV translations. On the other hand, since we also want to compare the systems, we select a set of highly dissimilar translations by picking up those whose longest common substring is shorter than half of the shortest translation. The dataset provided to annotators contains 250 similar sentences and 250 dissimilar sentence pairs, and the latter correspond to 500 translations (for dissimilar translations, each sentence pair is presented once, for the PBS and for the HS). In total, each annotator assessed 750 translations selected randomly from the test set of 1,562 sentences described in Sect. 7.2.2.3.

We ask annotators to focus only on the phrasal verb and its translation, ignoring the rest of the sentence. We use an adapted version of the BLAST system to provide a visual annotation interface (Stymne 2011a). The PV is highlighted, as well as its French counterpart, as shown on Fig. 7.1. The French counterpart is identified thanks to the word alignment information output by the MT systems. There are two dimensions on which a translation is evaluated: adequacy and fluency.

Adequacy

The annotator assessed a translated PV based on the extent to which the meaning of the original English PV is preserved in the French translation. The grade is based on how easy and precisely one can infer the intended meaning conveyed by the translation. The scale uses grades from 3 to 0, with 3 being the highest one.

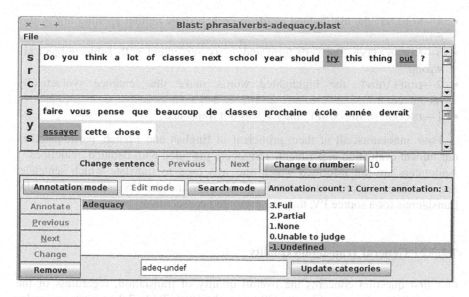

Fig. 7.1 Annotation interface using BLAST

- 3—FULL: the highlighted words convey the same meaning as their English counterparts.
- 2—PARTIAL: the meaning can be inferred without referring to the English sentence. The highlighted words sound clumsy, unnatural and/or funny, less relevant words might be missing or spurious words were added.
- 1—NONE: the meaning is not conveyed in the translated sentence. In other words, the meaning of the French highlighted words cannot be understood without reading and understanding the English sentence.
- 0—UNABLE TO JUDGE: There is a problem with the source English sentence, which prevents the annotator from understanding it.[9]

Fluency

The annotator assessed a translated PV based on its grammatical correctness in French, regardless of its meaning. The grade is based on how well the highlighted French words are inflected, specially regarding verb agreement in tense, number and gender. In this evaluation, the English sentence must be ignored. The scale uses grades from 4 to 1, with 4 being the highest one.

---

[9]Problematic source sentences were removed manually, but a small number of such cases accidentally remained in the test data.

- 4—FLUENT: the highlighted words in French show neither spelling nor syntax errors.
- 3—NON-NATIVE: the verb form and/or its agreement with subject/object are wrong.
- 2—DISFLUENT: the highlighted words make the sentence syntactically incoherent.
- 1—INCOMPREHENSIBLE: the PV was not translated.

Four annotators, all of them proficient in English and French, participated in our human evaluation experiment. They were provided with detailed guidelines.[10] Annotators are not informed which one was used to translate which sentence, and sentences are ordered randomly. If the PBS and the HS generate dissimilar translations for a source PV, they are presented consecutively.

7.2.3.2   General Translation Quality

Our first question concerns the overall quality of translation, regardless of the fact that it was generated by the HS or by the PBS. Table 7.3 presents examples of translations showing that translation quality is poor. For instance, the PV *boil down*, which means *reduce* or *come down* and should be translated as *résumer*, was translated literally as *bouillir descendu (boil went down)* by the HS and as *furoncle jusqu' (furuncle until)* by the PBS. The second example, *think through*, should be translated as *repenser* or *refléchir*, but was translated literally as *penser à travers (think through)*, which makes no sense.

An automatic sanity check, based on BLEU score, was performed for both systems on the PV set (2,071 sentences) according to the protocol presented in Table 7.1. PBS and HS systems obtained 29.5 and 25.1 BLEU points respectively (to be compared with 32.3 for Google Translate). This automatic evaluation shows that

Table 7.3 Examples of translated sentences

	*could **boil** this poem **down** to saying*
PBS	*pourriez **furoncle** ce poème **jusqu'** à dire*
HS	*pourriez **bouillir** ce poème **descendu** à dire*
	*he would **think** it **through** and say*
Both	*il **pense que** ça **à travers** et dire*
	*you couldn't **figure** it **out***
HS	*vous ne pouvais pas le **comprendre***
PBS	*vous ne pouviez pas le **découvrir***
	*Then we'll **test** some other ideas **out***
Both	*puis nous allons **tester** certains autres idées*

---

[10]The guidelines, labels and datasets discussed here are available at http://cameleon.imag.fr/xwiki/bin/view/Main/Phrasal_verbs_annotation

the PBS is better than the HS system. Even though both systems are outperformed by Google, we consider them as acceptable for our experiment, considering the limited amount of training data used (TED corpus only).

On Table 7.4, the first column shows the average score obtained by the PV translations. In a scale from 1 to 3, the translations obtain an average of 1.73 for adequacy and, in a scale from 1 to 4, an average of 2.57 for fluency. This means that roughly half of the translations present some meaning and/or grammar problem that reduces their utility. In proportion to the scale, adequacy problems are slightly more frequent than fluency problems. In order to have a better idea of how serious this problem is, we plot in Fig. 7.2 the proportion of each adequacy category in the dataset. The graphic shows that only 27 % of the PVs are translated as a French verb which fully conveys the meaning of the English PV. Around 20 % of the PVs are translated as a verb that is partly related to the original meaning, and the remainder 57 % of translations are useless. This is a clear evidence that these constructions are not correctly dealt with by our SMT systems.

7.2.3.3 Comparison of MT Paradigms

As shown in the second and third columns of Table 7.4, the PBS seems to outperform the HS for fluency and adequacy. However, the difference between both systems for adequacy is not statistically significant ($p = 0.5236$).[11]

However, in order to avoid the smoothing of category distribution generated by the presence of similar translations, we consider only those sentences for which different translations were generated. The average grade of each system on this set

Table 7.4 Average grades obtained by the systems

	Overall	PBS	HS	Similar	Different	PBS-Diff.	HS-Diff.
Fluency (1–4)	2.57	2.67	2.46	2.82	2.44	2.63	2.25
Adequacy (1–3)	1.73	1.75	1.72	2.07	1.56	1.65	1.48

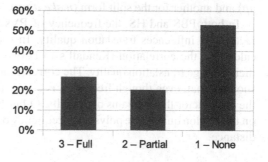

Fig. 7.2 Proportion of translations judged as FULL, PARTIAL and NONE for adequacy

---

[11]Statistical significance was calculated using a two-tailed t test for the difference in means.

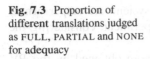

Fig. 7.3 Proportion of different translations judged as FULL, PARTIAL and NONE for adequacy

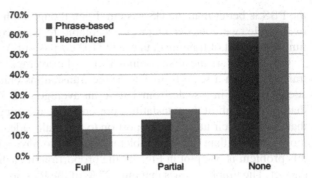

of different translations is shown in the last two columns of Table 7.4. In this case, the PBS performs significantly better than the HS in both fluency and adequacy. The distribution of adequacy classes for each system is broken down in Fig. 7.3.

An interesting finding of our analysis is shown in columns 4 and 5 of Table 7.4. We compared the average grades of sentences that were translated similarly by both systems with those translated differently. We found out that similar translations are of better quality (average grades 2.82 fluency and 2.07 adequacy) than different translations (average grades 2.44 fluency and 1.56 adequacy), and this difference is statistically significant ($p < 0.0001$). This result is a potentially useful feature in models to automatically estimate translation quality.

It is counter-intuitive that the PBS outperforms the HS in translating split PVs. These constructions have a flexible nature, and PBS systems generally enumerate all possibilities of intervening material whereas the HS can efficiently represent gapped phrases and generalise using non-terminal symbols. We provide three hypotheses for this surprising outcome. First, it is possible that the size of our training corpus is not sufficient for the HS to learn useful generalisations (notably, the language model was trained on the French part of the parallel corpus only). Second, possibly the standard parameters of the HS should be tuned to our language pair and corpus. Third, most of the time the intervening word is the pronoun *it*, and this can be efficiently represented as two bi-phrases in the PBS, one for the joint form (*make up*) and another for the split form (*make it up*).

In both PBS and HS, the frequency of PVs in the training data is one possible factor that influences translation quality. In order to validate this hypothesis, we calculated the correlation (Kendall's τ) between the frequency of verb types and their average translation quality. The correlations range from $\tau = 0.17$ to $\tau = 0.26$, showing that, even though frequency is correlated with translation quality, it is not the only factor that explains our results. Other factors that possibly have an impact on translation quality are polysemy, frequency of joint occurrences and verb-particle distance.

7.3 Summary

As a second evaluation of the `mwetoolkit`, we performed experiments on the translation of English phrasal verbs (PVs) like *give up* and *get by [a name]* into French, using SMT systems. The translation of PVs is a challenge because they present a wide syntactic and semantic variability. Modelling the complex syntactic and semantic behaviour of PVs using the flat contiguous word sequences of phrase-based SMT systems is not straightforward, so hierarchical SMT seem a natural choice.

The translation of English phrasal verbs (PVs) into French is a challenge, specially when the verb occurs apart from the particle. Our experimental results quantify how well current SMT paradigms can translate split PVs into French. We compare two SMT systems, phrase-based and hierarchical, in translating a test set of PVs. Our analysis is based on a carefully designed evaluation protocol for assessing translation quality of a specific linguistic phenomenon. We find out that (a) current SMT technology can only translate 27 % of PVs correctly, (b) in spite of their simplistic model, phrase-based systems outperform hierarchical systems and (c) when both systems translate the PV similarly, translation quality improves.

In short, the results presented in this chapter show that, even though SMT is nowadays a mature framework, flexible MWEs like PVs cannot be modelled appropriately. As a consequence, more than half of the translations have adequacy and/or fluency problems. The use of hierarchical systems does not seem to overcome these limitations, and generalisation over limited parallel data seems to be a current bottleneck.

References

Banerjee S, Lavie A (2005) METEOR: an automatic metric for MT evaluation with improved correlation with human judgments. In: Proceedings of the ACL 2005 workshop on intrinsic and extrinsic evaluation measures for MT and/or summarization, Ann Arbor. Association for Computational Linguistics, pp 65–72. http://www.aclweb.org/anthology/W/W05/W05-0909

Bolinger D (1971) The phrasal verb in English. Harvard University Press, Harvard, 187p

Briscoe T, Carroll J, Watson R (2006) The second release of the RASP system. In: Curran J (ed) Proceedings of the COLING/ACL 2006 interactive presentation sessions, Association for Computational Linguistics, Sidney, pp 77–80. http://www.aclweb.org/anthology/P/P06/P06-4020

Carpuat M, Diab M (2010) Task-based evaluation of multiword expressions: a pilot study in statistical machine translation. In: Proceedings of human language technology: the 2010 annual conference of the North American chapter of the Association for Computational Linguistics (NAACL 2003), Los Angeles. Association for Computational Linguistics, pp 242–245. http://www.aclweb.org/anthology/N10-1029

Cettolo M, Girardi C, Federico M (2012) WIT[3]: web inventory of transcribed and translated talks. In: Proceedings of the 16th conference of the European association for machine translation (EAMT), Trento, pp 261–268

Fraser B (1976) The verb-particle combination in English. Academic, New York

Gale WA, Church K (1993) A program for aligning sentences in bilingual corpora. Comput Linguist 19(1):75–102

Knight K (1999) Decoding complexity in word-replacement translation models. Comput Linguist 25(4):607–615

Knight K, Koehn P (2003) What's new in statistical machine translation. In: Proceedings of the 2003 conference of the North American chapter of the Association for Computational Linguistics on human language technology (NAACL 2003), Edmonton. Association for Computational Linguistics, p 5

Koehn P (2010) Statistical machine translation. Cambridge University Press, Cambridge, 488p

Koehn P, Och FJ, Marcu D (2003) Statistical phrase-based translation. In: Proceedings of the 2003 conference of the North American chapter of the Association for Computational Linguistics on human language technology (NAACL 2003), Edmonton. Association for Computational Linguistics, pp 48–54

Koehn P, Hoang H, Birch A, Callison-Burch C, Federico M, Bertoldi N, Cowan B, Shen W, Moran C, Zens R, Dyer C, Bojar O, Constantin A, Herbst E (2007) Moses: open source toolkit for statistical machine translation. In: Proceedings of the 45th annual meeting of the Association for Computational Linguistics (ACL 2007), Prague. Association for Computational Linguistics, pp 177–180

Lohse B, Hawkins JA, Wasow T (2004) Domain minimization in English verb-particle constructions. Language 80(2):238–261

Lopez A (2008) Statistical machine translation. ACM Comput Surv 40(3):1–49

Manning CD, Schütze H (1999) Foundations of statistical natural language processing. MIT, Cambridge, 620p

Och FJ, Ney H (2000) Improved statistical alignment models. In: Proceedings of the 38th annual meeting of the Association for Computational Linguistics (ACL 2000), Hong Kong. Association for Computational Linguistics, pp 440–447

Och FJ, Ney H (2003) A systematic comparison of various statistical alignment models. Comput Linguist 29(1):19–51

Och FJ, Ney H (2004) The alignment template approach to statistical machine translation. Comput Linguist 30(4):417–449

Papineni K, Roukos S, Ward T, Zhu W (2002) BLEU: a method for automatic evalution of machine translation. In: Proceedings of the 40th annual meeting of the Association for Computational Linguistics (ACL 2002), Philadelphia. Association for Computational Linguistics, pp 311–318

Ramisch C, Besacier L, Kobzar O (2013) How hard is it to automatically translate phrasal verbs from English to French? In: Mitkov R, Monti J, Pastor GC, Seretan V (eds) Proceedings of the MT summit 2013 workshop on multi-word units in machine translation and translation technology (MUMTTT 2013), Nice, pp 53–61. http://www.mtsummit2013.info/workshop4.asp

Shinozaki T, Ostendorf M (2008) Cross-validation and aggregated EM training for robust parameter estimation. Comput Speech Lang 22(2):185–195

Sinclair J (ed) (1989) Collins COBUILD dictionary of phrasal verbs. Collins COBUILD, London, 512p

Snover M, Dorr BJ, Schwartz R, Micciulla L, Makhoul J (2006) A study of translation edit rate with targeted human annotation. In: Proceedings of the 7th conference of the Association for Machine Translation in the Americas, Cambridge. Association for Machine Translation in the Americas, pp 223–231

Stolcke A (2002) SRILM – an extensible language modeling toolkit. In: Hansen JHL, Pellom B (eds) Proceedings of the seventh international conference on spoken language processing, third INTERSPEECH event (ICSLP 2001 – INTERSPEECH 2002), Denver. International Speech Communication Association, pp 901–904

Stymne S (2009) A comparison of merging strategies for translation of German compounds. In: Proceedings of the student research workshop at EACL 2009, Athens, pp 61–69

Stymne S (2011a) Blast: a tool for error analysis of machine translation output. In: Proceedings of the ACL 2011 system demonstrations, Portland. Association for Computational Linguistics, pp 56–61. http://www.aclweb.org/anthology/P11-4010

Stymne S (2011b) Pre- and postprocessing for statistical machine translation into Germanic languages. In: Proceedings of the ACL 2011 student research workshop, Portland. Association for Computational Linguistics, pp 12–17. http://www.aclweb.org/anthology/P11-3003

Tillmann C, Ney H (2003) Word reordering and a dynamic programming beam search algorithm for statistical machine translation. Comput Linguist 29(1):97–133

Chapter 8
Conclusions

At the beginning of this book, we asked ourselves three questions: what are MWEs, why do they matter and what happens if we ignore them? Through many examples, we illustrated that MWEs are a broad concept encompassing a large number of recurrent constructions in everyday language, like idioms, phrasal verbs, noun compounds and complex predicates. Due to the ubiquitous nature of MWEs, NLP applications dealing with real text should provide adequate MWE treatment, otherwise they will fail in generating high-quality natural output.

We have presented some linguistic theories for which MWEs are important, such as constructionism and meaning-text theory. There are many definitions for the term multiword expressions, but we chose to adopt a generic one that considers MWEs as word combinations that present some kind of idiommaticity and, at some point of linguistic processing, must be treated as a unit. We have discussed the notion of compositionality and idiomaticity, arguing that the extent to which a construction obbeys to general rules of the language varies in a multilevel continuum. We have also presented some important characteristics of MWEs such as arbitrariness, heterogeneity, recurrence and limited semantic/syntactic variability. Additionally, a MWE taxonomy can be useful when evaluating the acquisition, and we suggested a new one based on the morphosyntactic role of the MWE in a sentence and the difficulty to deal with it using computational methods.

MWE acquisition methods often use a common set of linguistic and statistical tools such as analysis software, word frequency distributions, n-gram language models and association measures. Therefore, we provided a brief overview of these foundational concepts before reviewing related work in MWE acquisition. Other tasks concerning MWE treatment, namely interpretation, disambiguation, representation and applications have also been illustrated. An important contribution of this book is this broad and deep review of the state of the art. This constitutes a significant step toward the consolidation of MWEs as a field in NLP.

After presenting this broad panorama on automatic MWE treatment, with a special focus on acquisition, we introduced a new framework called mwetoolkit.

© Springer International Publishing Switzerland 2015

C. Ramisch, *Multiword Expressions Acquisition*, Theory and Applications of Natural Language Processing, DOI 10.1007/978-3-319-09207-2_8

The main motivation for proposing this framework arose from the fact that most of the published research results in this area focused only on part of the acquisition pipeline, but there was no unified framework modelling the whole acquisition process. We have described in this book the modules of the methodology, with the most important ones being candidate generation and filtering. We also presented a toy experiment, which allowed us to discuss some technical details and practical aspects of MWE acquisition with the mwetoolkit. Finally, we compared the implementation of the proposed methodology with other tools performing similar tasks, showing that our tool obtains comparable results with increased customisation and flexibility.

While one of the principles in the conception of the mwetoolkit was to provide multiple techniques for solving a given sub-problem in MWE acquisition, we only implemented and tested a limited number of them. There are many possibilities to extend and adapt the methodology in order to compare different techniques, evaluate them in several acquisition contexts and propose new modules. The resulting software tool implementing the mwetoolkit framework is open software, freely available, and provides documentation to support future extensions. We intend to continue its maintenance, support and development in the future, as it is very important to improve its usability and quality based on user feedback. Some ideas for future developments and extensions are discussed in Sect. 5.1.3.

The evaluation of MWE acquisition being an open problem, we have proposed a theoretical framework which hopefully will shed some light on a possible structure for describing the problem. As for the extrinsic evaluation goals, we have demonstrated the usefulness of our methodology in the development of three different lexical resources. In addition, there are other applications of the mwetoolkit that were not included in the book (Villavicencio et al. 2012; Granada et al. 2012).

Throughout the book, a variety of languages, domains and types of MWE were investigated, and this analysis provided foundational knowledge about the behaviour of MWEs in texts. Given the availability of preprocessing resources and native speakers for evaluation, we focused on English, Portuguese, French and Greek. Languages whose writing systems have no word separators (such as Chinese, Japanese, Korean, Thai, Laotian and Khmer) have not been experimented with, but the mwetoolkit could handle them as any other language, once texts are preprocessed by one of the numerous word segmenters available.

In spite of a large amount of work in the area, the treatment of MWEs in NLP applications is still an open problem, and a very challenging one! This is not surprising, given that the complex and heterogeneous nature of MWEs has been demonstrated by numerous linguistic studies. At the beginning of the 2000s, Schone and Jurafsky (2001) asked whether the identification of MWEs was a solved problem, and the answer that this paper gave was: "no, it is not." More recent publications show evidences that this is still the case. For instance, the preface of journal special issues on MWEs (Ramisch et al. 2013; Villavicencio et al. 2005; Rayson et al. 2010) and of the proceedings of the MWE workshops (Kordoni et al. 2011, 2013) list several open challenges in MWE treatment such as multilingualism, lexical representation and application-oriented evaluation.

In our opinion, there are mainly two open challenges in automatic MWE processing: multilingualism and semantics.

1. **Multilingualism**. Machine translation is one of the most active research fields in computational linguistics nowadays. In this book, we stressed the importance of MWEs for MT through many examples. It seems clear that MWE processing should be one of the main goals of MT research in order to obtain better translations. However, MWE translations involve some hard sub-tasks for which there are no satisfying solution yet. First, there has been very little progress on bilingual MWE acquisition from parallel and comparable corpora. While some interesting constructions can be learnt from word alignments and phrase tables, such approaches often have limited coverage due to data sparseness, long-distance dependencies and the limited availability of parallel corpora. Second, it is unclear how one should successfully integrate existing MWE lexicons or models into current SMT systems. Simple heuristics like concatenation, extra MWE features and extension of the parallel corpus usually allow slight quality improvements. However, they are minor compared to the potential improvements, and usually the proposed solutions are specific to a given MWE type and language. We believe that it is important not only to integrate MWEs in current SMT models, but also to propose new SMT models, possibly enriched with higher-order linguistic information, that can naturally deal with fixed and syntactically flexible MWEs without requiring specific workarounds.

   The `mwetoolkit` does not currently support bilingual MWE acquisition. In spite of some promising preliminary results (de Medeiros Caseli et al. 2010; Ramisch et al. 2010; Villavicencio et al. 2010), we chose to focus on monolingual acquisition and its evaluation instead of focusing on bilingual acquisition. We would like to explore MWE acquisition from comparable corpora and from the web as a corpus. We would also like to investigate active learning or incremental methods to obtain cross-lingual correspondences for two monolingual MWE lists acquired independently from monolingual corpora. Related to our experiment with MT of asymmetric constructions, we would like to investigate techniques that explore cross-lingual asymmetries for bilingual acquisition. For instance, given that German compounds are concatenated together as single words, is it possible to detect their multiword counterparts in other languages automatically?

2. **Semantics**. One of the characteristics of MWEs in general is idiomaticity, and many MWEs present some degree of semantic idiomaticity. This means that it is not possible to simply use compositional rules to infer the meaning of the expression. As a consequence, some types of MWE require more sophisticated, semantic information, in order to be correctly identified. This is the case, for instance, of some phrasal verbs and idiomatic expressions. The non-compositional semantics of MWEs are a challenging problem for foreign language learners, and surely influence the performance of NLP tasks involving some degree of semantic processing. It is not even clear how one can accurately represent the semantics of words, let alone their composition in MWEs. Much advances in computational semantics have been made in the last years, including

evaluation campaigns like Semeval, dedicated conferences like *SEM, software tools and data-intensive models. However, the impact that the semantics and the semantic compositionality of MWEs have on the quality of applications like word sense disambiguation, textual entailment, lexical simplification and information extraction has not been researched thoroughly to date. Adequate treatment of the semantics of MWEs will not only help their correct interpretation in applications, but it will also enable their full integration into the underlying models. In the mwetoolkit, we have developed an integrated a stable experimental framework for MWE acquisition and evaluation. We would like to extend it by implementing and developing new methods for the automatic interpretation and disambiguation of MWE semantics. Similarly, we believe that fine-grained syntactic information, such as syntactico-semantic valency frames, can help obtain more precise acquisition results. The drawback of using this kind of information is that the method becomes quite language-dependent. However, distributional methods inspired on their semantic counterpart could be a good trade-off between linguistic precision and generality.

In sum, the mwetoolkit framework represents a significant step toward automatic acquisition of MWEs from corpora. However, given the complexity of the phenomenon, there is a constant need for improvements and it seems unlikely that, in the near future, a unified push-button solution will be proposed. It is crucial for the research community in computational linguistics to pursue research on MWE processing, since they constitute a major bottleneck for current language technology. The last decade has seen a rapid development of this field, and many advances have been made. However, most existing NLP applications do not perform MWE processing and fail to deal with these frequent constructions. In other words, while a significant first step has been taken, there is still a long road ahead before we can declare that we have found a definitive relief for this pain in the neck.

References

de Medeiros Caseli H, Ramisch C, das Graças Volpe Nunes M, Villavicencio A (2010) Alignment-based extraction of multiword expressions. Lang Resour Eval Spec Issue Multiword Expr Hard Going Plain Sailing 44(1–2):59–77. doi:10.1007/s10579-009-9097-9, http://www.springerlink.com/content/H7313427H78865MG

Granada R, Lopes L, Ramisch C, Trojahn C, Vieira R, Villavicencio A (2012) A comparable corpus based on aligned multilingual ontologies. In: Proceedings of the ACL 2012 first workshop on multilingual modeling (MM 2012), Jeju. Association for Computational Linguistics

Kordoni V, Ramisch C, Villavicencio A (eds) (2011) Proceedingsof the ACL workshop on multiword expressions: from parsing and generation to the real world (MWE 2011), Portland. Association for Computational Linguistics, 144p. http://www.aclweb.org/anthology/W/W11/W11-08

Kordoni V, Ramisch C, Villavicencio A (eds) (2013) Proceedings of the 9th workshop on multiword expressions (MWE 2013), Atlanta. Association for Computational Linguistics, 144p. http://www.aclweb.org/anthology/W13-10

Ramisch C, de Medeiros Caseli H, Villavicencio A, Machado A, Finatto MJ (2010) A hybrid approach for multiword expression identification. In: Proceedings of the 9th international conference on computational processing of Portuguese language (PROPOR 2010), Porto Alegre. Lecture notes in computer science (Lecture notes in artificail intelligence), vol 6001, pp 65–74. Springer. doi:10.1007/978-3-642-12320-7_9, http://www.springerlink.com/content/978-3-642-12319-1

Ramisch C, Villavicencio A, Kordoni V (2013) Introduction to the special issue on multiword expressions: from theory to practice and use. ACM Trans Speech Lang Process Spec Issue Multiword Express From Theory Pract Use Part 1 (TSLP) 10(2):1–10

Rayson P, Piao S, Sharoff S, Evert S, Moirón BV (2010) Multiword expressions: hard going or plain sailing? Lang Resour Eval Spec Issue Multiword Expr Hard Going Plain Sail 44(1–2):1–5. doi:10.1007/s10579-009-9105-0, http://www.springerlink.com/content/U07244R241063MV2

Schone P, Jurafsky D (2001) Is knowledge-free induction of multiword unit dictionary headwords a solved problem? In: Lee L, Harman D (eds) Proceedings of the 2001 conference on empirical methods in natural language processing (EMNLP 2001), Pittsburgh. Association for Computational Linguistics, pp 100–108

Villavicencio A, Bond F, Korhonen A, McCarthy D (2005) Introduction to the special issue on multiword expressions: having a crack at a hard nut. Comput Speech Lang Spec Issue MWEs 19(4):365–377

Villavicencio A, Ramisch C, Machado A, de Medeiros Caseli H, Finatto MJ (2010) Identificação de expressões multipalavra em domínios específicos. Linguamática 2(1):15–33. http://linguamatica.com/index.php/linguamatica/article/view/43

Villavicencio A, Idiart M, Ramisch C, Araujo VD, Yankama B, Berwick R (2012) Get out but don't fall down: verb-particle constructions in child language. In: Berwick R, Korhonen A, Poibeau T, Villavicencio A (eds) Proceedings of the EACL 2012 workshop on computational models of language acquisition and loss, Avignon. Association for Computational Linguistics, pp 43–50

Appendix A
Extended List of Translation Examples

The list of automatic translations (MT) in French (`fr`) were generated by Google Translate[1] on 2014/04/15. Multiword expressions wrongly translated are in boldface. Some sentences contain more than one MWE, but only one is highlighted to increase readability. Reference sentences were manually translated by native speakers.

en source	We only go out **once in a blue moon**
fr MT	Nous allons seulement **une fois dans une lune bleue**
fr reference	Nous sortons **tous les 36 du mois**
en source	The **dry run** went on smoothly
fr MT	Le **fonctionnement à sec** est allé en douceur
fr reference	La **répétition** s'est bien passée
en source	They **carry** my project **through** despite the crisis
fr MT	Ils **portent** mon projet **à travers** malgré la crise
fr reference	Ils **maintiennent** mon projet malgré la crise
en source	The children **ate** my cookies **up**
fr MT	Les enfants **ont mangé** mes biscuits **jusqu'à**
fr reference	Les enfants **ont mangé tous** mes biscuits
en source	My friend is always **chasing rainbows**
fr MT	Mon ami est toujours **Chasing Rainbows**
fr reference	Mon ami **fait** continuellement **des plans sur la comète**

---

[1]http://translate.google.com/

© Springer International Publishing Switzerland 2015
C. Ramisch, *Multiword Expressions Acquisition*, Theory and Applications
of Natural Language Processing, DOI 10.1007/978-3-319-09207-2

en source	The boy **is in** his mother's **black books**
fr MT	Le garçon **est dans les livres noirs** de sa mère
fr reference	Le garçon **n'est pas dans les petits papiers** de sa mère

en source	MWEs are a **pain in the neck** for computers
fr MT	MWEs sont une **douleur dans le cou** pour les ordinateurs
fr reference	Les EPL sont comme une **épine dans le pied** pour les ordinateurs

en source	MWEs are a **tough nut to crack**
fr MT	MWEs sont un **dur à cuire**
fr reference	Les EPL sont **un vrai casse-tête**

en source	I never get on **cable cars**
fr MT	Je ne suis jamais sur les **voitures de câble**
fr reference	Je ne monte jamais dans les **téléphériques**

en source	They **brought about** the boat
fr MT	Ils ont **apporté sur** le bateau
fr reference	Ils ont **fait demi-tour** au bateau

en source	He rarely **gets drunk** at work
fr MT	Il **se fait** rarement **bu** au travail
fr reference	Il **est** rarement **ivre** au travail

en source	The **workshop proceedings** are online
fr MT	Les **travaux de l'atelier** sont en ligne
fr reference	Les **actes de l'atelier** sont en ligne

en source	We can **count** Poland **in**
fr MT	Nous pouvons **compter** Pologne
fr reference	Nous pouvons **compter sur** la Pologne

Appendix B
Resources Used in the Experiments

B.1 Data

B.1.1 Monolingual Corpora

- **English**

  - *British National Corpus (BNC).* The BNC is a general-purpose corpus of British English, containing around 100 million words, mixing several genres like literature and newspapers It is one of the most popular corpora in NLP for English. It is annotated with POS.
  - *Genia corpus.* It is composed of a set of 2,000 English abstracts of scientific articles from the biomedical domain. It contains around 18K sentences and around 490K tokens. The corpus contains information about sentence and word boundaries, POS tags and terminological annotation with respect to the Genia ontology.

- **Portuguese**

  - *PLNBR-FULL corpus.* This corpus was built in the context of the PLNBR project (www.nilc.icmc.usp.br/plnbr). It contains 29,014,089 tokens of news text from *Folha de São Paulo*, a Brazilian newspaper, from 1994 to 2005. It can be considered as a general-purpose corpus of Brazilian Portuguese.

B.1.2 Multilingual Corpora

- *Europarl corpus (EP)* The EP corpus contains transcriptions of the sessions of the European Parliament. It contains around 50 million words of parallel text in 11 languages of the European Union, including Portugues, English and French,

© Springer International Publishing Switzerland 2015
C. Ramisch, *Multiword Expressions Acquisition*, Theory and Applications
of Natural Language Processing, DOI 10.1007/978-3-319-09207-2

plus around 10 million words for other languages of countries that recently joined the European Union. It can be viewed as a general-purpose corpus as it runs over more than 10 years and the political debates have a wide range of discussion subjects. It is one of the most popular resources for SMT. We used two versions: the older one, v3, consists of extracts from the proceedings of the European Parliament during the period Apr/1996–Oct/2006; and the more recent version, v6, contains the same texts as in v3 plus recent transcriptions up to Dec/2010. EP is publicly available at http://www.statmt.org/europarl/.

- *The web as a corpus.* The web contains a large amount of textual data in several languages. It can be used to overcome data sparseness in traditional corpora. It is not a parallel corpus, but comparable corpora may be extracted from the web. It can also be thought of as a set containing several monolingual corpora, each one with millions of words. It is practically impossible to crawl and download all the ever-growing text of the web, but search engines can be used to estimate the counts of words in the web. We use Google and Yahoo search APIs and the implementation of the mwetoolkit.

- *TED talks corpus.* It contains transcriptions of the TED conferences, covering a great variety of topics. Talks are given in English and translated by volunteers worldwide into many languages. We used the English-French portion, which contains 141 K sentences and 2.5 M words in each language. The corpus is freely available at the Web Inventory of Transcribed and Translated Talks http://wit3. fbk.edu.

B.2 Software

B.2.1 Analysis Tools

- *Europarl corpus tools.* The EP corpus comes with some scripts for text tokenisation, sentence splitting and sentence alignment. These were used in some experiments.
- *TreeTagger.* The TreeTagger is a free downloadable POS tagger available for several languages, and with a good performance for English. It performs not only POS tagging but also sentence splitting, tokenisation and lemmatisation of the text. The TreeTagger is freely available at http://www.ims.uni-stuttgart.de/ projekte/corplex/TreeTagger/. The tagset used by the TreeTagger in English is available at ftp://ftp.cis.upenn.edu/pub/treebank/doc/tagguide.ps.gz.
- *PALAVRAS parser.* This deep syntactic parsing tool of Portuguese was used for the analysis of Portuguese text It supports tokenisation, sentence splitting, POS tagging, lemmatisation, dependency parsing annotation and shallow semantic annotation. In most cases, only the first four features were used.
- *RASP parser.* The RASP parser is a free downloadable tool for the syntactic analysis of English text. It provides not only POS tagging but also constituent and dependency trees. It is available at http://www.informatics.susx.ac.uk/research/ groups/nlp/rasp/.

Appendix C
The `mwetoolkit`: Documentation

This appendix contains a snapshot of the `mwetoolkit` documentation. However, it is preferred to consult the latest and up-to-date documentation available on the website http://mwetoolkit.sf.net. This documentation was produced with the help of the people cited in Sect. C.8.

C.1 Design Choices

The `mwetoolkit` manipulates intermediary candidate lists and related elements as XML files. The use of XML as intermediary format has the advantage that it is readable and easy to validate according to a *document type definition* (DTD). It is also easy to import and export XML documents from and to other tools, as we describe in the next section. However, in terms of computational performance, the choice of an interpreted programming language like Python combined with a verbose file format like XML made some modules very slow and/or memory-consuming, requiring some optimisations. For example, the first versions of the indexing and candidate generation scripts were not able to deal with large corpora such as Europarl and the BNC. Therefore, some parts of the `mwetoolkit` were re-implemented in C. With the C indexing routine, for instance, indexing the BNC corpus takes about 5 min per attribute on a 3 GB RAM computer.

In the implementation, instead of using the XML corpus and external matching procedures, we match candidates using Python's built-in regular expressions directly on the corpus index. This avoids parsing a huge XML file and speeds up pattern matching. On a small corpus, the current implementation takes about 72 % the original time (using the XML file) to perform pattern-based extraction.

Our target users are researchers with a background in computational linguistics and with some experience using command-line tools. The method is not a push-button utility that acquires any type of MWE from any type of corpus: it requires

© Springer International Publishing Switzerland 2015
C. Ramisch, *Multiword Expressions Acquisition*, Theory and Applications
of Natural Language Processing, DOI 10.1007/978-3-319-09207-2

some manual tuning, pattern definition and parameter tuning. In sum, some trial and error iterations are needed in order to obtain the desired output.

Although no graphical user interface is available, we developed a "friendlier" command line interface. In the original version, one needed to manually invoke the Python scripts passing the correct options. The current version provides an interactive command-based interface which allows simple commands to be run on data files, while keeping the generation of intermediary files and the pipeline between the different phases of MWE extraction implicit. At the end, a user may want to save the session and restart the work later. Although it is not a graphical interface it is far easier to use than previous versions. In the future, we would like to develop a graphical interface, so that the toolkit can be used by researchers who are not at ease with the command line.

The mwetoolkit is a downloadable, freely available and open-source set of scripts. However, for more up-to-date documentation, as well as for downloading and testing the tool, one should prefer the official project website hosted at http:// mwetoolkit.sourceforge.net/.

C.2   Installing the mwetoolkit

C.2.1   Windows

Unfortunately, there is *NO WINDOWS VERSION AVAILABLE* of the mwetoolkit for the time being.

C.2.2   Linux and Mac OS

To install the mwetoolkit, just download it from the SVN repository using the following command:

```
svn co svn://svn.code.sf.net/p/mwetoolkit/code/
mwetoolkit
```

Once you have downloaded (and unzipped, in the case of a release) the toolkit, navigate to the main folder and run the command

```
make
```

for compiling the C libraries used by the toolkit. Do not worry about the warnings, they are normal. If you do not run this command, or if the command fails to compile the library, the toolkit will still work but it will use a Python version (much slower and possibly obsolete!) of the indexing and counting scripts. This may be OK for small corpora.

C.2.3 Mac OS Dependencies

In addition to mwetoolkit itself, you will need to download and to configure some specific libraries.

C.2.3.1 Coreutils Package (Through MacPorts)

To get this done is pretty simple, once you have MacPorts set up correctly (you can type man port and get a manual page), just run the following command:

```
sudo port install coreutils
```

If you don't have MacPorts yet, install it from http://www.macports.org/install. php/.

C.2.3.2 Simplejson (Python)

The Python installation comes with a handy utility called easy_install, which easily installs missing components: sudo easy_install simplejson

C.2.4 Testing Your Installation

The test folder contains regression tests for most scripts. In order to test your installation of the mwetoolkit, navigate to this folder and then call the script testAll.sh:

```
cd test ./testAll.sh
```

Should one of the tests fail, please send a copy of the output and a brief description of your configurations (operating system, version, machine) to our gmail, our username is mwetoolkit.

C.3 Getting Started

mwetoolkit works by extracting MWE candidates from a corpus using a set of morphosyntactic patterns. Then it can apply a number of statistics to filter the extracted candidates. Input corpora, patterns and candidates are stored as XML files, following the format described by the DTDs in the dtd directory in the distribution. The toolkit consists of a set of scripts performing each phase of candidate extraction and analysis; these scripts are in the bin directory.

mwetoolkit receives as input a corpus as a XML file. This file contains a list of the sentences of the corpus. Each sentence is a list of words, and each word has a set of attributes (surface form, lemma, part of speech, and syntax information, if available). To obtain this information from a plain textual corpus without annotations, usually a part-of-speech tagger is used, which takes care of separating the input in tokens (words) and assigning a part-of-speech tag to each word.

To obtain a XML corpus from a plain textual corpus, you can use a tagger program or parser, such as explained in Sect. C.5 and in Sect. C.6.

C.3.1 An Example

The toolkit comes with example files for a toy experiment in the directory toy/genia:

- corpus.xml—A small subset of the Genia corpus.
- patterns.xml—A set of patterns for matching noun compounds.
- reference.xml—A MWE reference (gold standard) for comparing the results of the candidate extraction against.

This directory also contains a script, testAll.sh, which runs a number of scripts on the example files. For each script run, it displays the action performed and the full command line used to run the script. It creates an output directory where it places the output files of each command.

Let's analyse each command that is run by testAll.sh. First, it runs index.py to generate an index for the corpus. This index contains suffix arrays for each word attribute in the corpus (lemma, surface form, part-of-speech, syntax annotation), which are used to search for and count the occurrences of an n-gram in the corpus. The full command executed is index.py -v -i index/corpus corpus.xml. The option -i index/corpus tells the script to use index/corpus as the prefix pathname for all index files (the index folder must exist). The -v option tells it to run in verbose mode (this is valid for all scripts).

After generating the index for the Genia fragment, it performs a candidate extraction by running:

```
candidates.py -p patterns.xml -i index/corpus >
candidates.xml
```

This invokes the candidate extraction script, telling it to use the patterns described in the file patterns.xml, and to use the corpus contained in the index files whose prefix is corpus (this is the same name given to the index.py script). Instead of using a patterns file, you could specify the -n min:max option to extract all n-grams with size between min and max.

Once candidates have been extracted, the counts of the individual words in each candidates are computed with the command:

```
counter.py -i index/corpus candidates.xml >
candidates-counted.xml
```

These counts are used by other scripts to compute statistics on the candidates. Word frequency cannot be computed directly from the XML file (it is done through binary search on the index). Instead of a corpus, you can count estimated word frequencies from the web, using either the Yahoo (option -y—DEPRECATED) or Google (option -w) search engine. You can also count word frequencies from an indexed corpus different from the one used for the extraction.

After word frequencies have been counted, association measures are calculated with the command:

```
feat_association.py -m mle:pmi:ll:t:dice
candidates-counted.xml >candidates-featureful.xml
```

The -m measures option is a colon-separated list specifying which measures are to be computed: Maximum Likelihood Estimator (mle), Pointwise Mutual Information (pmi), Student's t test score (t), Dice's Coefficient (dice), and Log-likelihood (ll, for bigrams only).

The association measures can be used in several ways. Here, we simply chose an association measure that we consider good, the t score, and sort the candidates according to this score, with the command:

```
sort.py -f t_corpus candidates-featureful.xml >
candidates-sorted.xml
```

The next script then works as Linux head command, cropping the sorted file and keeping only candidates with higher t score values. Finally, we compare the resulting candidates with a reference list containing some expressions that are already in a dictionary for the Genia biomedical domain. This is quite standard in MWE extraction, even though it only gives you an underestimation of the quality of the candidates as dictionaries are not complete. The command used in the evaluation is:

```
eval_automatic.py -r reference.xml -g
candidates-crop.xml > eval.xml 2> eval-stats.txt
```

The -g option tells the script to ignore parts of speech while the -r option indicates the file containing the reference gold standard in XML format. The final figures of precision and recall is in file eval-stats.txt. Remember that this is only a toy experiment and that with such a small corpus, the association measures cannot be trusted

For more advanced options, you can call the scripts using the --help option. This will print a message telling what the script does, what are the mandatory arguments and optional parameters. If you still have questions, write to our gmail address, username mwetoolkit, and we'll be happy to help!

C.4   Defining Patterns for Extraction

mwetoolit extracts MWE candidates by matching each sentence in the corpus against a set of patterns specified by the user. These patterns are read from XML files. This section describes the format of such files.

The root element of the XML patterns file is <patterns>. Inside this element comes a list of patterns, introduced by the tag <pat>. The candidates.py script will try to match each sentence of the corpus against each pattern listed:

```
<patterns>
    <pat>...</pat>
    <pat>...</pat>
    ...
</patterns>
```

C.4.1   Literal Matches

The simplest kind of pattern is one that matches literal occurrences of one or more attributes in the corpus. This is done with the tag <w attribute="value" ... />. For example, to match an adjective followed by a noun, one could use the pattern[1]:

```
<pat>
    <w pos="J" />
    <w pos="N" />
</pat>
```

C.4.2   Repetitions and Optional Elements

It is possible to define regular-expression-like patterns, containing elements that can appear a variable number of times. This is done with the repeat attribute of the pat tag and with the either element. Note that pat elements can be nested.

```
<patterns>
    <!-- Pattern for matching a simple noun phrase. -->
    <pat>
        <!-- optional determiner (appearing 0 or
            1 times) -->
        <pat repeat="?"><w pos="DT" /></pat>
```

---

[1] The actual part-of-speech tags depends on the convention used to tag the corpus, of course. Some tagging tools tag nouns with SUBST or NN, for instance.

```
         <!-- any number (including zero)
              of adjectives -->
         <pat repeat="*"><w pos="J" /></pat>
         <!-- one or more nouns -->
         <pat repeat="+"><w pos="N" /></pat>
     </pat>

     <pat>
         <!-- 3 to 5 adjectives -->
         <pat repeat="{3,5}"><w pos="J" /></pat>
         <!-- followed by the noun "dog" -->
         <w pos="N" lemma="dog" />
     </pat>

     <!-- A sequence of nouns or adjectives
          followed by a final noun -->
     <pat>
         <pat repeat="*">
         <either>
             <pat>
                 <w pos="N"/>
             </pat>
             <pat>
                 <w pos="J"/>
             </pat>
         </either>
         </pat>
         <w pos="N"/>
     </pat>
</patterns>
```

C.4.3 Ignoring Parts of the Match

You can discard parts of a match by specifying an `ignore` attribute to the `<pat>` element:

```
<pat>
    <!-- Match a determiner, followed by any number
         of adjectives, followed by a noun. The
         adjectives are discarded from the match. -->
    <w pos="DT" />
    <pat repeat="*" ignore="true"><w pos="J" /></pat>
    <w pos="N" />
</pat>
```

C.4.4 Backpatterns

It is possible to create patterns with backreferences. For instance, you can match a word that has the same lemma as a previously matched word. To do this, you assign an id to the first word, and use back:id.attribute as the value of an attribute in a subsequent word:

```
<pat>
    <!-- Match N1-prep-N1 compounds (e.g.,
         step by step, day after day) -->
    <!-- Match a noun, labeled n1 -->
    <w pos="N" id="n1" />
    <!-- Match a preposition -->
    <w pos="P" />
    <!-- Match a noun whose lemma is the same as
         the lemma of n1 -->
    <w pos="N" lemma="back:n1.lemma" />
</pat>
```

Previous versions of the toolkit used <backw lemma="n1" /> instead of <w lemma="back:n1.lemma" />. There was no way of specifying both a literal attribute and a backreference with the old syntax.

C.4.5 Syntactic Patterns

The toolkit supports corpora with syntactic annotations: the <w> element can contain a syn attribute, which contains a list of the syntactic dependencies of the word in the sentence, in the format deptype1:wordnum1;deptype2:wordnum2; ..., where deptypen is the type of the dependency, and wordnumn is the number of the word that is the target of the dependency (first word is 1). For example, <w lemma="book" pos="N" syn="dobj:4" /> in the corpus represents a noun, book, which is the direct object of the fourth word in the sentence. (Again, the syntactic tag will vary depending on the convention used in the corpus.)

You can specify a pattern with syntactic dependencies with the attribute syndep in the <w> element of the patterns file. First you assign an id to a word, and then you refer back to it with the syntax <w syndep="deptype:id">. This is so that the pattern is not dependent on the actual word numbers. For example:

```
<!-- Match a verb and its direct object, with possible
     irrelevant intervening material. -->
<pat>
    <w pos="V" id="v1"/>
    <pat repeat="*" ignore="true"><w/></pat>
    <w pos="N" syndep="dobj:v1" />
```

```
</pat>
```

Currently only "backward" syntactic dependencies are supported. Support for forward dependencies is planned.

C.5 Preprocessing a Corpus Using TreeTagger

This section explains how to use a POS tagger, TreeTagger, to obtain a XML corpus from a plain textual corpus.

C.5.1 Installing TreeTagger

To install TreeTagger, just follow the instructions in the "Download" section of TreeTagger's webpage.[2] In addition to TreeTagger itself, you will need to download parameter files for each language you wish to use the tagger with. We recommend that you add the path to TreeTagger to your PATH variable as suggested by the TreeTagger installation script, this will allow you to call it without using the full path.

C.5.2 Converting TreeTagger's Output to XML

After installing TreeTagger, you can run it by running `path-to-tree-tagger/cmd/tree-tagger-language input-file`, where language is the language of the input file. TreeTagger will read the corpus from `input-file` and print each word, together with its lemma and part of speech, as a separate line to standard output.

mwetoolkit comes with a script, `treetagger2xml.sh`, which takes TreeTagger's output and converts it to XML. All you have to do is feed TreeTagger's output to it:

```
path-to-tree-tagger/cmd/tree-tagger-english
corpus.txt |
python path-to-mwetoolkit/bin/treetagger2xml.py
>corpus.xml
```

From there on you can process the XML corpus using mwetoolkit tools, such as is shown in Sect. C.3.

---

[2]http://www.ims.uni-stuttgart.de/projekte/corplex/TreeTagger/

C.6   Preprocessing a Corpus Using RASP

This page explains how to use a parser, RASP, to obtain a XML corpus from a plain textual corpus.

C.6.1   Installing RASP

RASP doesn't need to be installed. Just download it from RASP Download.[3]

C.6.2   Converting RASP's Output to XML

After downloading RASP, you can run it by running `path-to-rasp/scripts/rasp.sh < input-file`. RASP will read the corpus from `input-file` and print for each sentence it's words, together with surface form, lemma and part of speech. Then, it will print the grammatical relations, which can be viewed as a kind of dependency tree.

mwetoolkit comes with a script, `rasp2mwe.py`, which takes RASP's output and converts it to XML. All you have to do is feed RASP's output to it:

```
path-to-rasp/scripts/rasp.sh < corpus.txt |
python path-to-mwetoolkit/bin/rasp2mwe.py >corpus.xml
```

From there on you can process the XML corpus using mwetoolkit tools, such as is shown in Sect. C.3.

C.7   Examples of XML Files

Figure C.1 shows an example of sentence in a XML corpus file. There are four possible attributes that can be defined at the word level: `surface` for the surface form, `lemma`, `pos` for the part of speech and `syn` for the dependency syntactic relation. Syntactic relations are represented as a pair `type:parent` where the first element is the type of syntactic relation and the second element is the position of the parent word on which the current word depends. This example sentence was parsed using the RASP parser. Word indices start at 1. The corresponding tree representation would be:

---

[3]http://ilexir.co.uk/applications/rasp/download/

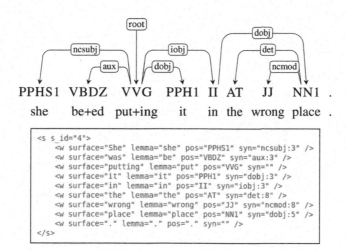

Fig. C.1 Example of sentence in a corpus

C.8 Developers

The mwetoolkit was developed and is maintained by:

- Carlos Ramisch
- Vitor De Araujo
- Sandra Castellanos
- Maitê Dupont
- Alexander Kobzar

Appendix D
Tagsets for POS and Syntax

D.1 Generic POS Tagset

The parts of speech described below compose a minimal, generic, coarse-grained set of tags used in Chaps. 5–7. They are not standard and were created only to explain the MWE extraction patterns using the same tags in all languages.

- **CC** conjunction
- **DT** determiner
- **J** adjective
- **N** noun
- **P** preposition
- **R** adverb
- **V** verb

D.2 RASP English POS Tagset

The tagset used by the RASP for English POS tags is available at http://ucrel.lancs. ac.uk/claws2tags.html, reproduced below.

- **!** punctuation tag— exclamation mark
- **"** punctuation tag— quotation marks
- **$** Germanic genitive marker—('or 's)
- **&FO** formula
- **&FW** foreign word
- **(** punctuation tag—left bracket

- **)** punctuation tag— right bracket
- **,** punctuation tag— comma
- **-** punctuation tag— dash
- **——** new sentence marker
- **.** punctuation tag— full-stop

- **...** punctuation tag— ellipsis
- **:** punctuation tag— colon
- **;** punctuation tag— semi-colon
- **?** punctuation tag— question-mark

© Springer International Publishing Switzerland 2015
C. Ramisch, *Multiword Expressions Acquisition*, Theory and Applications
of Natural Language Processing, DOI 10.1007/978-3-319-09207-2

- **APP$** possessive pronoun, pre-nominal (my, your, our etc.)
- **AT** article (the, no)
- **AT1** singular article (a, an, every)
- **BCS** before-conjunction (in order (that), even (if etc.))
- **BTO** before-infinitive marker (in order, so as (to))
- **CC** coordinating conjunction (and, or)
- **CCB** coordinating conjunction (but)
- **CF** semi-coordinating conjunction (so, then, yet)
- **CS** subordinating conjunction (if, because, unless)
- **CSA** 'as' as a conjunction
- **CSN** 'than' as a conjunction
- **CST** 'that' as a conjunction
- **CSW** 'whether' as a conjunction
- **DA** after-determiner (capable of pronominal function) (such, former, same)
- **DA1** singular after-determiner (little, much)
- **DA2** plural after-determiner (few, several, many)
- **DA2R** comparative plural after-determiner (fewer)

- **DAR** comparative after-determiner (more, less)
- **DAT** superlative after-determiner (most, least)
- **DB** before-determiner (capable of pronominal function) (all, half)
- **DB2** plural before-determiner (capable of pronominal function) (e.g. both)
- **DD** determiner (capable of pronominal function) (any, some)
- **DD1** singular determiner (this, that, another)
- **DD2** plural determiner (these, those)
- **DDQ** wh-determiner (which, what)
- **DDQ$** wh-determiner, genitive (whose)
- **DDQV** wh-ever determiner (whichever, whatever)
- **EX** existential 'there'
- **ICS** preposition-conjunction (after, before, since, until)
- **IF** 'for' as a preposition
- **II** preposition
- **IO** 'of' as a preposition
- **IW** 'with'; 'without' as preposition
- **JA** predicative adjective (tantamount, afraid, asleep)
- **JB** attributive adjective (main, chief, utter)

- **JBR** attributive comparative adjective (upper, outer)
- **JBT** attributive superlative adjective (utmost, uttermost)
- **JJ** general adjective
- **JJ** general comparative adjective (older, better, bigger)
- **JJT** general superlative adjective (oldest, best, biggest)
- **JK** adjective catenative ('able' in 'be able to'; 'willing' in 'be willing to')
- **LE** leading co-ordinator ('both' in 'both…and…'; 'either' in 'either…or…')
- **MC** cardinal number neutral for number (two, three…)
- **MC$** genitive cardinal number, neutral for number (10's)
- **MC-MC** hyphenated number (40–50, 1770–1827)
- **MC1** singular cardinal number (one)
- **MC2** plural cardinal number (tens, twenties)
- **MD** ordinal number (first, 2nd, next, last)
- **MF** fraction, neutral for number (quarters, two-thirds)
- **NC2** plural cited word ('ifs' in 'two ifs and a but')

- **ND1** singular noun of direction (north, south-east)
- **NN** common noun, neutral for number (sheep, cod)
- **NN1** singular common noun (book, girl)
- **NN1$** genitive singular common noun (domini)
- **NN2** plural common noun (books, girls)
- **NNJ** organization noun, neutral for number (department, council, committee)
- **NNJ1** singular organization noun (Assembly, commonwealth)
- **NNJ2** plural organization noun (governments, committees)
- **NNL** locative noun, neutral for number (Is.)
- **NNL1** singular locative noun (street, Bay)
- **NNL2** plural locative noun (islands, roads)
- **NNO** numeral noun, neutral for number (dozen, thousand)
- **NNO1** singular numeral noun (no known examples)
- **NNO2** plural numeral noun (hundreds, thousands)
- **NNS** noun of style, neutral for number (no known examples)
- **NNS1** singular noun of style (president, rabbi)

- **NNS2** plural noun of style (presidents, viscounts)
- **NNSA1** following noun of style or title, abbreviatory (M.A.)
- **NNSA2** following plural noun of style or title, abbreviatory
- **NNSB** preceding noun of style or title, abbr. (Rt. Hon.)
- **NNSB1** preceding sing. noun of style or title, abbr. (Prof.)
- **NNSB2** preceding plur. noun of style or title, abbr. (Messrs.)
- **NNT** temporal noun, neutral for number (no known examples)
- **NNT1** singular temporal noun (day, week, year)
- **NNT2** plural temporal noun (days, weeks, years)
- **NNU** unit of measurement, neutral for number (in., cc.)
- **NNU1** singular unit of measurement (inch, centimetre)
- **NNU2** plural unit of measurement (inches, centimetres)
- **NP** proper noun, neutral for number (Indies, Andes)
- **NP1** singular proper noun (London, Jane, Frederick)
- **NP2** plural proper noun (Browns, Reagans, Koreas)

- **NPD1** singular weekday noun (Sunday)
- **NPD2** plural weekday noun (Sundays)
- **NPM1** singular month noun (October)
- **NPM2** plural month noun (Octobers)
- **PN** indefinite pronoun, neutral for number ("none")
- **PN1** singular indefinite pronoun (one, everything, nobody)
- **PNQO** whom
- **PNQS** who
- **PNQV$** whosever
- **PNQVO** whomever, whomsoever
- **PNQVS** whoever, whosoever
- **PNX1** reflexive indefinite pronoun (oneself)
- **PP$** nominal possessive personal pronoun (mine, yours)
- **PPH1** it
- **PPHO1** him, her
- **PPHO2** them
- **PPHS1** he, she
- **PPHS2** they
- **PPIO1** me
- **PPIO2** us
- **PPIS1** I
- **PPIS2** we
- **PPX1** singular reflexive personal pronoun (yourself, itself)
- **PPX2** plural reflexive personal pronoun (yourselves, ourselves)
- **PPY** you
- **RA** adverb, after nominal head (else, galore)

- **REX** adverb introducing appositional constructions (namely, viz, e.g.)
- **RG** degree adverb (very, so, too)
- **RGA** postnominal/adverbial/ adjectival degree adverb (indeed, enough)
- **RGQ** wh- degree adverb (how)
- **RGQV** wh-ever degree adverb (however)
- **RGR** comparative degree adverb (more, less)
- **RGT** superlative degree adverb (most, least)
- **RL** locative adverb (alongside, forward)
- **RP** prep. adverb; particle (in, up, about)
- **RPK** prep. adv., catenative ('about' in 'be about to')
- **RR** general adverb
- **RRQ** wh- general adverb (where, when, why, how)

- **RRQV** wh-ever general adverb (wherever, whenever)
- **RRR** comparative general adverb (better, longer)
- **RRT** superlative general adverb (best, longest)
- **RT** nominal adverb of time (now, tommorow)
- **TO** infinitive marker (to)
- **UH** interjection (oh, yes, um)
- **VB0** be
- **VBDR** were
- **VBDZ** was
- **VBG** being
- **VBM** am
- **VBN** been
- **VBR** are
- **VBZ** is
- **VD0** do
- **VDD** did
- **VDG** doing
- **VDN** done
- **VDZ** does
- **VH0** have
- **VHD** had (past tense)
- **VHG** having
- **VHN** had (past participle)

- **VHZ** has
- **VM** modal auxiliary (can, will, would etc.)
- **VMK** modal catenative (ought, used)
- **VV0** base form of lexical verb (give, work etc.)
- **VVD** past tense form of lexical verb (gave, worked etc.)
- **VVG** -ing form of lexical verb (giving, working etc.)
- **VVN** past participle form of lexical verb (given, worked etc.)
- **VVZ** -s form of lexical verb (gives, works etc.)
- **VVGK** -ing form in a catenative verb ('going' in 'be going to')
- **VVNK** past part. in a catenative verb ('bound' in 'be bound to')
- **XX** not, n't
- **ZZ1** singular letter of the alphabet: 'A', 'a', 'B', etc.
- **ZZ2** plural letter of the alphabet: 'As', b's, etc.

D.3 RASP English Grammatical Relations

The set of grammatical relations used by the RASP in English is available at http://www.cl.cam.ac.uk/techreports/UCAM-CL-TR-662.pdf, reproduced below. It is organised as a tree of more generic to more specific relations. Underspecified relations may be assigned when the parser cannot disambiguate a construction.

- **dependent** : underspecified dependence
- **ta** : text adjunct
- **arg_mod** : underspecified argument or modifier
- **det** : determiner (articles, quantifiers, partitives)
- **aux** : auxiliary verb
- **conj** : coordination
- **mod** : underspecified modifier
- **arg** : underspecified argument
- **ncmod** : non-clausal modifier
- **xmod** : predicative modifier
- **cmod** : clausal modifier
- **pmod** : prepositional modifier
- **subj** : underspecified subject
- **ncsubj** : non-clausal subject
- **xsubj** : predicative subject
- **csubj** : clausal subject
- **subj_dobj** : underspecified subject or direct object
- **comp** : underspecified complement
- **obj** : underspecified object
- **dobj** : direct object
- **obj2** : second direct object (for double object verbs)
- **iobj** : indirect (prepositional) object
- **pcomp** : prepositional complement
- **clausal** : underspecified clausal
- **xcomp** : predicative complement
- **ccomp** : clausal complement

D.4 TreeTagger English POS Tagset

The tagset used by the TreeTagger in English is available at ftp://ftp.cis.upenn.edu/pub/treebank/doc/tagguide.ps.gz, reproduced below.

- **CC** Coordinating Conjunction
- **CD** Cardinal Number
- **DT** Determiner
- **EX** Existential there
- **FW** Foreign word
- **IN** Preposition or subordinating conjunction
- **JJ** Adjective
- **JJR** Adjective, comparative
- **JJS** Adjective, superlative
- **LS** List item marker
- **MD** Modal
- **NN** Noun, singular
- **NNS** Noun, plural
- **NNP** Proper noun, singular
- **NNPS** Proper noun, plural
- **PDT** Predeterminer
- **POS** Possessive ending
- **PRP** Personal pronoun
- **PRP$** Possessive pronoun
- **RB** Adverb
- **RBR** Adverb, comparative
- **RBS** Adverb, superlative
- **RP** Particle
- **SYM** Symbol
- **TO** to
- **UF** Interjection
- **VB** Verb, base form
- **VBD** Verb, past tense
- **VBG** Verb, gerund or present participle
- **VBN** Verb, past participle
- **VBP** Verb, non-3rd person singular present
- **VBZ** Verb, 3rd person singular present
- **WDT** Wh-determiner
- **WP** Wh-pronoun
- **WP$** Possessive wh-pronoun
- **WRB** Wh-adverb

Appendix E
Detailed Lexicon Descriptions

E.1   Sentiment Verbs Extracted from Brazilian WordNet

List of sentiment verbs extracted from the Brazilian version of WordNet. We intend to investigate the relation between these verbs and the complex predicates extracted in Sect. 6.2.

abalar	apreciar	desadorar	desprezar
abominar	arrasar	desagradar	distrair-se
aborrecer-se	assanhar	desagradar-se	doer
abrandar	atormentar-se	desagradecer	embaraçar
acalmar	atraiçoar	desalentar-se	emburrar
acalmar-se	atrair	desangustiar	encantar
acender-se	atrapalhar-se	desanimar	encantar-se
acovardar-se	babar-se	desapoquentar	encorajar
adorar	cativar	desassossegar	enfurecer
afligir	chatear	desconfortar	enfurecer-se
agitar-se	cobiçar	desejar	enlouquecer
agradar	comover	desemburrar	enlouquecer-se
alarmar	comover-se	desemburrar-se	enlutar
alarmar-se	compadecer-se	desencabular	enlutar-se
alegrar	conciliar	desencorajar	entristecer
aliviar	confortar	desenjoar	entristecer-se
alterar	conquistar	desesperar-se	entusiasmar
alucinar	consolar	desfazer-se	entusiasmar-se
alvoroçar	consolar-se	desiludir	envaidecer-se
animar	consumir-se	desinteressar	envergonhar
antipatizar	decepcionar	desmotivar	espezinhar
apiedar	decepcionar-se	despertar	estimar
apoquentar	deleitar-se	despreocupar	estimular-se

© Springer International Publishing Switzerland 2015

C. Ramisch, *Multiword Expressions Acquisition*, Theory and Applications of Natural Language Processing, DOI 10.1007/978-3-319-09207-2

exasperar	impacientar-se	magoar-se	pirraçar
exasperar-se	incomodar	malucar	preferir
excitar	inferiorizar-se	nublar	preocupar-se
expectar	inquietar-se	nublar-se	rebaixar-se
expiar	intimidar	obsequiar	simpatizar
fascinar	intimidar-se	orgulhar-se	sossegar
frustrar	invejar	penitenciar-se	temer
fustigar	irar-se	perrengar	torturar
horrorizar	irritar-se	perturbar	venerar
horrorizar-se	irromper	perturbar-se	zangar
humilhar-se	lastimar		

E.2   Sentiment Nouns

List of Brazilian Portuguese nouns expressing sentiments. These nouns were identified using the morphosyntactic patterns described in Sect. 6.2.1.2 and manual validation.

admiração	coragem	instinto	rancor
adoração	culpa	interesse	receio
ambição	curiosidade	inveja	rejeição
amor	desejo	irritação	remorso
angústia	desespero	mágoa	repugnância
ansiedade	desprezo	medo	repulsa
antipatia	devoção	moleza	respeito
apego	dificuldade	necessidade	responsabilidade
apelo	disposição	nojo	sabor
apreço	dó	nostalgia	saudade
asco	dor	obsessão	segurança
aspiração	dor-de-cabeça	ódio	sensação
atração	dúvida	orgulho	sentimento
bronca	esperança	paciência	simpatia
carinho	expectativa	paixão	sintoma
certeza	fadiga	pâ nico	suador
cheiro	falta	pavor	suspeita
choque	fascinação	pena	tentação
ciúme	fobia	piedade	tranquilidade
compaixão	fome	prazer	trauma
complexo	frio	predileção	tristeza
confiança	gosto	preguiça	vergonha
consciência	horror	preocupação	vontade
constrangimento	ímpeto	pudor	
convicção	impressão	raiva	

Printed in the United States
By Bookmasters